Democratic Discourse of a Satrap

Biju Patnaik

Democratic Discourse of a Satrap
Biju Patnaik

Satya Prakash Dash

SHIPRA

₹ 1500
US$ 60.00
ISBN: 978-81-7541-872-1

First Published in India in 2022

Democratic Discourse of a Satrap: Biju Patnaik

Published by:
SHIPRA PUBLICATIONS
LG 18-19, Pankaj Central Market
I.P. Ext., Patparganj, Delhi 110092, India
Tel.: +91 11 2223 5152/6152; 96500 28065
E-mail: info@shiprapublication.com
www.shiprapublication.com

Preface

The book brings out thc political, economic and social thoughts of the late legendary leader Biju Patnaik on different aspects of nation-building and presents it for wider dissemination and further research purposes. Biju Patnaik needs no introduction and this book is a humble attempt to present his ideas and philosophy in a systematic and concise manner so that the succeeding generations visualize and understand the vision of this dynamic statesman. The post-independent politics of the twentieth century was dominated by Biju Patnaik among others, both at the national and state level. He was a store-house of knowledge and wisdom who had command over varied subjects and disciplines starting from international relations to grass-root level Panchayti Raj institution; from defense technology to security issues; from fiscal federalism to agricultural labour economics. His intelligence is unmatched, and such persons are never diplomatic in nature, but straight forward dare-devil type of attitude that Biju Patnaik really was. He had the democratic quality to patiently listen and analyze what others are saying, even his opposition parties, and then would give his opinion. The chapters in the book depict his thorough knowledge that reflects the justification of him being branded as a *statesman* and not a politician.

Devdas Chhotaray in his book *Bijubabu* (2021) in Odia, writes about his visit to *Navin Niwas* (residence of Biju Patnaik in Bhubaneswar) sent by late Prof. Shreeram Chandra Dash, Head, Department of Political Science, Utkal University, to invite him for the Political Science Department Annual Seminar in 1969. Chhotray then writes that he heard Biju Patnaik ordering his secretary Darbesh, from inside, to put him to Nixon. They were all stunned, as Nixon was none other than American President. He further writes that in 1969, Biju Patnaik was out from power-politics and Rajendra Narayan Sighdeo was the Chief Minister of Odisha. No one dared to invite Biju Patnaik at that time, but Professor Dash, without caring for it, intentionally sent them to invite Biju Patnaik to the Political Science Department. Biju Patnaik agreed to attend Seminar, and the topic he chose was *War: From Hannibal to Ichhogil Canal.* Chhotaray writes that the topic itself made them spellbound. It spread from third century BC anti-Roman General Hannibal to 1965 India-Pakistan War and the re-capture of

Ichhogil Canal by the 9th Battalion *Madras Regiment* under the command of Lieutenant Colonel B. K. Satyan. The *extempore* speech that Biju Patnaik delivered showed his deep understanding of the historical sequence of war, defense policy, and political confusion. I, myself, heard about the richness of the speech, later from the mouth of my father, late Prof. Shreeram Dash. Can anyone imagine any political personality of today speaking on such a vast and varied topic? This was the wisdom of the great personality that Biju Patnaik was.

The only concern that Biju Patnaik had was the development .of his state, Odisha, and the Odia people. He was a great enthusiast of federalism and believed that with the development of the states, can only India develop. The chapters in the book vividly describe his ideas and philosophy in this regard. He had a strong desire to build the Odia identity, the identity that Emperor Kharavela heralded in the ancient times, and was always proud of Odisha, even though it was considered to be a backward and tribal state in the second half of the twentieth century. He very successfully set-up his Kalinga Industrial empire in Odisha in the late 1940s.

The book has been divided into three chapters that contain Biju Patnaik's discourses on the political, economic and social issues, covering the period of his membership in different Houses of Assembly, Lok Sabha and Rajya Sabha. The discourses have been clubbed so that it clearly marks the views and opinions of this Statesman on the concerned issues. The name of Odisha has been kept unchanged, though during the period of Biju Patnaik, it was spelled as Orissa. The conclusion is also based on his speeches and deliberations on various issues, and it also contains some of his personal matters as narrated by him in the House.

I convey my deep sense of gratitude to Sri Dasharathi Satapathy, IAS, Secretary, Odisha Legislative Assembly (OLA), for the idea and conception of the book. Many valuable inputs have been incorporated from his rich experience in administration and legislative matters. My thanks are due to Bijay Krushna Palit, OLA, Jayashree Janmejaya Jena, and Siba Prasad Sahoo for collection of data. I also thank all who extended their cooperation and support, directly or indirectly, and also the authors whose references have been used in completing this work. However, I am solely responsible for any error and omission in the volume. My thanks to Mr. D. Kumar, Shipra Publications, for agreeing to bring out the volume in a short span.

Contents

1

Biju Patnaik
From Aviation to Politics

Rarely a leader emerges among the mass who due to his unparalleled contribution leave an indelible mark in the state, national and international level. A leader who hardly remained in power-politics for a decade, as the Chief Minister of Odisha (1961-63, & 1990-95) and as a Union Minister (1977-80), but had a tremendous influence and aura in national political dynamics and was a *phoenix* in Odisha politics, simply due to his dare-devil, and more importantly with a do-or-die attitude. Biju Patnaik was associated not only with the freedom struggle of India, but also of Indonesia. He also contributed in the democratic movement of Nepal against the Rana regime in 1951, and also helped the Russian Air-Force in the Second World War. He closely associated with all the political luminaries of India till his death on 17th April 1997. It is a strange correlation that both Netaji Subash Chandra Bose and Biju Patnaik were born in Cuttack City, and both had very similar natural traits and sense of immense patriotism and love for the nation. Biju was revered as Biju *dada* by his contemporary national political brethren cutting across political parties. In Odisha, the intellectual and political class revered him as Biju babu, while the common-man refer him fondly as 'Biju', and the tribal called him 'Biju Patt'. No matter whatever is his political power incumbency, he was always forthcoming to help the needy and the poor. His personality was such that no one ever dared to speak-up in front of him. "He is addicted to authoritarian methods and will stop at nothing in his pursuit of power. He won repute in Congress, by retrieving the party's fortunes in the 1961 mid-term elections in Orissa" (Hangen, 1963; 100).

Biju Patnaik was born on 5 March 1916 at his ancestral home named Anand Bhawan, Cuttack. His father was Laxminaryan Patnaik and mother was Ashalata Devi. He was married to Gyan Devi in 1939, who herself was also a fearless spirited lady and accompanied Biju Patnaik during his rescue flight mission to Indonesia against the Dutch air-force attacks. They are blessed with two sons, Prem Patnaik and Nabin Patnaik and a daughter Geeta Mehta. Unlike the politicians who are eager to bring their off-springs to politics, Biju Patnaik never practiced it, and it was only after his death that his son Nabin Patnaik reluctantly entered into public life due to the pressure from the party unit of Odisha.

Biju Patnaik passed his Secondary examination from Ravenshaw Collegiate School, Cuttack, in 1927, and Higher Secondary in Science from Ravenshaw College, Cuttack. He discontinued graduation study in Science from Ravenshaw College and took up training as a Pilot at Aeronautical Training Institute of India, and Delhi Flying Club. During his student days, he went from Cuttack to Peshwar on a cycle. He started his career with his entrepreneurial skill under the brand name of *Kalinga*. All his commercial activities were branded as Kalinga Airlines, Kalinga Tubes, Kalinga Refrigerators, Kalinga Iron Works, Kalinga Newspaper. These were very successful entrepreneurial venture with a huge turnout in the decades of 1940s and by the end 1950s it came to a sudden end with the meteoric rise in Biju Patnaik in Congress party. He also instituted the popular Kalinga Prize for popularization of Science in 1951 with a grant from his Kalinga Foundation that is given by UNESCO annually.

Biju Patnaik rose to national prominence due to his aviation skill. He joined the Royal Indian Air Force in 1936, and during the Second World War, eventually becoming the head of air transport command. He flew air transport to Burma, to help the British forces fighting the Japanese in the Second World War. Biju's adventure in flying extended to "flying missions to resupply the Soviet Red Army, which was besieged by German forces in Stalingrad" (theweek.in). His stellar role in flying his plane to the erstwhile Soviet Union during the Second World War to help the war efforts against Hitler commanded respect in the international arena (Sahu, 2021). The then Prime Minister I. K. Gujral in his obituary reference on 21st April 1997 in Lok Sabha, said, "For flying across to the embattled Soviet troops during the Second World War, a grateful Russia conferred honour upon Shri Biju Patnaik for the overtime services to the country, 50 years ago in 1945". He was an excellent pilot, and this excellence and contribution to freedom struggle brought him close to many freedom fighters including, Dr. Ram Manohar Lohia, Jaya Prakash Narayan, Aruna Asaf Ali, Achyut Patwardhan, etc. He was supporting the freedom struggle due to his nationalist and patriotic fervor. His collusion with the India's freedom struggle ultimately landed him in prison from 1943 to 1946 by the British. By the time he was released he had contact with Nehru that went on till the latter's death. "Not surprisingly, most obituaries by international publications on the death of Biju Patnaik in April 1997 referred to his deeds as a pilot. *The New York Times* called him a 'daring pilot-patriot of India', while the UK's *Independent* noted he was 'a buccaneering pilot, whose feats during and after the Second World War were legendary'. *The Economist* wrote about Biju Patnaik's exploits, noting 'he gave Indian politics a rare flash of colour'. 'His great pleasure was flying, and his exploits as a pilot provided his career with a metaphor that endured from the frolics of his youth to his ambitions as a politician and an industrialist: he was, everyone said, a high flyer', *The Economist's* obituary on Biju Patnaik read" (www.theweek.in).

The year 1947 bore a significant relevance in the career graph of Biju Patnaik. Two very important events took place that had much wider ramifications in international politics. The first event happened in July 1947, when Nehru told Biju Patnaik to help the Indonesian people in their fight against Dutch control over Indonesia for the second time. The Dutch had taken control of the Indonesian archipelago, even though they were driven out by the Japanese during the Second World War, and with the fall of Japan, Indonesia became independent on 17th August 1945. President Sukarno insisted that Vice-President Mohammad Hatta and Prime Minister Sultan Sjahrir must leave Indonesia to gather support of the international community against Dutch excesses and eventually leading to Indonesia's independence. President Sukarno and Nehru had a good relation, and so upon the request of the former, Nehru handed over the responsibility to Biju Patnaik for bringing the leaders from the Dutch-controlled Indonesia. As an avid reader of the history of Kalinga, Biju knew how Kalinga and Indonesia had a long-standing cultural link in the past and the opportunity now at hand to render some service to the people of Indonesia at their crucial hour of need should never be lost sight of (Das, 2005; 55). With exceptional accuracy and brilliant aviation skill, Biju Patnaik was able to fly back from Yogjakarta, safely bringing the two leaders Vice-President Mohammad Hatta and Prime Minister Sultan Sjahrir to New Delhi via Singapore on 24 July 1947. These leaders addressed press briefings in New Delhi, and spoke about the Dutch control over a free Republic. US threatened to cut post-war aid to Holland, and finally the Dutch handed over power to a sovereign Indonesia in April 1949. Later, Indonesia conferred Honorary Citizenship with the title of *Bhoomi Putra* to him. The obligation of Indonesia was further extended when Biju Patnaik was conferred the highest civilian award *Bintang Jasa Utma* during the Golden Jubilee Celebration on Indonesia's independence in 1996. Biju Patnaik also named President Sukarno's daughter as Meghawati. Nehru wrote in 1947, "I pay a tribute to the very gallant Indian airman who brought Dr. Sjahrir to Delhi. He has been known to us for a number of years not only for his great efficiency in flying but also for his adventurous and daring spirit" (https://frontline.thehindu.com). With this successful endeavour, it was quite certain that Biju Patnaik acquired an enviable status in the inner-core of Nehru and remained his trusted lieutenant.

Biju Patnaik's aviation skill was again relied upon by Nehru in October 1947 during the accession of Kashmir to Indian Union. The Pakistani raiders were fast marching into Srinagar, and Indian troops had to be sent urgently to take control of Srinagar. Biju Patnaik made much flying in his

Dakota DC 3 transport plane from Safdarjung Airport since the morning of 27th October 1947 and transferred troops to Kashmir, and also brought back 17 soldiers of 1 Sikh regiment under the command of Lt. Col. Dewan Ranjit Rai. Upon reaching Srinagar Airport, he flew the plane very low so as to ensure the absence of enemy raiders in the Airport. There was strict instruction from the Prime Minister's Office not to land the plane in case of enemy presence. On 6th August 2019, during the debate on bifurcation of Jammu & Kashmir (J&K) and abrogation of Art. 370, in the Lok Sabha, this commendable role of Late Biju Patanik was raised by Pinaki Mishra, Member from Puri Lok Sabha constituency. He also demanded conferment of *Bharat Ratna* posthumously to Biju Patanaik for his contribution towards nation-building. Biju Patnaik also played a key role in helping the people of Nepal against the atrocious Rana regime of that country, and in the democratic movement of 1953.

Prime Minister Modi in a tweet on the Biju Patnaik's 104th birth anniversary, on 5 March 2020, shared a 'classified' IB letter written by its Deputy Director G. Ahmed on 27 September 1945 that states,

> It can be argued that Patnaik may still be a danger so long as conditions on our eastern border do not return to normal — but that would be to state a hypothetical risk. In the circumstances we do not feel that we can urge, on strong security grounds, that Patnaik should be prevented from flying.... The Indian National Airways (INA) can be persuaded through Mr Cambridge, the Managing Director not to take Patnaik back. But if the INA do not re-employ him, Tatas probably will, because he is an excellent pilot.

It was these two indelible accomplishments that perhaps laid the foundation of the towering personality of Biju Patnaik. The events also happened within a short span of three months that made him an indomitable leader in the inner circle of Nehru, increasing his proximity to Nehru. The personal equation between them was of very high order, and this made it possible for institution-building in Odisha during the formative years. During the decade of 1950, Biju Patnaik was elected to the Odisha Legislative Assembly, twice in 1952 and 1957. In the 1961 mid-term election, Congress, under his Presidentship, got huge majority in Odisha Assembly and Biju Patnaik became the Chief Minister on 23rd June 1961 till 2nd October 1963. It is irony that he had to resign from Chief Minister under the Kamraj Plan of the Congress party, "... attributed to Biju Patanaik, the Orissa Chief Minister, Kamraj, the Madras Chief Minister, and Nehru himself" (Zachariah, 2004; 254).

Nehru period has been analysed by Brass (1994; 37) as "state and central politics were largely autonomous" with central leadership in Congress party, known as 'High Command' playing "arbitrating and mediating roles" with state Congress leaders. Brass (1994) further writes, "Moreover under Nehru, a strong central government coexisted with strong states and powerful state leaders in a mutual bargaining situation in which ultimate authority existed in Delhi". This was the political condition, under which Biju Patnaik was functioning with a strong will to develop and prosper Odisha during the post-independent period. During this period the strong central leadership of the Congress party made the regional satraps revolve around it, but simultaneously maintaining distinct identity in each of their states. The personality cult of Jawaharlal Nehru and Indira Gandhi was phenomenal to curb any desire or design to challenge it, thereby making all submissive to its leadership. Those leaders who challenged did not get any great success in their political career.

The international UNESCO Kalinga award for popularization of science and technology was set-up in 1951, and since been awarded. He took active interest for the infrastructural, industrial, scientific, and educational development of Odisha, and it was solely due to his efforts, among other institutions, Paradeep port became a reality, for which Nehru laid the foundation on 3rd January 1962. He had the plan to set-up the second steel plant after the Rourkela Steel plant, as he visualized the prosperity of the Odia people through the path of industrial development also, apart from the irrigational facilities for agricultural purpose. The state, long one of the poorest and most backward in India, has become in effect another department of Patnaik's giant Kalinga Enterprises (Hangen, 1963; 100).

Biju Patnaik was instrumental for holding the Bhubaneswar session of the Indian National Congress that was inaugurated by Prime Minister Nehru on 6thJanuary, 1964. On 8th January 1964, Nehru rose to spoke but had a near-fall as he was immediately supported by Indira Gandhi who was also in the podium. Nehru had a mild heart-attack, and he was partially paralysed on the left side. Katherine Frank (2001; 240-41) writes, Congress leaders like Biju Patnaik, the former Chief Minister of Orissa, urged Indira to take over as Deputy Prime Minister immediately despite the fact that not only was she not a member of the cabinet, she did not even hold an elected position in the government, but Indira refused. Earlier, Hangen (1963; 178) quoted Indira Gandhi who said with finality, "Orissa needs a jolt. And under Patnaik it is getting one". She could probably count on Patnaik's support for Prime Minister as per Hangen.

It was during the period 1966-67, when there was high drama in the political scene over the issue of the 1967 election and the Congress party candidate selection. Dissidents and defections and break-away from the Congress in Odisha appeared with the formation of Jana Congress by Hare Krushna Mahtab in June 1966. The Chief Minister of Odisha then was Sadasiva Tripathy, after the resignation of Biren Mitra on 21st February 1965, a friend and contemporary of Biju Patnaik. Morris-Jones (1969; 40) writes, "The busy Bijoyananda ('Biju') Patnaik under a clout at the centre, but continuing to enjoy a place in the Orissa sun, first made trouble for his former friend, the Chief Minister (Biren Mitra), and Congress President K. Kamraj had to step in to prevent Patnaik's men from bringing down the government". Later rivalry between Biju Patnaik and the then OPCC President, Anand Pani, was reported to have held-up candidate selection for a while.

Rudolph and Rudolph (2008; 70-71) with supporting data of NCERT 'Educational Statistics District wise 1960-1' showed that the state of Odisha is "fifth in terms of enrollment for technical/vocational", while it ranks "thirteenth in per capita income and fifteenth in level of development". They write the following, quoting from Alan J. Sable (1967) and Richard P. Taub (1969), on the pro-industrial policy of the then Chief Minister Biju Patnaik:

> The answer lies to a considerable extent in the policy pursued by former Congress Chief Minister Biju Patnaik, who believed that, in the face of the state's overall backwardness, technical/vocational training was a 'leading sector' and could spur the state's industrialization (Sable, 1967); to a lesser extent he also believed in the biases of Orissa's leading civil servants who, not unlike their counterparts elsewhere, show a marked preference for 'modern' industry-related programmes, and show a marked dislike for those related to agriculture, villages, and their needs (Taub, 1969; 116-18).

The Hon. Speaker P. A. Sangma in Obituary Reference in Lok Sabha on 21 April 1997, said, "In the sixties, when he was Chief Minister of Orissa for the first time, along with Governor Ayodhyanath Khosla, he launched a *Decade of Destiny* and ushered in an era of industrialisation in the State. Somnath Chatterjee, in his reference said, "Biju Patnaik believed that unless the states become strong, India can never be a strong nation and that is why, when he fought for Orissa's development, it was not by reason of any narrow consideration but to make India stronger as a whole". This is what is exactly pursued by the present Prime Minister Narendra Modi, who wants to develop the eastern part of India expeditiously, as the states in the eastern part are lagging behind the states of western part in India. India as a whole can develop and progress when the states share an equitable development process and contribute in the national productive output. Somnath Chatterjee also said, "His commitment to parliamentary democracy, his commitment to the development and progress of the country through industrialisation, his concern for the development of the States and his belief in true federalism gave us not only food for thought but also plan for action. Indeed, he was the maker of modern Orissa and the architect of industrialisation in Orissa. He was himself a successful industrialist and brought Orissa into the map of industrial India". This statement of Chatterjee is very accurate and has been very rightly observed for this great Parliamentarian, and it is also evident from the discourses made by Biju Patnaik.

Biju Patnaik played a significant role during the Chinese war of 1962. It was said that he was the *unofficial* defense adviser to Prime Minister Nehru and the only civilian who was given office at North Block and free access to Teen Murti Bhawan (official residence of Prime Minister). During the war with China, he flew cargo planes to some high-sensitive border areas which other pilots feared to venture (Modi, 2020). It was the period when the then Defense Minister and Nehru's trusted, V K Krishna Menon was the Defence Minister, and after the gains of China in Ladakh and NEFA, due to tremendous criticism, Menon had to tender resignation on 28th October 1962, but was made Minister for Defense Production, and was retained in the Cabinet. Search was on for a new person of equal significance to take charge of Defense Ministry. On 4th November 1962, the National Development Council (NDC) had a meeting and in the evening, five Chief Ministers, viz, Biju Patnaik of Odisha, K. Kamraj of Madras, Pratap Singh Kairon of Punjab, Sanjiva Reddy of Andhra Pradesh and Y. B. Chavan of Maharashtra, attended a meeting in the Prime Minister's Office in the South Block, and conveyed the resentment of the party and the country over the continuance of Krishna Menon in the Cabinet (Pradhan, 1999; 10). Later, Nehru decided that the new Defense Minister will be Y. B. Chavan of Maharashtra. However, Chavan initially was reluctant, as he had no experience of national level politics, and, secondly, he had been the Chief Minister of newly carved out state of Maharashtra, on 1st May 1960, but later acquiesced. Chavan made arrangements for his successor in Maharashtra, and came to Delhi on 19th November. On the same day late night, Biju Patnaik visited Chavan. Chavan could not say no to meet him, and spent almost an hour. Pradhan (1999, 17-18) writes that Biju Patnaik asked Chavan, "Why have you come all the way to Delhi? The Chinese are moving in with such speed that they may even reach Bombay very soon". The next day, Chavan told to Pradhan, his Private Secretary, "Even before I have assumed office, a good friend has already started lowering my morale". The Prime Minister had himself told Chavan that Biju Patnaik was lobbying hard to succeed Krishna Menon. May be he had not given up his efforts, wrote Pradhan. This indicates that Biju Patnaik had an inclination to join the Union Cabinet, but conditions were not favouring him. "His most serious liabilities are his reputation for shady business deals and his dependence on primitive Orissa as a political base. Nevertheless, Patnaik is a man to watch" (Hangen, 1963; 279). It is quite intriguing that inspite of such a great degree of reciprocity between Nehru and Biju Patnaik, and with the international and national prominence, Biju Patnaik was never inducted into the Union Cabinet neither by Nehru, nor by his daughter Indira Gandhi!

During the Chinese aggression, the IB Director B. N. Mullick, in November 1962, requested Nehru to establish a secret service on the pattern of Second World War *Special Duties Service* (SD). This would be assisted by CIA of America with small Lysander aircraft, training to Tibetan persons to collect secret information, with other support. Agreeing to the proposal, Nehru appointed Biju Patnaik as the political point person in charge of dealing with the Americans. Patnaik had carte blanche in this regard, and it was up to him how to steer the relationship away from any domestic political fallout (Malhotra, 2021; 301). In December 1962, Biju Patnaik along with an officer of IB, R. N. Kao, went to Washington DC and met with Robert 'Moose' Marrero, former US Marines aviator and present CIA air operations specialist. As the two pilots conversed, they recognized the need for a thorough review of the airlift requirements for clandestine warfare in the high Himalayas (Malhotra, 2021; 302). The success of the meeting resulted with an intelligence cooperation agreement between CIA and IB, with the establishment of the *Aviation Research Centre* (ARC) on 4th June 1963 at Charbatia in Odisha, code-named as 'Oak Tree'. During his stay in Washington, Biju gave interviews to *Baltimore Sun* and *Washington Post*, in which he said that he had come to seek both ground-to-ground and air-to-air missiles along with radars, which could conceivably be tied to a network of the South East Asian Treaty Organisation (SEATO) (Kanungo, 2005; 90-91). This gave a chance of alleging 'impropriety' on his part by the Opposition in Indian Parliament, but Nehru strongly defended Biju Patnaik.

After the sudden death of Prime Minister Lal Bahadur Shastri, in January 1966, the Congress 'Syndicate', (as it was then referred to the powerful group of senior Congressmen that included Biju Patnaik among others) reposed faith on Indira Gandhi to be the next Prime Minister, over other aspirants including, Morarji Desai, Gulzarilal Nanda, S. K. Patil, Y. B. Chavan, Sanjiva Reddy, and Kamraj himself. In 1967 general elections, the Congress gained majority in Lok Sabha, but lost majority in seven states, including Odisha. In the 1967 general election, not only Biju Patanik from Odisha, but also other prominent members of the Congress, who formed the Syndicate within Congress lost, like Kamraj in Madras, S. K. Patil in Bombay, Atulya Ghosh in Bengal, and for Indira, all these were "sweet defeats" (Frank, 2001; 271). Indira Gandhi in the Parliamentary Board meeting on 27 February 1967, remarked "it was triumph of youth over age" and she referred triumph to all those who were planning to oust her after the elections. Indira Gandhi had an authoritarian style of functioning and she was not in favour of working under the 'old guards'. Subsequently, in the 1969 President election, Indira Gandhi supported V. V. Giri, and told Congress leaders to vote as per 'conscience', thereby going against the official nominee of the Congress, N. Sanjiva Reddy. On 20 August 1969 V. V. Giri was declared to have won the President election, and on 13 November 1969, the Congress split into Congress (R) under Indira Gandhi (R being Requisitionist) and Congress (O) under the Syndicate members, (O being

Organisation). Biju Patnaik remained in the Congress (R) till in May 1970, when he left and formed Utkal Congress. In 1971 Assembly election, he was defeated by Hare Krushna Mahtab from the Bhubaneswar Assembly seat, but he made an alliance with R. N. Singhdeo, leader of the Swantra Party, and together they won the state Assembly election and formed government under Bishwanath Das in Odisha. In 1974, all the members of Utkal Congress merged with Bharatiya Lok Dal under Charan Singh.

Emergency and Janata Party

Biju Patnaik was included in the first group of leaders who were arrested in the wake of Emergency under the *Maintenance of Internal Security Act* (MISA) in June 1975. He was lodged in Rohtak Jail, and was released from detention early in November 1975, along with, Charan Singh, Piloo Mody, Ashoka Mehta, Surendra Mohan and Jayaprakash Narayan. Indira Gandhi's opponents began small steps toward resolving policy and organizational issues even during the late autumn of 1976 (Austin, 1991; 396). In February 1976, Indira Gandhi postponed the general election and extended Emergency. Biju Patnaik wrote a letter in March 1976, to his party Chairman Charan Singh, "praising the gains of the Emergency, expressing his elation over Young Sanjay's exhortation to his party workers, and stressing the need to stop political quibbling for some time to get on with the task of nation-building at the grass-roots level" (Chandra, 2003; 213). This indicates that Biju Patnaik was somehow inclined to make compromise with the ruling regime under Indira Gandhi. Further, Vasant Sathe in Lok Sabha refereed to a written statement of Biju Patnaik to the Press on 16th October 1976, alleging the later to be a sycophant, as follows:

> The Bharatiya Lok Dal leader, Mr. Biju Patnaik said here today that extraordinary powers assumed by the Government had brought in distinctive gains. Highlighting the gains of Emergency, Mr. Patnaik said that nearly ₹2000 crores of floating money had been brought to account, trade balance had improved to ₹1100 crores in spite of steep rise in international oil prices the buffer food-stocks had risen to an all-time high quantity worth $ 2.5 billion, smuggling curbed, galloping inflation arrested and rupee made stringer day by day. In addition, general discipline had been enforced and thousands of inept officials removed. He described the 20-point economic programme as a healthy socio-economic programme which has been floated and backed by unusual Government instance on its implementation (*Lok Sabha Debates*, 11.5.78; 94-5).

However, Biju Patnaik retorted to the above statement of Vasant Sathe in Lok Sabha debates on 11th May 1978, and said, "Please read the whole lot. It says that some good things may have been done by this kind of dictatorship but it cannot carry on. Did not believe that Mrs. Indira Gandhi would be a dictator, but she proved me wrong, not only proved me wrong but she tried to be and she continues to be".

On 18th January 1977, Indira Gandhi announced the general elections will be held within two months time, and subsequently it was held on 16th March. After much deliberations, the various opposition parties, Congress (O), Bharatiya Lok Dal (BLD), Jan Sangh, and Socialist Party, finally agreed on 20th January 1977, to merge and formed Janata Party under a common symbol and projected Morarji Desai to be their unanimous leader. On 2nd February 1977, a splinter group of the Congress, under the leadership of Jagjivan Ram, broke away from it and formed the Congress for Democracy (CFD). The other leaders in this party, were H. N. Bahuguna (former UP Chief Minister), and Nandini Satapathy (former Odisha Chief Minister). The CFD, along with CPM, Akali Dal, and DMK made seat alliance with Janata Party. The results of the elections brought Janata Party to power, and together with CFD, the alliance had won 299 seats and Congress won 153 seats in the Lok Sabha. Biju Patnaik became the Union Minister for Steel and Mines in the Morarji Desai Cabinet, and when Chaudhury Charan Singh became the Prime Minister, he became the Union Minister for Steel, Mines, and Coal. However, Charan Singh government that was formed on 15th July 1979, lasted till 22nd August 1979, when President dissolved, and fresh elections were declared to be held in January, 1980.

After assuming office, the Janata government dissolved ten state Assemblies where the Congress was in power, and hold fresh elections in June 1977. This dissolution was a big controversy then and it went upto the Supreme Court giving a favorable order on 29th April 1977. On the same day, leaders of the Janata Party met at the Dupleix Road residence of Prime Minister Desai. Austin (1991; 446) writes as per an interview by Ramkrishna Hegde, the General Secretary of Janata Party told that Desai, Jagjivan Ram, Shanti Bhusan, H. M. Patel were against the dissolution of the state Assemblies, but the then Home Minister Charan Singh was adamant joined by H. N. Bahuguna and Biju Patnaik. Finally, Desai yielded to the pressure and the state Assemblies were dissolved. Elections were held in June 1977, and the Janata party was elected to power in seven states, UP, Bihar, Haryana, Odisha, MP, Rajasthan, and Himachal Pradesh. In Punjab, the party formed coalition with Akali Dal. In Tamil Nadu, AIADMK under M. G. Ramachandran was elected to power.

In September, 1979, Biju Patnaik ventured to accomplish a merger between the Dravida Munnetra Kazhagam (DMK) led by Karunanidhi and the Anna Dravida Munnetra Kazhagam (ADMK) led by M. G. Ramchandran, in the state of Tamil Nadu. He visited both the leaders, on 12th September, and persuaded them to merge, with the proposition that M. G. Ramchandran would continue to be the Chief Minister of Tamil Nadu, and Karunanidhi to become the head of the unified party. Anil Dhir quotes from the autobiography of Karunanidhi, titled, *Nenjukku Needhi,* and it was he who referred Biju Patanaik as *Uyarnta Manithan* (Tall Man). Biju Patnaik made the two great leaders agree to the merger during their talks at the Chepauk Guest House, where DMK General Secretary Prof. K Anbazhagan and AIADMK's Nedunchezhian and Panruti Ramachandran met in the sidelines. However, the merger that would have brought tremendous effect on Tamil Nadu politics could not transform into a reality, and it remained an unsuccessful attempt on the part of Biju Patnaik. The motive of Biju Patnaik to bring a merger between these two dominant parties was to cease the poll alliance between Congress and the DMK in the forthcoming elections to the Lok Sabha and Assembly. Pranab Mukherjee (2016; 16) writes that, in May-June 1980 elections, the Congress came to power in some states except Tamil Nadu, where the Congress–DMK alliance failed to dislodge the AIADMK from power.

Prime Minister Vajpayee, during the discussion on the Motion of Confidence, on 27th May 1996, alleged that he remembers the day when Biju Patnaik split the Janata Party and took Chaudhury Charan Singh to South Block, in July 1979. Biju Patnaik, however, retorted that he had burnt three letters In front of Choudhary Charan Singh and that he did not engineer any split in Janata Party. If what Vajpayee said is correct, then one can contemplate Biju Patnaik's influence and hold over the contemporary national political scene.

To the above allegation of Vajpayee, Nilamoni Routray, former Chief Minister of Odisha and former Union Environment and Forest Minister in V. P. Singh government, and a close associate of Biju Patnaik, has written in his autobiography, *Smruti O' Anubhuti* (1986; 716) that people did not vote the Janata (S) party in the 1980 Lok Sabha election as they knew about the deep internal conflict of the power-hungry leaders who broke the Janata party and the government. He writes that Biju Patnaik did not contemplate the dissatisfaction of the public for his and Rabi Ray's (the then Union Health Minister in Desai government) involvement in breaking the party and government, and forming Janata (S) party and government under the leadership of Chaudhury Charan Singh in July 1979. After the defeat of Janata (S) in the 1980 Odisha Assembly election under the leadership of Biju Patnaik, he realized the misnomer of his popularity. Further, Basanta Das (2017; 287) writes about the involvement of Rabi Ray in taking four Members of Lok Sabha and making them join in the break-away group of Janata (S) under Raj Narayan. Later, Biju Patnaik, George Fernandes, and H. N. Bahuguna also joined Janata (S), along with Charan Singh. He also had a good link with Karpoori Thakur of Bihar.

Sundarlal Patwa, addressing the Motion of Thanks on the President's address on 3rd March 1997 had said that Biju Patnaik made him the Chief Minister of Madhya Pradesh for the first time on 20th January 1980, in the

Janata party government. Patwa also said that at that time "Biju Patnaik was his leader, but he left us". Patwa remained as Chief Minister till 17th February 1980.

Biju Patnaik as Union Minister

Biju Patnaik had a desire to join the Nehru cabinet after the resignation of V. K. Krishna Menon as Defense Minister. However, with all accessibility to Prime Minister Nehru, this could not happen. Subsequently, after Nehru's death, Biju Patnaik gradually faded out in Congress politics under compelling circumstances, and thereafter it was not feasible for him to return to the Congress fold again. He then consolidated his base in the non-Congress politics with the culmination of the Janata party in 1977, and after the Lok Sabha election, Morarji Desai became the Prime Minister, and Biju Patnaik was made the Union Cabinet Minister for Steel and Mines in the Janata government. During this period, he overtly supported the Sanjay Gandhi's Maruti car project (Biswas, 1993). Biju Patnaik had a dream to make a second steel plant in Odisha, after the Rourkela Steel Plant. He had made demonstration before the then Prime Minister Indira Gandhi for the second steel plant in Odisha. Hence, the allocation of the Steel Ministry flared up his desire for the second steel plant, and he was looking for the opportune moment to grab it.

Biju Patnaik got the golden opportunity for his cherished desire to establish the second steel plant in Odisha when there was a proposal for a heavy steel industry to be set-up in Salem. He cleverly changed it to a small stainless steel manufacturing company and created the stage for setting-up the heavy steel industry at Paradip Port City. The justification behind the change to Paradip in Odisha was also a valid point, as the raw materials was available in Odisha and Bihar (now Jharkhand), and thus would considerably reduce the transportation cost thereby the price of the steel also. This proves the intelligence of this person and his dedication for the industrialization of his state of Odisha. Nilamoni Routray (1986; 678) cites a news-report, "Biju's Manipulation", in the communist newspaper *National Democracy* published from Bombay, of 4th October 1971, where it was reported that "Biju Patnaik through deft manipulation transferred the integrated special steel plant proposed for Salem into a simple stainless steel plant.... Mr. Patnaik was keen to make out a case for another steel plant for his home state of Orissa at Paradip". However, the second steel plant never became a reality as the subsequent Congress government shifted the site of the plant from Paradip to Daitari, and later it was shelved. He played an important role in taking forward the cause of the Vizag steel plant, the first shore-based one in India (Sahu, 2021). Whatever it may be, Biju Patnaik was the founder of the conceptualization of establishing *Port-based Steel Plant* (Routray, 1986; 680).

Nilamoni Routray (1986; 676-77) describes the role of Biju Patnaik as Steel Minister and his contribution for the industrial development of Odisha. The Crossbar Telephone Factory in Bhubaneswar was finalized to be set-up in Bhubaneswar and during the talks with the concerned Union Minister Shri Brijlal Verma, Biju Patanik always accompanied with the then Chief Minister of Odisha, Nilamoni Routray. However, after the fall of the Janata government, the same factory site was shifted to Rae Bareilly at the instance of Indira Gandhi. Biju Patnaik took active interest for the establishment of aluminum factory in Koraput district, as it was rich in bauxite deposits. Due to his initiative, the *Bharat Aluminum Company* (BALCO) made agreement with Alumina Pachinery French, for the establishment of a 1200 crore aluminum complex in Koraput district of Odisha in June 1979. However, the foundation stone of the factory was laid by Indira Gandhi after she became the Prime Minister in January 1980.

National Front Government 1989

In the 1989 Lok Sabha elections, the Janata Dal won 16 seats with their pre-poll alliance partners in Odisha, the CPI and CPM, won one each seats. The combined seat tally was 17 out of the 21 Lok Sabha seats from Odisha. However, at the national level, none of the major political parties could win enough seats to form the government. The Congress party under the leadership of Rajiv Gandhi was the single-largest party, but it refused to form the government. Now the onus to form the government at the Union level came to the pre-poll alliance partners named as National Front (NF) consisting of 13 parties, dominant being Janata Dal, which fought the election projecting V. P. Singh as an alternative to Rajiv Gandhi. However, Chandrasekhar was more interested to be the Prime Minister, and opposed V. P. Singh's candidature, if Devi Lal does not agree to be the consensus nominee. A compromise formula was adopted that was kept as secret. This was on 1 December 1989, when the events were chalked out at Odisha Bhawan in Chankyapuri, personally supervised by none other than Biju Patnaik, for the selection of the Parliamentary Party leader. At Odisha Bhawan, Biju Patnaik was waiting with V. P. Singh secretly, and Arun Nehru brings in Devi Lal. Together it was agreed to unfold the events that would become history. Devi Lal then invites Chandrasekhar to Odisha Bhawan. The Janata Dal finally convened its parliamentary board meeting at 3:15 p.m. on December 1 in Parliament's Central Hall to elect its leader and the next prime minister of India. The meeting was presided by Madhu Dandavate, and V.P. Singh proposed the name of Devi Lal to be the leader that was seconded by Chandrasekhar. Since there was no other name, Dandavate declared Devi Lal to be elected. Then Devi Lal thanked V. P. Singh, and expressing his inability said that the election result was really a fight against the corruption of the Rajiv Gandhi government and the leading warrior was V.P. Singh. Hence, I propose the name of V. P. Singh to be the leader that was immediately seconded by Ajit Singh. Singh was declared to be elected by Dandavate. Ajit Singh was earlier briefed over telephone by Arun Nehru. This was the dramatic turn of events and V. P. Singh was destined to be the Prime Minister. In the whole process Biju Patnaik earned the distinction of becoming 'King-Maker'. Though the government continued, but with the whole lot of leaders and parties, differences and conflicts were a recurrent feature, and Biju Patnaik was immediately relied upon to solve the tension within the National Front government, as he was the Chief Minister in Odisha and had no direct role in the Union government. His frequent role as solving the crisis in the National Front government from 1 December 1989 to 7 November 1990 earned him the acronym of PCM (Principal Crisis Manager). During this period, major political decisions were taken in *Odisha Bhawan*, where Biju Patnaik used to stay when he visited New Delhi.

The major conflict between the leaders occurred when Devi Lal the Deputy Prime Minister, declared to hold a mega farmers rally at Boat Club in New Delhi in August 1990. Prior to this announcement, there were differences between Devi Lal and V. P. Singh. Singh viewed the mega farmers rally as a direct threat to his leadership and in anticipation of any adverse step by Devi Lal, he announced the implementation of the recommendation of the Mandal Commission for 27% job reservation for 'other backward castes' on 7 August 1990. This decision was the turning point of the National Front government that finally led to withdrawal of support by the BJP to the NF government. Biju Patnaik, initially, did not support the Mandal Commission recommendation implementation, and was dissatisfied with the Prime Minister. He criticized the hastiness with which V. P. Singh acted. "Orissa, Chief Minister Biju Patnaik raised the first standard of revolt, angrily accusing the Prime Minister of inciting caste violence..... But when more than a dozen MPs from Orissa called on Singh and told him they were opposed to Biju's outburst, he sensed an incipient revolt in his own house, and within 24 hours had softened his own stand (Chawla, 1990). Saba Naqvi (1990) writes, "Chief Minister Biju Patnaik does not need V. P. Singh's help to create a vote bank. He has a clear majority in the Assembly, one reason why he has turned out to be the rare Janata Dal Chief Minister who has not merely decided against implementing the report but also come out publicly against caste-based reservations. In a letter to the thenPrime Minister, Biju Patnaik wrote that if the lot of backward classes has not improved despite reservations in the past so many years, they would be no better in next generations too". During a discussion in the Lok Sabha, Hon. Member K. P. Reddaiah Yadav from Machalipatnam, said "it is not a matter of fact whether Shri Biju Patnaik has negatived the proposal or Congress people have negatived the proposal.... If the Congress party or the Biju Patnaik government is mistaken about the consciousness that is created in the minds of the backward classes, I am sure they are going to eat their mud" (https://parliamentofindia.nic.in).

United Front Coalition 1996

After the resignation of the Prime Minister Vajpayee in 1996, United Front coalition of 13 parties formed the government with Devegowda as Prime Minister, supported by the Congress and the CPM from outside. As per Dilip Ray, former Union Minister and close associate of Biju Patnaik, in an interview to *Kanak* TV (Youtube.com), during the government formation talks, Biju Patnaik had proposed the name of Jyoti Basu to be the Prime Minister of the United Front government, and himself was interested in Defense Ministry. However, the CPM politburo was against joining the government, and due to a vigilance charge-sheet, Biju Patnaik's name was dropped from Ministry. According to Dilip Ray, the vigilance charge-sheet was a conspiracy by a leader of the Janata Dal in Odisha, and was facilitated by the then Congress Chief Minister of Odisha. Earlier, in 1962 also, Biju Patnaik was interested to be the Defense Minister after the resignation of Krishna Menon.

Ray also said that he had suggested Biju Patnaik to form a regional party and make alliance with BJP for electoral gains in Odisha, and that initial level talks had started with Atal Behari Vajpayee and L. K. Advani, mediated by Pramod Mahajan, just before his demise. To supplement it, during the *Motion of Thanks* on 3 March 1997 in Lok Sabha, Sundarlal Patwa referred an interview of Biju Patnaik in newsprint and *Home* TV where he "termed the United Front Government as a group ridden with infightings among its constituents. He has suggested that in case the Congress and the CPM join the Government, it will be delivering the goods in a better way". Hence, it is evident that Biju Patnaik was dissatisfied with the functioning of the United Front government, and with the Janata Dal party. This aversion and the version of Dilip Ray correlate very much. However, in his initial period in the Congress party, he favoured left-wing rather than the right-wing politics within the Congress party. He was more akin with the Socialist brand of politics of Ram Manohar Lohia, Jaya Prakash Narayan, and their young follower Madhu Limaye. At the party's annual session in Bhubaneswar, leftist spokesmen such as Menon, Bijoyananda Patnaik and K. D. Malaviya urged more nationalization in all sectors, while S. K. Patil and Morarji Desai for the right rejected it (Rudolph and Rudolph, 2008; 335-6).

Biju Patnaik was elected to the Odisha legislative Assembly and Lok Sabha and Rajya Sabha as per the details given below in tabular form. He was a Member of the Rajya Sabha for a short period from 13 May 1971 and resigned 6 October 1971.

Odisha Legislative Assembly

Sl.	Year	Constituency	Party	Position	Term
1	1946-52	Central Cuttack Sadar	Congress	Member	Pre-Period
2	1952-57	Jaganath Prasad	Congress	Member	1st
3	1957-61	Suruda	Congress	Member	2nd
4	1961-67	Choudwar	Congress	Chief Minister (till 1 Oct. 1963)	3rd
5	22/9/71-73	Rajnagar (bye-election)	Utkal Congress	Leader of Opposition (Feb-March 1973)	5th
6	1974-77	Rajnagar	Utkal Congress	Leader of Opposition	6th
7	1980-11/6/80	Patkura (Resigned)	Janata (S)		8th
8	1985-90	Bhubaneswar	Janata Dal	Leader of Opposition	9th
9	1990-95	Bhubaneswar	Janata Dal	Chief Minister	10th
10	1995-20/5/96	Bhubaneswar (Resigned)	Janata Dal	Leader of Opposition	11th

Source: https://odishaassembly.nic.in/memberprofile.aspx?img=379, 19.3.20223

Lok Sabha

Sl.	Year	Constituency	Party	Position	Term
1	1977-80	Kendrapara	Bharatiya Lok Dal	Minister	6th
2	1980-84	Kendrapara	Janata Party	Member	7th
3	1984-25.3.85 (Resigned)	Kendrapara	Janata Party	Member	8th
4	1996-17.4.97 (Expired)	Aska	Janata Dal	Member	9th
5	1996-97 (Resigned)	Cuttack	Janata Dal	Member	9th

Source: https://odishaassembly.nic.in/memberprofile.aspx?img=379, 19.3.2022

The following chapters discuss the discourses made by Biju Patnaik in the Lok Sabha, Rajya Sabha, and Odissha Vidhan Sabha. The speeches delivered by the late leader Biju Patnaik has been selected and mapped according to the relevance of the topic and has been placed accordingly. This can enable an interested reader to get the information on the views and opinions of Biju Patnaik on the specific topic instantly. Some of the subjects have been placed in the miscellaneous section as the frequency of the said topic is very less. While reading through the pages, one can easily grasp the phenomenal knowledge and wisdom the leader had on a wide range of subjects starting from international relations to grassroots level politics. He was a nationalist to the core and wanted to see the growth and development of his State of Odisha and the Odia people. While reading the pages, one can also realize how relevant his ideas and plans are even in the twenty-first century, and it also has a close resemblance to any Government that seriously contemplates for the developmental issues and causes. What best can describe the significance of the contributions of this legendary leader than to quote *The Economist* obituary that mentions, "Itis worth writing about Biju Patnaik for at least two reasons. His long life can be read as something of a history of India back to the time when the country was run by Britain. And he gave Indian politics a rare flash of colour" (www.theeconomist.com). "Bijubabu remains a uniquely mixed bag of impulses: peacemaker, stormy petrel, patriarch, pioneering entrepreneur, Nehruvian socialist. Through it all survives the passion for his state" (Biswas, 1993).

2

Political Issues

The discourse on the political issues forms the crux of the subject matter and varies from the freedom struggle, nation-building, democracy, to political party, role of opposition, etc. It also contains his views and opinions on the Panchayati Raj institution, a subject very dear to him, and for which he was really committed, as it involves peoples' participation in the administrative and governance process. The political issue that Biju Patnaik is deliberating in the Houses is really not simple discourses, but his sentiments and emotions that is echoing from his heart. There is no pretension is what he says or desires to achieve. His speech is always unidirectional from the beginning of his political career upto the end. A leader with real dedication and commitment who understood the pulse of the people and who himself had a thorough understanding of the international politics and world leaders.

Freedom Struggle

During the Budget discussion of February 1960, he reminded about the situation during freedom struggle and said, "Sir, permit me to get you back to the year 1942, when this country was in the throes of a great struggle of liberation when a great leader of the moment, like Mahatma Gandhi made millions of men, out of clay, few heroes and through the assistance of millions of men, thousands of whom faced bullets and guillotines and millions of whom were prepared to go to prisons and sink in jails and got this country its much cherished independence. That was an age of sacrifice. That was an age of emotion when nothing mattered. That was an age when fanatics cropped up from the paddy fields and from the various cities. Yet, at that time also in this country a large section of people who were oblivious to the country's momentous requirement and who were pursuing their own avocation, whatever it may be, were totally detached from the country's requirement and its ambition at that time. At that time we used to dream of a brave new India that we are going to have and that we have got today. Year after year, we dreamt of a land flowing with milk and honey, which was stopped only by the Britishers. That was reason for our fight. We were a revolutionary party. At that time only one wing of our party which was away from us originally, i.e. the Communist party took a different view and supported their parent organization. We, in the Congress, were at that time a purely revolutionary party. It is true that they did not take part in this movement and nobody, no one than the Congress party was keenly aware of the fact that there were 600 and odd Rulers in this country who gave their fullest, individual and collective support to the British Government. Sir, I am forcing this point only to counteract the view forcefully expressed by my previous speaker, the Hon'ble friend from Nimapara, when he went on attacking the Rulers of this State who happened to have joined the coalition party. No one than the Congress party is more aware of the part the Rulers played. The Congress party is made of big men, only powerful men and not of small men that exist in the Communist party today, who even do not know their own minds. From day-to-day they betray the country in days of great insecurity and of national emergency. I should not take any cognizance of the views expressed by the Communist party because I take it that none else than the Congress party brought this independence, and it is on the basis of our judgment. We had, in fact some Rulers who supported us in our struggles and who have come and joined the Government in the State, the Government of the country; and think alike other citizens in this State and in the country and who have a right to prove that they can also be of great service to the millions. As I said before, we dreamt of a brave new world when we were a revolutionary party then. In our over-enthusiasm, without knowledge, without fair knowledge of economic theories, without fair perception of administrative efficiency, we at that time rightfully thought that all the ills of India rested with the British administration. We promised the people of our land, land of millions, that we would face bullets, sacrifice ourselves in the jails for achieving independence. You would appreciate, we really faced bullets, and we could do it because that amount of enthusiasm was in us to justify the hope with which the people were looking forward to us. We really believed in what we did. As the time went on we tried to be Ministers of country in the Centre as well as in the States. We came across walls after walls of ignorance, walls of inefficiency, walls of lack of patriotism, and so on so forth. It took time, months and years, to demolish them and before they are demolished, more walls sprang up in those places. We as Congress party are wedded to democracy and if we dare just to speak in this House, there is only one definition of democracy which says that, 'I in the name of God may not believe what you say, but I shall lay down my life holding it up and to save it'. Having given a social Constitutional democracy, we allowed the whole country to go ahead without any fear complex. But today, Sir, after 14 years of Government, we still find, whether we are in the Treasury Benches or in Opposition that we have not yet developed a clear economic thinking. Things jumble up and we have in our midst conservative thought, monopolistic thinking, feudal minds and extremist thought. We have in our party fluctuating minds inside us. Therefore, we cannot forge ahead with clear economic independence. Sir, lately the Congress party has determined that finally the Congress party shall emerge as a Socialist party based on socialistic economic theories. It is now the article of faith of the Congress party and when my Hon'ble friend from Nimapara talked about the coalition Ministry, let me remind him that when the leader of the *Ganatantra Parishad* joined the Congress, it was on the basis that he shall carry on the directive socialistic policy of the Congress party. So, Sir, now we have to come to a stage where in this House within the scope of our budget, we have to analyse how to practice this socialistic pattern of society (*OLA Debates*, Vol. IV (5), 23.2.60; 20-2).

He said, "Nearly 40 years ago from today, when we were released from jail-at that time we were under arrest. In Cuttack, we were not allowed to go out 30 miles radius. We were in jails for three years from 1942 to 1945. During that time, within 30 miles there were two places in Cuttack and one was Choudwar. I was thinking that there was necessity to start some industry there; our people are working outside, etc. To give employment to people and to increase their productive power, we emphasized on labour-intensive and less on capital-intensive, excepting for key industries, heavy industries for which industries started. When I started, at that time, Mahatma Gandhi issued a statement that this is not correct, only to make clothes using handloom and spinning wheel. At that time Birla was given three licenses to set-up three industries in Odisha. I remember at that time Mahtab Babu was the Chief Minister, and he said that Birla can do their industries. We said it cannot be done. Under our pressure, Birla had to close down. Birla had the license of Kalinga Airlines since long. He told me to take the air license and to give textiles to him. I said, I will run both the Kalinga Airlines and the textiles. I will not handover anything to you, even though, I will press the Government for taking it over, but I would like to bring to your notice that we had approximately seven thousand employees. I will only request that taking and then retrenching the labourers will deliver no result. It is our duty and also the duty of the State that the objectives should not only run the industry but also to provide jobs to all and to expand it also. Hence, I would request that as all Members have approveed this Ordinance to take-over Odisha Textile Mill by Government and to regularize it. They have also point-out that those who have lost their jobs, what will happen to them. When State management has come in, then there should be more investment, what is the problem? The Government should consider it" (*OLA Debates* Vol. I(6), 21.3.1985; 17).

Speaking on the days of freedom struggles during the Obituary Reference to Dr. H. K. Mahtab, he said, "Dr. H. K. Mahtab, a great son of India has passed away and many things have been told about him. He is practically the maker of the Modern Odisha with assimilation of all the

States and various other developmental activities which have been written about and spoken about him. I was very intimately known to him as early as 1945, when he came out of Jail after three years. I was doing the underground movement along with Jayaprakash Narayan and Ram Manohar Lohia. Dr. Mahtab and Mr. N. K. Choudhury, in April 1945, came secretly to have a meeting with me in the upstairs of my Cuttack house. You know why. Sir, the thinking still was that the British would not leave us; we may have to go through a battle with British people, so we may have to gather guns and ammunitions, to fight the British force. After discussion we came to a conclusion, as suggested by Dr. Mahtab, that we must create an underground go-down where all these guns and ammunitions could be stored. So we thought of how to give coverage to it and that is how the idea of a Textile Mill came into being and a Company in the name of Orissa Textile Mill Ltd was formed where Dr. Mahtab, Mr. N. K. Choudhury and myself were associated. That was the beginning of the Orissa Textile Mills. But wheels of fate moved differently. By September, I took Dr. Mahtab with me in my private aeroplane from Bhubaneswar to Delhi and he stayed with me in my house at Delhi. There we talked to the Secretary to the Chancellor of Exchequer Mr. Blake, he was in the Air-Force-we had become very friendly during the Second World War. Dr. Mahtab and myself then stayed at Delhi to have our own secret deal. Subsequently, I invited all of them to *Roshaman's Club*. It is still written in the club book about the visit of these personalities in 1945. You may recollect that Mr. Wavell, who was then the Governor-General, announced Mr. Mahtab's name as a member in the interim Cabinet. These are the things which are unknown to many people. When it was mentioned to Panditji, he called me and I met him in the house of Asaf Ali and he asked me how I knew Mr. Cripps. I told him how I knew him through his Secretary, a friend of mine. That is quite interesting, Panditji told me, you tell Mahtab that he should go back to Odisha and become Chief Minister. So I flew to Odisha with Dr. Mahtab and he became the Chief Minister. This is how he became the first Chief Minister of Odisha after independence. He is my political *Guru*, till his death, he fought for the right of the man" (V (1), 23.2.1987; 15).

Recalling his past involvement during the freedom struggle and British India, he said, "We had to fight for the nation's independence. We suffered for it; our family suffered for it. One of my brothers was shot dead by the British and a young boy of 14 years was sent to *Kalapani* for 16 years. I was put for 3 years in jail. We had some hopes, some dreams when we spent days and years in British jail that someday the nation will become free because that day nobody was thinking that the nation will be free. Much later came Cripps Mission. I was well acquainted with Sir Stafford Cripps and I had a pleasure to invite Sir Stafford to my club at Delhi way back in 1945, exactly 50 years ago. I went to him; he was staying in the President

Bhawan at that time one wing was given to them. I was invited there. I remember that there was a map, India map hanging around with all great pieces of Rajas and Maharajas. Sir Stafford and James Corner came from London from the White Hall. As a young man, a flying man I spent 3 years in British prison. Sir Stafford through his Secretary Bakr, who was with me in Air Force asked me, well my boy what kind of India do you want? 600 pieces of India were there, I said, no, the whole lot, the entire lot of India should be ours and that should be the India. The Britishers laughed. This story I told you remember a man like Biju Patnaik has an experience of his stories who wins and losses, somewhere some seats were won, Government was made on earth, matters of minor significance" (*OLA Debates*, Vol. II (22), 27.7.1995; 175).

Biju Patnaik during the *Motion of Thanks to President's address* in Lok Sabha on 3rd March 1997, had replied to Sundar Lal Patwa on the reference to Kashmir issue by saying that you talk of nationalism, but do you know what nationalism is? He said, "When Vajpayee ji went out after making his submissions, did anybody say anything at that time...(Interruptions). We are fighting for Kashmir for the last fifty years and you people say that you will not claim Kashmir. Thousands of our people have sacrificed their lives during the last fifty years for Kashmir. He said to accept the Line of Actual Control. What is the problem with you..... In 1947 I flew down in a plane. None of you came. I contained the Pakistan Army there. You are continuously discussing the Kashmir issue. You are trying to make it an issue of Hinduism. Please talk about the country and not Hinduism". This was his view on the Kashmir issue *vis-à-vis* the BJP's stand, in the perspective of nationalism and Hinduism.

Nation-Building

On the dream of building the nation, Biju Patnaik said, "When we made our country independent, we fought with the Britishers, both inside and outside mixing with Subash Bose. No one told us to make independence. Lakhs of youth participated, army participated, air-force participated, Subash Bose participated in foreign. Independence was achieved with everybody's participation. We have seen many youths were hanged and shot. I am sitting here today as the Chief Minister, then I was sitting with chains in hands and feet- Thousand days and thousand nights. I was dreaming of a brave new India where there will be no pain, no sorrow for anyone. When the country became independent, one Constitution and rules accordingly was required, otherwise how will the country run? The country has now run for years. We constructed a Government structure according to the 1935 colonial Act. IAS was made in place of ICS. That structure remained. Because of the Administration, there was no change, but we thought that we did the right! Since a new country came in with the amalgamation of

525 Princely States, we thought of making a structure, that will be Central Authority, which we called later as Union Government. Hence, Central Authority was made, but the Constitution framers had it in mind that India should be a Federal country or Federal State or Federation of States. For this, Art. 1 states, 'India is a *Union of States*'. But it was thought it will be a *Federation of States*, which I mention in-between. Instead of calling India as *Union of States*, we should call it *United States of India*. It connotes the same idea" (*OLA Debates*, Vol. V (8), 20.9.1991; 193).

On the nation-building, he said, "When we swear in the name of the Constitution for oath taking as MLA or MP, but in the mean time the Constitution has got 73 amendments. There was nothing sacrosanct. The Constitution provides the way of life, and we should examine that way of life. The Constitution has been made for the last 40-45 years, and many things have happened since then. Pakistan has been separated, Bangladesh has been separated, and whatever left from the pieces is called as Bharat by us. During the last few years certain fissiparous tendencies are seen.... Because our Constitution has undergone several changes according to the needs of the time and the policy that is needed to be changed from time to time. We are changing it in every field" (*OLA Debates*, Vol. V (8), 20.9.1991; 194).

Showing the diminishing quantity of land due to development, he said, "Your population is growing. Take the case of land. Everything that you build on land reduces the cultivable land. You build a road, you cut on the land. You build a factory, you build a city, you cut the land. So the land is decreasing and the population is increasing. Therefore, we have to make that land more productive so that industries, more fertilizer plants, more of this and more of that and you put more on the cultivator. So all these are problems. We, who are sitting on the mountains of iron-ore, we have special duty to perform for the nation and for us also" (*OLA Debates*, Vol. X(7), 26.2.1993; 117).

On the people's movement, he said, "Merely by armed forces you cannot suppress the movement and recommend that we shall be a separate country. Russia is the example which is only relevant to that extent, nothing else. Yugoslovakia division is to that extent nothing else. Different ethnic people clubbed and counter clubbed into one or the other arrangement by victory and formed the federal nation. These are all the histories of last few years. If Lithuania, the northern Baltic State, merged with Russia at that time, they have arranged for federal nation and so on and so forth. These are the histories of the last 50 years. But in our case, already we have division of India. Do we want further divisions? The answer is no. This needs careful thinking" (*OLA Debates*, Vol. V (8), 20.9.1991; 195).

On the question of nation, he said, "Are we a nation? I charge this idea to the thinking of people of India that we have ceased to be a nation. Just waving a flag does not make a nation. Is is the will of the people that makes a nation.

Where is that will? We have lost all sense of will and therefore, we have lost all sense of direction. How proud India would be or could be if with all its brain power it can develop all the machines today that we have to import from Europe, America, or Japan? One little rocket which our Engineers have developed, i.e. *Pruthvi* or *Agni*, or whatever you call it, a medium distance rocket is eulogized by everybody that a wonderful thing has been done by India. We import Aeroplanes and we ride them. We import oil because they are used in the cars, vehicles and trucks. When I was made a Chairman of the Committee for Reducing Costs, I said, reduction in cost can only be done by a nation, and I told the Prime Minister, you the Prime Minister of India or the President of India or a Governor or the Chief Ministers or the Speaker, MLAs, MPS, live in a style, in a manner which is totally foreign to our State. When Gandhiji said a Minister cab serve the people with ₹500 a month, when Gandhiji said the Presidential Palace should be converted into a children's park, he was correct. Then I asked Panditji, why you live in this palatial house? You are alone. Why do not you live in a single room within the periphery? He agreed that is a good idea. He asked the Chief Engineer to draw a plan and by the time the Chief Engineer did the plan, the value of the building came to ₹2 crores at that time. He must see visitors, he must see VIPs, all that and all this and the place became as big as the British Commander-in-Chief's house. We lost Gandiji and along with Gandhiji, we lost directions. That is why this petty World Bank, IMF, dictates us. All these countries that has become rich, they so managed without any troubles to themselves that this country became poor. When we started with a population of 300 millions and now India has 900 millions, which country can survive with such a huge population" (*OLA Debates*, Vol. XIV (6), 2.3.1994; 98).

He further said, "The whole thing is collectively the nation from 1947 till date has started declining. As the hon. Member from Brajarajnagar tried to put it. I do not think he explained it adequately. I got his idea. It is declining because the nation has lost its courage. Courage to stand, courage to fight this, courage to hold up this view. That's why Sir, I always say to the people, wherever I go, I am Kalinga, not Odisha, I am Kalinga. Kalinga is *sahasik* (Brave). Kalinga is *sahasikata* (Bravery)" (*OLA Debates*, Vol. XIV (6), 2.3.1994; 98-9).

On the then present situation of India, he said, "Now, after 45 years. What did we miss? We have missed one great thing in this nation that we have no pride in ourselves. We no longer could be proud of our independence. That we can sing *Jana gana mana*; go in march-past with splendor on the Republic Day parade. That we have lost one great value-the Human value, and for that we are no longer proud of ourselves. This is what Gandhiji tried to teach us. He has said one thing, whatever you do-yes, do it, but whatever you buy from outside, you provide jobs, works for them and ultimately you keep your own people in hunger and unemployment.

This is exactly what is happening to this country today" (*OLA Debates*, Vol. XIII (3), 24.12.93; 103).

Expressing concern for the country, in the obituary reference to Khan Abdul Gaffar Khan, he said, "I would like to add that Khan Abdul Gaffar Khan, termed himself as *KhudaiKhidmadgar*, meaning 'servants of God', *Khudai* means 'belonging to God' and *Khidmadgar* means 'servant'. Not only was he a great stalwart who fought for national independence, but in later years, after Gandhiji died, he had come to India often and had expressed, at various places, his great anguish in the manner in which India was shaping. He was shocked over the internal strives based caste, religion, etc. He often said that this was not what Gandhiji dreamt of India. He had never accepted the division of India and till the end of his life, as much as he could, resisted the forming of Pakistan by the then imperialists who were ruling our country. Sir, on his death I would say, the freedom movement of India has lost one of its greatest son" (VII (!), 24.2.1988; 12).

On the allegation of Biju Patnaik misusing Governor's House in Tamil Nadu, he clarified and said, "They said that I had misused the Governor's House in Madras for discussing party matters. Wherefrom he (Government Chief Whip) got that information, I do not know. Why not you send for the records from the Governor's House, Madras as to how many times I visited and for what purpose? Let me for enlightening this House, tell this, I visited the Governor's House in Madras only on three occasions. The first occasion was to utilize a wing of that Governor House for holding a committee meeting called *National Integration Committee's* meeting of which I happened to be a Member. This Committee was appointed by Prime Minister Jawaharlal Nehru with 7 Members. For his education, I may tell him that the other Members were, Mr. Kamraj, Chief Minister of Madras, Mr. Chavan, Chief Minister of Maharashtra, Mr. Bimal Chaliha, Chief Minister of United Assam, our Deputy Chairman of Planning Commission, Mr. Ashok Mehta, and one other Member. We held a committee meeting there to assess the opinions of eminent persons like Shri C. Rajgopalchari among others. We were holding examinations of these great personages as to how the nation has to be integrated. The second time was when I went to meet one eminent national leader like Mr. Acharya Kripalini because he was not well and he wanted to see me for some reason or other. And the third time was when we discussed this matter between two eminent persons, the existing Chief Minister of Tamil Nadu Mr. M. G. Ramachandran and Mr. Karunanidhi, who was Leader of Opposition. But in this case, it is a sad thing that the Governor of Odisha permitted his residence which is sanctified because he is supposed to be neutral, but he allowed the Congress Party to use it as it'sbattle-ground. This is what I objected to" (V (2), 24.2.1987; 75-6).

Speaking on the Obituary Reference of Dr. Rajendra Prasad, Former President of India, he said, "In Rajen Babu's passing away we have lost a pearl amongst men and these words were used by no less a person than the Father of the Nation while describing Rajen Babu. He was indeed a pearl amongst men; a man of great character, of great learning, of great devotion to duty and a relentless fighter for the cause of India's freedom and progress. During his student career he was known to be a person who always stood first, while the Universities in his time comprised of four States of Bengal. Bihar, Odisha, and Assam. While he was going to be appointed as a Judge of the High Court, he spurned it under the British rule and preferred to join Gandhiji and the Congress as simple volunteer and worker. Such was the character of the man even from earlier days. He was a pearl amongst men because millions of men respected him, respected his integrity, his feeling for the down-trodden and the poor. The House would be surprised to know that when the Bihar earthquake took place in 1934, Rajen Babu's relief fund far exceeded the Viceroy's relief fund. He was the first President of the Republic of India and he fulfilled his task as the first President for long years with distinction and dignity. Earlier as a Member of the Constituent Assembly and one of the architects of the Constitution, he ushered into the country a Constitution which gave us democracy, which gave us freedom of thought and action, which made us all free to work as we like, to think as we like. Yet today the duties incumbent on us by the society and of the requirements of our motherland-he created in us while he was the President of India and that Constitution of India became the tradition of India. He brought light to the entire life and functions of Indian society; a man of great tolerance, he tried to explain to the people how to solve disputes; as a great disciple of Gandhiji his entire life has been a life of renunciation. Such men are rare and when such men pass away it leaves a great void in the public life of a country" (*OLA Debates*, Vol. IV (4), 1.3.1963; 22).

Democracy and Democratic Principles

Speaking on the Congress party and its contribution to promoting the democratic principles, he said, "The Congress has a background and a history of which not only we are proud of but I would go a little further and say that the Members of the Opposition parties will be proud to belong to that party. They should not forget the fact that Congress has bestowed the privilege, has produced that sense of democracy in this country which says, 'I may not agree with what you say, but I will certainly lay down my life to uphold your right to say'. Therefore, it does not behave the Members of the Opposition more especially the leaders of the Opposition parties who have never lifted their little finger to bring about democracy in the country to talk about this party, the Congress party, which is the greatest Democratic Party in the world" (*OLA Debates*, Vol. II (8), Part II, 26.3.58; 26-7).

On democracy, he said, "I am proud that democracy is functioning in our different States in a manner that when urgency comes the Opposition parties and the Government party function together and they become one party. The consideration was to look to the best interest of the two parties, the interest of the entire nation and in keeping this interest in view the decision was arrived at in a manner that there is happiness in Andhra Pradesh and there is happiness in Odisha which means justice has been done to both" (*OLA Debates*, Vol. III (11), 5.9.62; 48).

On democracy and the accusations of the Opposition party Members of destroying it, he said, "The Leaders of the Opposition groups after their extraordinarily violent speeches-not always in the best tradition of parliamentary democracy or the prestige of the House-have always wound up their speeches with a plain note that democracy must be saved, Opposition may be allowed to flourish, that Congress party must take upon itself the task of nourishing, supporting and creating an opposition for the purpose of maintenance of democracy. The Hon'ble Member from Khunta said that at the end of his speech, the Member of the Communist party, ultimately even the Opposition Members who have claimed some independence and the main opposition group-Swatantra, all quoted the same not a request, an urgent request to the Congress party that please do not destroy the Opposition and thus eliminate the democracy. I can assure the Hon'ble Members of the Opposition that it is farthest from our thoughts that opposition should be demolished. While we prepared the Constitution for India, we declared to make it a democratic one. The Constitution of India is primarily, if not entirely, a creation and construction of the Indian National Congress. We not only provided for a democracy with opposition, but with a pious hope there would come a time in this country when there would be a combined opposition on certain basic economic theories and such opposition should at one time and from time to time be able to take over the governance of the country. Today's greatest danger to democracy is not the Congress party. The greatest danger to India's democracy is the total absence of Opposition. There are few Members here and there is different forms and in different groups and a few stray independents. I do not know for what reason they come to this House, because they represent nothing, they project nothing, they believe in nothing, they do not sustain democratic thought or democratic procesa...." (*OLA Debates*, Vol. V (13), 18.9.63; 38-9). To this Hon'ble Member Harihar Patel objected by saying, "This remark is derogatory to the Hon'ble Members. On a *point of order*, Sir. Can you say why the Members come to this House"? To this Biju Patnaik said, "It is not a *point of order*. I only wish that the Hon'ble Member should not disturb my thought because it may lead to volleys of reaction. I am trying my best to be polite. Now, as I said, Sir, it is the Congress party which brought out democracy in this country and after independence gave this nation a Constitution on democratic principles. It hardly lies in the mouth of Hon'ble Members from the Opposition to say that we are not democratic.

It sounds like a whine the Hon'ble Members from Sundargarh says that the Congress is trying to destroy the democracy. It is like the whimpering agents who not being sure of their own position, not being sure of the status which has been provided to them by the Congress, begin to attack the hand that feeds them, begin to bite the hand that gives them food. Now who has given them the food for democracy? It is the Congress. Who are the Members of the Opposition that are sitting today in the Opposition Benches? They are the out-come of democratic thought process given to them by the Indian National Congress. It is these gentlemen who are here for us today as the preachers of democracy. It does not lie in the mouth of one section of the House to say to another section *thou hath destroyed democracy in the country*. (*Interruption*) The group leaders of the Opposition parties have, as I said, claimed the right to exist as opposition. They said it was necessary in a democracy to avoid growth of tyranny, to correct despotic tendency. I expect that these are the tenets of democracy that we have assigned in our Constitution. But never for a moment, Sir, I can assure you, when the Members of the Constituent Assembly framed this Constitution could have portrayed even in the darkest thoughts a type of opposition that we see today before us. These are the groups completely divested from any combined thought process of a nation, little mushrooms creating and nursing themselves for their own conveniences with no patterns of thought for the growth of a people. They are few groups and individuals who have gathered together with the sole purpose of loading abuses on individuals and the Congress party, a few groups who have no other purpose in life, who have no other purpose for survival excepting to abuse. When Members of these groups, the leaders of these groups, claim the right to exist as an Opposition. I would say it was not the intention of the Constitution makers that when Opposition is allowed to live, an assembly of a group of unidentified people would call themselves as opposition. Therefore, such are the credentials of this Opposition that at all times they quote only the Congress leaders, only the tenets of the Congress, the declarations of the Congress and the resolutions of the Congress. The Hon'ble Member from Bhadrak says something about our leaders. He himself in his speech, I understand has declared that he is the *dhol-pita* (beating drums) of the Congress party. He said, *my business is dhol-pita against the Congress*. Yet, he says that he talks lightly and in a disparaging manner about our leaders, whereas he also extols some Congress leaders. He says that this Government is against what he calls as *Mahtab Gosthi* (Mahtab group). It is the figment of their imaginations. We have our difference of opinion because we are a democratic party not only in words but also in practice. We may have violent difference of opinion. That is our business, because we have not only given democracy to the nation but we are also a democratic party. It must always be remembered that whatever be our quarrels, that is a quarrel of a democratic party. Congress is a voluntary body and an association of people who formulate ideas, who create revolutions and who create Governments. When it becomes necessary, they have the capacity to destroy the Government. But they always remain a democratic party. There are differences, there are quarrels, but ultimately, they are always settled democratically inside the party. There are no groups. Therefore, this fond desire of the Members of the Opposition parties that by mentioning this name or that name of the Congress-not of themselves because they have no leaders, they may sow some seeds of discord is rather prone to dismal failure as it always has been. Let me assure them. This Opposition in the House claims the right to exist. I say they have the right of existence provided they are a responsible Opposition, provided they develop into a responsible Opposition, capable of taking over and running the administration. Now, how does one judge that capacity of taking over and running a Government? One judges it from its leading Members, from their speeches, from their conduct, from their assessment of a States future-a people's requirements, focusing budgetary attentions on the Government and from the varieties of facts. From all these, people judge the Members, judge their parties, judge the capacity of the Opposition parties" (*OLA Debates*, Vol. V (13), 18.9.63; 38-41).

On the democratic functioning of the House and Opposition conduct in it, regarding the convention and conduct of the Members of the House, he said, "Debates can be of violent nature when vital issues are concerned, when we in this House-members of different parties, different groups having different convictions, different economic convictions, social convictions, frame our policies. Therefore, it is natural that when a House starts a debate on issues which are vitally opposed to each other, the debates and the tempo of discussions can be somewhat of violent nature, but that does not mark any interruption. What I wish to bring to your notice, Sir, is that violence in discussions, violently expressing views, does not mark a healthy tradition of a debate. What spoil the whole thing is personal attacks and counter attacks. What spoils the whole thing is continuous day-in and day-out accusing an individual Minister on various things. What is required is constructive approach and trying and framing issues and debating on that and assisting Government in a manner so that Government is forced to change its policy. Mere personal attack and continuously doing so would naturally close the mind of the Government. It will not receive anything, it will not change. That is not the purpose of democracy. In democracy, parties in Opposition, through their intelligent suggestions, through their sharpened attack can change the policy of Government. If the Government of the majority closes its mind finally and makes up its own mind to attack Opposition irrelevantly and irresponsibly though isis not worth consideration. I can assure you, Sir, this House will be turned into a House of tyranny of majority. Therefore, in democracy when opinions are sought, opinions are valued, opinions are accepted and policies are changed by virtue or by logic of opinions, it becomes the bounden duty of the Opposition who feel themselves, for the party and for the House. I do not propose to lay down any law or principle or code for the Members of the Opposition because they are intelligent enough, capable enough, to evolve their own course for the same purpose and for the purpose of tradition. Sir, I must admit, as indeed any one would admit, we have vast improvements to make in every facet. I can assure the Members of the House that it cannot be the business of only the Government to do so. It is in the field of good administration, intelligent support of the Opposition becomes an essential factor. It must be a support of honest criticism; it must be a support of guiding Government, based in facts. It must be a type of support which, while disagreeing with Government must demand respect from Government. By this kind of criticism, they can defy Government, they can control Government, and they can force Government to change its policy, however small they may be. It is a question of clash of intelligence, over-powering by superiority.... So, if the Opposition wishes to get results, they have to become psychologists, they have to treat individuals in the Government or in the Treasury Benches, according to the capacity of taking or giving it back. If they wish to get results, they should do to the reverse of what they are doing now. Therefore, as I said originally, there should be convention, there should be tradition, in the House and we have to frame our own code of conduct. I have no doubt, Sir, that we will get glorious things" (*OLA Debates*, Vol. V (18), 25.9.1963; 32-5). Furthering on the role of the Opposition, he said, "The Opposition should and must always stand their ground. They must under no circumstances, give in. If they give in under any pretext, they will fail in their duty as Opposition. Therefore, Sir, I must admit before I close my speech, that I have a very great liking for the Opposition. If the Opposition were not there, whom shall I call? If the Opposition were not there would have no fun, if the Opposition were not there, whom I could deal and destroy. Therefore, Sir, I adore them. I hope that, in retrospect, they will not love us too much, but love us a little. I would now request that in the process of democracy, in the process of give and take, in the process of crossing of swords and rapiers, we also carry on the business of the House" (*OLA Debates*, Vol. V (18), 25.9.1963; 35).

On a Resolution for setting up Ombudsman, delegated legislation, he said, "I am grateful to the Hon'ble Member from Sundargarh to have brought up this Resolution to the House which invokes the basic and fundamental thoughts. From the time human society was constructed, men and women tried to frame rules to maintain their society. Through the evolution of men in different countries, different rules have been framed and when the society changes, the rules change. It always falls on the men who think and who administer, the responsibility of watching over these rules ensuring their implementation and modifications wherever necessary. Different institutional growths also fall in this category. It is always said, commonly said, that people get the Government they deserve or it also can be said that people develop institutions that they deserve. Will these institutions, mentioned by the Hon'ble Member from Sundargarh have reached a certain level of operational efficiency and national dignity in these countries? It will be interesting for the Hon'ble Members to know in effect how it functions even in these highly developed countries like Sweden, where the national consciousness has been stupendous, where individual consciousness is of very high caliber, where technology surpasses and social security is highest in the world. Even there, you will be surprised to know, Sir, out of about a thousand complaints received by this institution, Ombudsman, in 1959, out of these thousand complaints 803 warranted no action, even in a place like Sweden. Here we are in the framework of a social structure at a more considerably different level than that of Sweden. You may call it lower level or higher level but apart from using comparative words of that nature, I would say we are on a different level. Our individual consciousness of our own rights and responsibilities very low indeed because individual consciousness needs a historical growth. In our country we have just got out from slavery of foreign yoke. We have not yet got out of slavery from various systems like feudal system, caste system, both religious and irreligious, which in practice tried all the time the exploitation of man by man at different ladders of the society. If you have to practice these institutions of Ombudsman, it is not only in terms of administration of justice to be given to the people but also social justice to be given to the people different ladders of the society that still exists in terms of caste, se and various things. We are having separate judiciary. In Sweden, the judiciary also comes in the orbit of the executive. We have in our Constitution tried to provide safeguard at the top. We have provided Parliament. We provided independent judiciary under the Constitution. We provide the third ladder-Audit of Accounts under the Constitution. So new have three tiers; the first one is the Parliament, which gives the Government; the second is judiciary which is protected by the Constitution and the third is Auditor-General of India and Accountant-General in the States, which are again protected by the Constitution. These are ideal institutions. We are functioning under these idealistic conditions. Now what we sought to achieve in the Indian society? In framing this Constitution, we want to get requirements of a socialistic structure that India wanted to live in. It declared that India should be governed by rule of law. It declared that its Government should be of representatives of the people. It declared that the expenditure of Government and accounts must be checked and audited by independent body. It also declared that Government can also be tried like individual citizens in the court of law. Such were the safeguards that the Indian

Constitution tried to give to the Indian citizens. We operate under these Constitutional limitations and Constitutional safeguards and Constitutional checks and balances. But we know, each one of us knows-whether in the Government, whether in the Opposition, whether in the Administration or whether outside the orbit of these three-we all know that our society is not a perfect society. What we sought to achieve through our Constitution, we have not only achieved but a long way from it. We know, executive makes serious errors and blunders at all levels. We have separated judiciary, but we also know, just because we have a separate judiciary, all the functions of the judiciary have not certainly become flawless. We have a separate Auditor-General and Accountant-General; how much do we know how efficiently they carry out their duties. These are the doubts that must come upon us when we, in Houses like this, consider and consider seriously how to reframe our rules and laws and what kind of society we want to create or recreate or reconstruct. When we delve into these deep roots of social structure, naturally thoughts of millennium ideal society, a society where every man can live outside the scope of oppression from any quarter arise in our minds. We hopefully want some kind of apparatus which would do the maximum good to society, some kind of apparatus which would ensure social justice to the little man. In projecting the same thought, we have to make the little man conscious; how to make the little man appear proud of his labour; if we give him the knowledge of urban research, how do we give him the sense of responsibility that he is also somebody in the whole structure of the society, whole structure of administration and whole structure of the development of society? Out of our attempts to reach that kind of mind, the reframing of the little man's mind, was born the great idea of Panchayati Raj. Some structure was given to this Panchayati Raj; rules and laws were framed; a skeleton was prepared. How to administer it? But we as nascent free people who have not the convention of freedom for centuries, who still live and work under many psychological handicaps, we have a habit of thinking that the moment we pass an Act, the society has undergone a change; we have a habit of assuring ourselves, quite mistakenly, that the moment we have debated a problem here, that problem is no longer there and all of us in this House, from which you have given yourself the Government, they too, coming out of the same class of mind, may think, and again quite mistakenly, that the moment they pass an order on the file, the whole thing is implemented in the field. We all know how mistaken these notions are and those notions are indeed the outcome of our immature mind, both in the Legislation and in implementation, which together is called administration; which reflects in other fields of administration like the judiciary, like the audit, like the Parliament and all other fields of activity and in every instrument of society that we now-a-days have prepared to govern ourselves. Therefore, there is no millennium to social evils; there is no readymade apparatus which would overnight remove the causes of these evils. But we must constantly try to evolve such apparatus which would indeed put a definite curb against our weaknesses, against our attitude of becoming little dictators and at the same time would curb also all irresponsible thinking. I do believe, and I have seen in the last 16 years in this Assembly, that steadily we are proceeding towards greater responsible thinking although at times we fly at each other's throat which must happen in human affairs; we have also developed an undercurrent of responsible debates of pin-pointing issues which affect the lives of men. We also in this State have undergone various pressures-all kinds of pressures, democratic pressures, undemocratic pressures, dictatorial pressures, economic pressures, pressures of technology-all kinds of pressures we have seen and gone through during the last 16 years in our State and through the apparatus of this House. When we started this Assembly, Sir, we had hardly 300 kw power in the whole of the State; we were frightened to think in terms of lakhs of kw. Today, we think in terms of millions and millions kw of power. We are the same man, but only the mind has gone through the process of evolution, the capacity and confidence in our own creative activities, capacity and confidence in our ability to face criticism and not to be frightened by it, not to be frightened by the mistakes of our ability to rectify as we grow up. That is why we are able to conceive the geometrical growth, as was pointed out by the Hon'ble Member from Sundargarh and quite rightly he said that as we grow, as our activities grow in geometric progression, as technology provides us with greater productivity and greater services, as the society's hunger for amenities provides far greater stress and strain out of their collective demands then it was feasible, say in federal society of Rajas and Maharajas or foreign rules, as these human stresses go up, the society must adjust itself by its rules and laws and by its activities, unless it wishes to face a total destructive revolution. Therefore, when we have decided in our Constitution that we shall be a people governed by law, must be wise enough as people's representatives to continuously improve upon our existing systems and continuously be watchful so that we do improve our existing systems to take care of this stress and strain of the society that we have created the society that we are going to create and the society that we wish to live in. After so many years in this Legislature, Sir, I cannot be one of those who are cynical enough to say or stupid enough to say that everything is wonderful in our society. I would not be cynical enough to say that everything is wrong nor would I be stupid enough to say that everything is right. As long as human society exists, there would always be rights and wrongs and consequently we do have taken upon ourselves to be the watchdogs of the basic philosophy of the society which we ourselves have created by the Constitution. It is our business indeed to ensure the implementation or creation of suh an apparatus which would atleast satisfy the requirements that we have professed ourselves. The Constitution of Sweden during the last so many years has evolved a society which today for us is a far-off dream. Whether their methods could be applicable here is a matter of debate, whether the same instrument or the same apparatus would at all be applicable to our society is also a matter of debate. But there is no doubt that there must be some instrument or instruments or changes in the existing instruments to ensure that what we have set out to do ourselves we are able to achieve. Since this thought has been evoked in this House, I congratulate the mover of the Resolution. But as I said, it is a matter of debate whether and how and what sorts of machinery we should form within our State, within our development structure and within our socialistic structure" (*OLA Debates*, Vol. V (10), 13.9.1963; 38-42).

On the redesigning of the administrative apparatus of the Panchayat Raj, he said, "It is the inherent right of the Opposition to level their attacks against the inefficiency of the Government; I think it proper to read through the entire analysis of our inability to do so, what they would expect us to do. I would like to point out to you, Sir, that in the last twenty years of this Assembly I have not found yet any constructive creation of thought process which would enable us collectively in this House to attempt even at redesigning of our administrative apparatus. This is the first piece of legislation that the treasury benches with the assistance of the Opposition tried to create, the first piece of legislation we tried to frame and tried to implement, the first piece of legislation for diversification of responsibility, a new Government, a new administration of the people, for the people and by the people, which we thought in the context of democracy before that with this Panchayat Raj democracy would read at the source. We have seen ourselves how difficult it is to prepare this piece of legislation, we have seen ourselves how more difficult it is to implement it and we have also found against that it is most difficult to get the result out of it. As we thought, as we devised it and as we implemented it, we found thousand of flaws, we.found hundreds of weaknesses of human mind at different levels of the Panchayat Raj which defeats the very purpose for which this legislation was sought. Such is the difficulty of human affairs. When you prepare a legislation, when you try to implement it in the field, you want to frame rules and regulations but the officers from top to bottom cannot understand the spirit of the resolution and by the time it comes to the form of circulars and reaches down the villages you have seen yourself how the whole character, the impetus, the direction and the thought process has undergone a very substantial change so that the spirit of this House by the time it actually reaches the fields, the villages is set at naught" (*OLA Debates*, Vol. VII (25),

31.3.1965; 34-5). He said that this has also been analysed in the *Kamraj Plan* as follows:

> We have deliberately chosen the path of democracy knowing its strength and weakness. We in India have valued the dignity of man for thousands of years, and that has been the foundation of Indian Culture. It is because of this that Mother India gave birth to great thinkers, administrators, generals and patriots. She also put into the world great sages, writers, poets, artists and engineers. All this was possible only because individual liberty of thought and expression was never sought to be suppressed in this great country. Even today, with the new concept of modern democratic State, we have enshrined in our Constitution continuance of these eternal values of man......Thus, by the will of the people of India, we have abhorred and declared any form of institutional growth within our nation which would smack of Fascism or dictatorial tendencies. We have decided to give ourselves a Parliamentary demcocracy, i.e., Government by Constitution. Inspite of this, when India has launched on the process of developing her economy and her strength, it is important that for consolidation of the pillars of democracy, the Congress party must also take upon itself the unpalatable task of development of a responsible Opposition (*OLA Debates*, Vol. VII (25), 31.3.1965; 35).

The *Kamraj Plan* also discussed how to develop healthy responsible Opposition, and quoted from it as follows:

> Looking around the Indian horizon, we find that there is hardly any opposition to the Congress worth the name. Some Opposition parties always accuse the Congress of remaining in power by improper means of use of authority or money-lender or both. Such accusations are the outcome of immature political understanding and lack of affinity with the hope and aspiration of the people. Here and there, the Opposition groups register small success, but in the nation's body politic, these parties present only a few isolated spots. Obviously, these parties largely created by individual whims and fancies, totally divergent and opposed to each other, can never constitute themselves into one of the major pillars of democracy, i.e., a responsible Opposition capable at a point of time to take over the Government of the Nation (*OLA Debates*, Vol. VII (25), 31.3.1965; 36).

He said, "In our democratic set-up, may I say with all humility that Opposition has not done enough. I ask Opposition how many hundred years they do take to build up a truly national organization to become real Opposition in the democratic Government. I submit that they have not. They have to look into themselves and make their own interpretation. They have to look into themselves and make their own interpretation. They have to examine themselves where lies the fault. Cannot people look forward to them at a point of time to change over Government from the Congress to the national Opposition as a whole? If they cannot do it, I submit they have failed in their duties and responsibilities as responsible Opposition in the democratic set-up" (*OLA Debates*, Vol. VII (25), 31.3.1965; 36). He quoted from the *Kamraj Plan* and said the following:

> While Congress may consider general support to a process which would develop a healthy Opposition party, it must not lose sight of one fundamental fact that for all these years, it has held the nation together. If, today, Congress were to weaken, and different warring groups form Governments in different States and inevitably a weak centre follows, there is no doubt that the nation would be disintegrated and democratic institutional growth in India would *perish* (*OLA Debates*, Vol. VII (25), 31.3.1965; 36).

While suggesting the Opposition in the Assembly, he said, "Congress continues to rule as pointed out by the Leader of Opposition by hook or crook, by *priyaprithitosan* (appeasement), by *durniti* (corruption) is not a fact. May I point out again with all humility if Opposition at all wise to hear the advice of the leader of the Swatantra party who is supposed to be an intelligent person, if they care for my intelligence let me come forward to give a piece of advice. Let then listen to the piece of advice: stop talking against Congress. That is the great disadvantage for them. When they talk about Biju Patnaik, Biren Mitra and Congress, we are known throughout the country in length and breadth through the agencies of the Opposition. If I would have been in the Opposition, I would have ceased talking about Congress, I would have been talking about me programme, my leader, my party, etc." (*OLA Debates*, Vol. VII (25), 31.3.1965; 36).

On the issue of defections with reference to the then State Government, he said, "If the Government feels unstable, it is because of their own action. There is a saying in *Bible*, 'I do not want you to die today, tomorrow or day-after-tomorrow'. The Government which has been formed by defection has no business to stay there. They cannot stay long. The number of members will dwindle and immediately they will be relegated to my position. I do not lay any blame on them as this Government is sustained by those people who belonged to my Party and the parties which we had captained. So you should not expect loyalty from them you will not get it. You may get some expedient action from them. When the expediency expires, your life also expires. This may be your sorrow, but the people will not be sorry because you have proved nothing, sheer nothing in this speech for which the people of Odisha and the unemployed youth will not tolerate to see you in saddle. But you will break under your own steam, under your own weight" (*OLA Debates* Vol. V (2), 12.2.1973; 29).

The Governor in his address in 1985 had said, "The people of Odisha have elected my Government to office with a massive majority and my

Government will spare no effort to fulfill the expectations of the people, etc." To this, he said, "Did the people of Odisha elect this Government to Office? The people of Odisha gave majority votes to the Congress (I) party headed by Shri Rajiv Gandhi. People of Odisha voted in an enormous way for the Party because of the sympathy raised in the hearts of the people not only of Odisha, but he whole of India on the cruel killing of our former Prime Minister Indira Gandhi. The people of Odisha as well as people of India also did not approve the theory of federal structure which was proposed by the Opposition at the national level. These are the factors which brought the Congress (I) party to power with extra votes. So, the people of Odisha have elected this Government with massive majority is not a fact, is an incorrect statement" (*OLA Debates* Vol. I (2), 15.3.1985; 8).

On the democratic performance, he said, "It is a democratic country. Everybody has a right to move, to hold public meetings, etc. Why should anybody inform the Government? I would like to know from the Minister why the law and order situation has deteriorated in the State.... I want to know from the Minister whether the Press and the Opposition have the right of dissent or not. Anybody who has a dissenting voice is suppressed by this Government. They are the critics, not sycophants. But this Government makes sycophants of everybody. You have got a sycophant class of officers. We have to make men out of these officers" (*OLA Debates*, 19.3.1986; 88). He also said, "I want to know from the Chief Minister whether the press and the Opposition have a right of dissent or not. As far as we see anybody who raises a dissenting voice is being suppressed by Government or by the machinery of the Government. These are the things which I would request the Chief Minister as the Head of Government to study very carefully. I know you will give the assurance, but your assurance has no value. Your instructions are not being carried out by your administration (*OLA Debates*, 20.3.1986; 103).

On the democratic method of discussion in Assembly, he said, "Government should not take any discussion in the Assembly as a bor. It may be trying on the officials while without getting any reply. But in a democratic set up like ours, it is the people's representatives who matter and the administration is merely there to follow the policies of the Government and implement them. What we discuss here, when we attack the Minister, we not only attack the Minister but the administration and part of the administration of which the Minister is the head. We point out the Minister for the weaknesses, omissions and commissions of his department. We do not wish to name anybody of the department because he is not here to defend. We attack the Minister. So when we attack the Minister, it is not personal, it is for the inefficiency and omissions of the departmental officers. Therefore, I believe and I hope that in future enough time should rightly be given for full discussion of all subject matters which come for discussion. The Members place many problems in the House and the views expressed by them in the House are reproduced in the Newspapers. This process is essential in a democratic set up" (V (29), 9.4.1987; 60).

On the issue of coming to power, he said, "Only two instances are required-time and scope-to come to power. It is regrettable that you (J. B. Patnaik, Chief Minister) have not utilized the time. Had you utilized that time with prestige and dignity then we would have had the second Steel Plant in Odisha. Rajiv Gandhi is dominating this State, but not the Chief Minister of the State. We have no dignity in ourselves" (*OLA Debates*, Vol. IX (2), 22.2.1989; 99).

On the issue of reduction of voting age to 18 years, he said, "Long ago, Madhu Dandavate brought a Bill in Parliament where he wanted to reduce the age of voting to 18 years. In Madras, 15 lakhs of people gathered for National Front, the biggest ever rally and you are saying age-limit will be 18 years. Now you are saying, who did 18 years of age for voting; who else than Rajiv Gandhi. Not that Rajiv Gandhi wanted. Entire country wanted that. It was catapulted by the Opposition. A Bill came to the House by Madhu Dandavate and Government said, we have brought a Bill and you please withdraw. That is why we have withdrawn" (*OLA Debates*, Vol. IX (2), 22.2.1989; 99).

On the issue of democratic functioning, he said, "We have some valuable systems of democratic norms where every expression is free and no expression should be suppressed. How did you then suppress the Opposition when you went round the State? Why you get them arrested everywhere? Now who opposes you, arrest them under what law and by what means of the democratic norms Mr. Chief Minister? Are you proud of that? In a democratic country you cannot take the law into your own hand Mr. Chief Minister? Think about those things, because these are basic norms of democratic functioning" (IX (2), 22.2.1989; 95). Again, on democratic values, he said, "If the same thing (emergency) would have continued in the country, we could put Indira Gandhi behind bars. Would she have liked it? No, we made you free, we made the press free, we made the speech free and you are trying to negate the democratic values by arresting all the people of Opposition at a time when you are touring somewhere. Don't you think that people are revolting" (*OLA Debates*, Vol. IX (2), 22.2.1989; 96).

On the functioning of democratic Government in Odisha, he said, "Only here (Odisha), nowhere in the non-Congress (I) Governments, wherever the Chief Minister goes to, Opposition are arrested. Is that your habit or instruction? Our MLAs are being arrested, are they criminals? Our party leaders are being arrested. Is this the way a democratic Government functions? Wherever the Chief Minister goes, all the Opposition leaders are arrested. We had a Chief Minister in Karnataka. Shri Jyoti Basu goes alone in a car all over the State and also Shri N. T. Rama Rao, and Shri Devi Lal, what is there? Why this special thing here that he should be cordoned in all the places, everybody should be arrested. I told you last time if you go on provocating people, a day will ome when you will be nowhere" (*OLA Debates*, Vol. X (3), 11.9.1989; 136).

Speaking on the role of the Governor and Raj Bhawan, he said "Last 9 years of so-called stable Government of Congress (I) in Odisha, is it not a fact that the Governor's residence has been virtually converted into Congress (I) office for the Congress (I) dignitaries hodling meetings, conferences in that August House, which is supposed to be over and above Party considerations. Sir, you talk here about the rules but you had a Governor who was a part-time Governor of the State by reducing the status of Odisha. More peculiar is the fact that the Governors are being transferred like Class III employees. Yesterday only the Governor took over the charge as full-time Governor" (*OLA Debates*, Vol. IX (2), 22.2.1989; 95).

On the role of general people and the preceding Congress government in Odisha, he said, "People are the supreme power in a democratic set-up. Please remember that. The whole of Russia has been collapsed. People revolted. Look Lithuania, getting independence against the mightiest emperor. It is the power of the people. Let us be afraid. We need to bow down a little. Let us put all our heads together to work jointly. All that I say, you have collectively failed to serve the nation" (*OLA Debates*, Vol. I (4), 21.3.1990; 52).

Commenting on his massive mandate in the 1990 Assembly elections, where his Janata Dal got 119 seats out of the total of 147 seats in the Assembly, he said, "It is true that people have given us a massive mandate. It is not that they have given us the mandate; the people have decided to throw away a bunch of servants to whom they thought corrupt, inefficient and murderers, etc., and they have brought another set of servants of which I am the Chief. I don't need bodyguards or car procession. No Police arrangement for the Chief Minister. This is a radical change. It is the question of beginning of people's Government. We are elected in a democratic state and as such we should forget to have 10 cars in front and back moving around the elected representatives. This we have inherited from the colonial power. I would like to remind the House and also the people of India that the black has not replaced the white master. White has come out itself" (*OLA Debates*, Vol. I (4), 21.3.1990; 50).

On the principles of democracy, he said, "Do not encourage confrontation. As a democratic leader, it is not foul, it is not only undemocratic but it is a crime against democracy. Do not encourage violence. By suppression, you only encourage violence, why is it? Wherever I go, I do not see any black flag, whereas, wherever the Congress men go, they are thrown stones and shown black flags. You must know how to deal with young people, do not aggravate them" (*OLA Debates*, Vol. IX (2), 22.2.1989; 100).

On democratic rights of the people, he said, "Someone said that *Ganatantra Adhikar* (democratic rights) was suppressed to build Hirakud

Dam. I admit that. Otherwise, Hirakud would have never been built. What is *Ganatantra* (democracy)? It is a benefit of few or benefit of large number? It is a question of voting rights for which we are here. We are here in this side because our number is more and you are in that side because your number is less. *Ganatantra Adhikar* does not mean advantage of a few. Advantage of few is not *Ganatantra*" (*OLA Debates*, Vol. VII (23), 26.3.1992; 100).

On the democratic tradition, he said, "Sir, another track record of the Government I must appreciate and I am sure, the House will appreciate that any conference, meeting, by any Opposition leader has not only been thwarted but encouraged, we want democracy to function. Also, I like to be abused by Opposition, it does not matter. It is for the people to decide ultimately how much of the abuse they will take and how much of the abuse they will get, I know it. For example, this is to express their opinion is to exercise their lawful political rights under the democratic system. And this Government or this State will never, never, never oppose it. I can give you some illustrations. Illustrations are peaceful meetings by Sri Vajpayee, Sri Advani, Smt. Uma Bharati, Govinda Acharya of BJP, Balaram Jhakad, Ahmed Patel, Miss Mamata Banerjee, M. S. Bitta of Congress (I), and Chandrasekhar of Janata (S)" (*OLA Debates*, Vol. XVI (4), 1994; 72-3). He again said, "One thing, I think, this Government is proud of that we have given equal opportunity to all political parties. This is a thing that this Government has done. Now for example, whether it is a meeting by the BJP by Sri Vajpayee or Youth Congress young man Sri Bitta or Sri Chandrasekhar of Janata (S) or the Communist Party, whoever it is, they are free to hold their conference and meeting without fear and also they will have the police protection to ensure that nothing untoward incident happen to them. I think, atleastin one point Opposition should encourage this Government" (*OLA Debates*, Vol. XIV (13), 16.3.1994; 121).

On the democratic election process in Bihar, Biju Patnaik "raised a matter of great public importance on what is happening in Bihar. It is a National issue. The Central Government is involved, the Prime Minister is involved and the Election Commissioner is involved" (*OLA Debates*, Vol. I (6), 29.3.1995; 8). He said, "I have mentioned in this House that the deferment of the election by nearly six weeks by the Election Commissioner is quite uncalled for, which is quite unconstitutional and unnecessary. That apart, what has happened in Bihar now? I had mentioned that issue and said in the discussion, three months delay in holding the elections, continuous delay in holding the elections. It is not only unconstitutional, it is objectionable and improper and the Election Commission has been engaged into this impropriety and defeating the Constitutional propriety. The Central Government headed by Mr. Narasimha Rao in collusion with the Election Commission also planned to defer the counting of votes till tomorrow which brought a situation where the Central Government had to intervene for passing Vote-on-Account Budget, so that the Government of Bihar can be ousted. At 11.30 am they passed a Resolution in the Cabinet knowing that the election will be completed by 5 pm. There was another meeting of the Cabinet and they proposed President's Rule in Bihar. So, this negated the entire election process, the entire democratic process in the nation. Sir, this is so reprehensible that we the Members of the Janata Dal are very much shocked by the conspiracy between the Prime Minister and the Election Commission to defeat the total election process. It is unfortunate. Therefore, we do not want to create any problem here. We only wish to stage a walk-out. It is a serious problem" (*OLA Debates*, Vol. I (6), 29.3.1995; 8-9).

On the democratic pattern, he said, "Janata Party truly wants a democratic pattern in this country. Two major parties are functioning as the two wings of the nation's welfare Government. That is why, Sir, in the first meeting of the Cabinet, we proposed that the leader of the Opposition shall be of Cabinet rank and given the facilities of Cabinet Minister. We wish to give them honour, dignity, in spite of the fact, they tried to dishonor us, reduce us to the dust mentally, psychologically and physically and we are here in spite of them and because of the great people of India, It is to them we salute. That is why it is their express desire that democracy must function in this country and the instrument of democracy must also function responsibly" (OLA; 55-6).

On democracy, Biju Patnaik while criticizing the Opposition, said, "You bow and scramble like a pack of slaves. We do not do that to our Prime Minister, we do not do that to Shri Jagjivan Ram, we do not do that to Shri Charan Singh. We take them as equals and talk to them as equals. When we take decision as a Government, it is always one decision as you may have noticed to your great discomfort" (*Lok Sabha Debates*, 10 May 1978; 391-2). He also said, "If you were united, you would have got a majority in Maharashtra. Now you have got a minority tottering Government in Maharashtra. You have lost in Assam. You have got only two Governments in two States. Let us see how long you survive there. But that is beside the point. We are never going to dismiss. You will do it yourself. I trust and rely on you to do that as you have done it here" (*Lok Sabha Debates*, 10 May 1978; 394).

On political revenge and democracy, Biju Patnaik in an Adjournment Motion, said, "We have people here with us who fought the British government, a unitary power to bring about Constitutional democracy in this country. They are seriously worried whether we have not reverted to the same position of British imperialism, whether we have only exchanged black master for white masters. The moment somebody comes to power, he starts taking revenge on political opponents only from political motivations. I would say that for such acts, the democracy in India stands murdered.

Therefore, whenever a Government in power in a democratic set-up wishes to exercise total authority as has been provided in Acts, like MISA, the Government in power is to think ten times what would be the public reaction and if there is even a slightest doubt that it would be construed as politically motivated. A democratic government should desist from it.... I say even the British Government thought ten times before they took away the freedom of a man because the Britishers are born under the background and training and history of the *Magna Carta* and an Indian administrator is born with a slave mind with a feudal mind. Any Indian who is in authority wants to exercise feudal authority. Democracy in India has to grow from inside. Democracy is not natural to us. Therefore, when we have democratic institutions like this Assembly, like democratic Governments and the citizens, the exercise of democratic options has to be taken great care of before you start taking away the freedom of the citizens. In 1942, people like us, I myself spent 3 long years in jail, *haatha re bedi, goda re bedi pindhi* (chain in hands, chain in legs). That was the democracy then in India. Democratic actions are taken with care, generosity and fairness. What do we see now? What are the charges? These are frivolous charges" (*OLA Debates*, Vol. III (1), 9.12.1974; 114-5).

On the democratic process, he said, "By enjoyment of property. I mean accumulation of property, in the hands of few. This accumulation of property cannot be eliminated in a day or month or year, as the Prime Minister has herself put it. It will take years to remove this disparity. Really, it is not a simple thing, only one of the most preliminary steps that the Government or Parliament is taking to eliminate the control of a few over many. If the majority wants to do something we should allow it to be done. So it is the majority of the people in the Parliament which is the sovereign body in the country that have decided to do this and we have therefore to accept it. If the Parliament decides to take certain steps, I do not think it is fit and proper for us to object to it. We, in this House should support it because we are democrats. The whole structure of our Parliamentary democracy is based on it.... Government should be more democratic minded, more vigilant and more careful to ensure that the intention of the measures are not misused, and the people are not unnecessarily harassed (*OLA Debates*, Vol. III (6), 10.1.1972; 49-50).

On the democratic principle, he said, "I recall once again that we should work hand in hand in all matters with a view to develop our State. For the growth and development of the State this House as one body shall function. There is no matter whether you are in Opposition benches or with the Government. Our intention is one and the same for all-round development of our State. If any where something wrong is committed, there the role of the Opposition is to criticize the Government. But in all good works they should lend their whole-hearted support. That is the principle of democracy.

We are the people who will execute and they are the people who are the critics. That is manner of democratic Government which we have provided in our Constitution. But when there comes the people's demand, when there is need in Odisha for a certain thing, the people of Odisha are one" (*OLA Debates*, Vol. III (33), 6.4.1972; 36).

As the Leader of Opposition, responding to Governor's Address, Biju Patnaik said that it contained a new thing called *Democratic Society* that none of the previous governments in the last 29 years mentioned. It seems democratic society is a new study book. He refereed from the address, "While dissent is natural in a democratic society, we all have to ensure that this does not generate into unruly conduct or intolerance towards persons professing different opinions or faiths" (Vol. IV (2), 1975; 89), and said that this has been approved by the Cabinet also. He said that the Congress and the Communists have together formed the government and bring a policy, and if we as opposition party oppose it, then what is the action of the government? What is referred above, or if the government wants to suppress through police force, lathi, tear gas or bullets or MISA or try to suppress through the 'draconian' laws drawn under the aegis of an autocratic coterie, then to who will the referred quote be applicable? Those in government "must treat with tolerance the opinion of the Opposition". He also said, "What the government has spoken and what the government is doing are totally contradictory". He said, "A democratic society aims at creating conditions in which all citizens, irrespective of their political and religious belief, can live without fear of persecution"(*OLA Debates*, Vol. IV (2), 19.2.75; 89). He cited the murder case of Parshuram Satapathy of Bolangir, which was "a clear case a political murder" (*OLA Debates*, Vol. IV (2), 19.2.75; 90). He said, "Here is a government which acts totally undemocratically, which is demolishing democratic conscience every day and like Devil quoting scripture, likes to repeat the definition of democracy" (*OLA Debates*, Vol. IV (2), 19.2.75; 90). He referred to a judgment of Supreme Court that "unseated a Congress Member of Parliament (MP) because he spent more money or his party spent more money than what was allowed under the People's Representation Act" (Vol. IV (2), 1975; 90). The government of the day "cared a fig for that judgment and countermanded it by issue of an Ordinance which later on became the law...The intention was that unless that Ordinance was issued and later on become law, 170 MPs of the Congress Party would have been unseated including the Prime Minister of India. Their brute majority takes away the minimum of the fundamental rights granted by the Constitution to the poor man to be able to contest the election who has no relations, no party or anything. This is how democracy is functioning" (*OLA Debates*, Vol. IV (2), 19.2.75; 90).

While participating on the Representation of the People (Second Amendment) Bill, on 26th July 1996, Biju Patnaik suggested certain note for future guidance. First, he suggested making "every voter" or "every vote" to be "mandatory", and if a person does not vote being a voter, has to pay a substantive fine? Secondly, for somebody to get elected, he must also get 50 per cent of the votes. Thirdly, he spoke of state funding of elections, as many candidates are spending crores of rupees to get themselves elected to this House. He said that it is absolutely imperative that money power has to be curbed totally. In his own words, on this serious issue, he said, "if this cannot be done, the terrible sickness with which the electoral process is suffering from cannot be remedied. I would request that the House take up instead of going into the details and legal questions of various sorts, the House should apply its mind to honour two or three points with which alone our democratic process can survive". State Funding is a must whether it has ₹1000 crore or ₹2000 crore, whatever it is.

Biju Patnaik also agreed to the amendments brought by George Fernandes, when he suggested that one person should not be allowed to contest in more than one constituency instead of proviso of two constituencies, as per the Bill. Fernandes gave the examples of three leaders, viz: Biju Patnaik, Atal Behari Vajpayee, and Narasimha Rao, who were victorious in both constituencies, and had to resign from one, in the present House. By this, the constituency remains without being represented, and secondly it also involves huge expenditure.

Government

About Government, he said, "Government shall work as a most powerful instrument. It must contain persons of great capacity, great ability, to whom administration will respect" (*OLA Debates*, Vol. IX (27), 31.3.1989; 60-1). On Government, he said, "The entire Government machinery should be linked with the people for their development.... I presume, that to maintain law and order is one of the main functions of the Government" (*OLA Debates* Vol. I(2), 15.3.1985; 16).

On the matter of Government order and its obeisance, Biju Patnaik had said, "I am not talking of the validity of the order or otherwise, all that I am saying is that Government order has not been carried out by a subordinate agency. OSEB may be a different corporation or a different agency, but they are subordinate to the Government and the Legislature.... Government order is a Government order and that must be carried out by every agency in the State... Government authority in respect of governance of the State is supreme and it cannot be abrogated. That is the principle of Government" (*OLA Debates*, Vol. III (9), 19.12.74; 114-15).

On minority government, Biju Patnaik said, "When we formed the Government, there all component party were in the Government. It was a coalition Government. In your case you are a minority party. You do not enjoy the majority of 50 per cent of the House.... On the mercy of the Communist Party, the Congress ministry has been formed. Congress does not have majority in this House. For this I said minority. For this I want to say that what the Chief Minister says and what I am saying is not irrelevant.... The Chief Minister is saying we have got the mandate of the people, I say it is wrong; you have not got the mandate of people. Mandate means majority of the people. The Indian Constitution has provision that even with fewer votes more members in the Parliament and Assembly can come. That is not the mandate of the people. That is number one, number two, minority government – as you do not have 74 Members out of the total 146 Members. You have formed Government with the support of others. If Congress and Communist Party would have formed coalition government, it would have been a majority Government. This is the difference between the two" (Vol. I (3), 1974; 74-5). Biju Patnaik said, "I refuse to concede 35 per cent of the mandate of the people.... Yesterday the Leader of the CPI Party said that they have given the conditional support to the Government. It is not unconditional support. He has said this and it is in the proceedings" (*ibid*, 76).

On the performance of his Government, Biju Patnaik mentioned what the then Chief Minister of West Bengal Shri P. C. Sen in his letter dated the 17th January 1965 wrote to the then Prime Minister about the fiscal policy of Odisha. He wrote, "It is true that for long years business monopolies of Calcutta have thoroughly exploited Odisha. There was need for some drastic thinking for Odisha if she were to come to her own. In fact, Biju's policy and the mechanism by which he steadily developed this though led to what has now become widely accepted policy of rural industrialization and development of local trade under the name of Orissa Panchayat Industries system" (Vol. I (3), 1974;88).

On the issue of Government rules and laws not being adhered to in large projects, he said, "We are dealing with very large works involving tens of crores of rupees. There have been slight defects in the methods of operation. There were certain methods of audit which has nothing to do with the framing of rules by the State Government. The rules are not like the Ten Commandments of the Bible that the money shall not be spent unless it gets the administrative approval. When a job has to be done quickly as a measure of emergency and when it is given high priority, Government decides to waive its own created rules and orders (for the Chief Engineer) to go ahead with the work. It is the business of the audit to point out that the proper administrative approval has not been taken. It is equally the business of Government to decide and say that it is the Government orders by which this was done. This is perfectly natural. The business of the audit is to bring out any departure from the established rules prepared and authorized by Government. Of course, Government can change the whole set of rules overnight. But Government does not wish to change all these rules. Government's deviation from the rules according to certain standard under Government's own orders temporarily for the time being becomes Government rules" (*OLA Debates*, Vol. V (18), 25.9.1963; 34).

On the Government and its performance through the Governor's Address, he said, "The Hon'ble Member from Dhenkanal who was the mover of the Motion of Thanks, took great pains to try to teach us the gospel that this in effect is not the speech of the Governor, Governor is only a mouthpiece of Government and all these facts and figures are written and told by the Government to the Governor and he speaks on their behalf. I can assure the Hon'ble Member that we are well aware of this, we understand this" (*OLA Debates* Vol. V (2), 12.2.1973; 22). He continued to say, "A Government in position never claims itself to be tottering; a Government in position never talks of its own instability. It only shows what is in their minds. It is from their camp that news goes out to Press and other places that this Government is going to be disjointed, this Government is going to expand Ministry to avoid a disaster. It is never from our side that the Opposition is going to displace the Ministry or the Opposition would try to dissolve the Ministry.... Because if they are unstable and they plead that the Opposition should assist them to keep them stable, I can only assure the Leader of the Government that the Opposition would consider it on its merit, on the ability of the Government to govern. There was a time when I myself welcomed the present Leader of Government with the hope that she while remaining in Delhi in charge of a Department must have learnt a great deal and my assumption was later substantiated by the Finance Minister of India, Shri Chavan, during Cuttack election, that if the present Leader of the Government wins the seat, money will flow for the resurrection of Odisha.... Sir, the matter was taken up in Parliament. There was debate in the Parliament. Shri Chavan preferred to keep quite unlike our Leader. So I thought that when the Government is headed by a person who claims to be appointed as Subedar of Indira Gandhi as is noted in a piece of letter thrown round in the streets of Cuttack town during the last bye-election, 'I Shrimati Indira Gandhi appointed Shrimati Nandini Satapathy as Subedar in Odisha to bring about socialism and socialist progress'.... The main plank of that Party is *Garibi hatao, Bekari hatao*, (remove poverty, remove unemployment) suppress rising prices, increase production in fields and factories and ensure social justice for the low income group and down trodden *adibasis* and *harijans* and to ensure nutrition to children, employment to unemployed. But I find in this statement not a small paragraph has been written about it even though this is a budget speech which is projecting Government policy for the coming year. If these things would have been incorporated in the statement, I would have personally wished to let the present leadership continue for 10 years more. But the report before us is very shallow" (*OLA Debates* Vol. V (2), 12.2.1973; 23). It does not contain anything about roads that would have been given high priority, and nothing about the labourers. "It is rather sad that I had to point out this fact to a Government who profess minimum value of socialism. I do not know what they understand by socialism but there is a so-called socialistic Finance Minister who has not provided even a paragraph about the labourers in this speech" (*OLA Debates* Vol. V (2), 12.2.1973; 23-4). He listed out some of the necessities for governance and said, "If you want to improve agriculture, irrespective of the ceiling that may be finally fixed by this House, consolidation of holdings is of the highest priority. If we want to introduce any modern method of farming, whether it be pump, whether it be modern implements or any other means of ploughing, the most urgent task is to introduce consolidation of holdings. An Act has been passed to this effect, but it is regrettable that nothing has been done in this regard so fair.... Time has come and we must ensure that minimum of 5 acres is given to the deserved landless, i.e., a man who has depended on land and then if there is surplus that can be distributed to other people. So that land can be a source of income. Land must be worked out on scientific methods. If you cannot do that, we will take you to task, we will not excuse you. This is scientific reorganization of land on the basis of social justice. Neither the Government nor the Opposition would be able to take undue advantage of it on the platform or in the public. I would like the Government to discuss the whole thing with the Opposition and decide the whole thing in close consultation with the Opposition.... I do not want to blame any previous Government or Governments. All I wish to present to this Government, this is a huge task; no Government has even completed 5 per cent of the programme. A close examination, even one or two items, will expose the hollowness of Government. I do not want to expose Government. I have been here in this House for over 25 years. We have not made any headway. We are 15 years behind the other States. I want to ask this simple question, are we to go their back or are we to develop ourselves; will we not stand on our own legs. It is not Indira Gandhi who will come to our help, it is our attempt that will help us rise, which no Prime Minister can prevent.... The Chief Minister and the other Ministers say that Biju Patnaik and Mahtab are setting up people against them. I can assure the Chief Minister and other Ministers that we are here to see to the interest of the people but we are least interested on any person. If the Government has lost confidence of the youth then they have to reap their consequences but not others" (*OLA Debates* Vol. V (2), 12.2.1973; 24-6). While concluding, he spoke on the role of the Government, and said, "We the people of the independent India should not remain poor for all of our lives. Nobody should stand between our prosperity and make full use of our internal resources so that our legitimate and reasonable standard of growth would be cast aside. With the possession of resources at our disposal with collective vision and with intelligent vision in the interest of the people some result takes place. If the Deputy Minister for Defense has mentioned that ship building yard will not be removed, that is due to the pressure of the Opposition, but not from Government.... We should have the collective responsibility to see the growth of Odisha. At least, in this House we can cease to be battling with each other and try to raise the moral of the people, the standard of the people and think how to built up collectively. It is not that I fight with the Leader of the House or Leader of the Government. What all I say is either you do it or allow us to do it.... We have enough resources, we have got the raw materials and we can have money from outside and manage it as a commercial venture. Either the Government of India do it themselves or give the State Government, if necessary, limited validity to do it, and I can assure the Chief Minister it is possible; it is not such a big thing that cannot be done.... Government is a continuous affair. If there is an arrangement between the Centre and the State Government there is no reason why that should not be implemented" (*OLA Debates* Vol. V (2), 12.2.1973; 24-8).

Criticizing the then state government, he said, "Government has failed to develop the country. You are the government. You are not doing any development. Therefore, for all these reasons, I always say that this government is not competent to deliver the goods in terms of their own promises" (*OLA Debates*, Vol. III, No. 11, 20.12.74; 86). He also said, "I have asked the Minister not to politicize the Police force, not to politicize the Army. These are stable forces in the country and no attempt should be made as fear is expressed in the House that Police force is being appointed for political consideration. That was the charge.... What is the policy of government, as passed in the Assembly, is the law of the land and that policy must implement whatever be the law. But politicization for political consideration was the charge in the House which needs to be discouraged" (*OLA Debates*, Vol. III (11), 20.12.74; 115).

On the poor performance of the State Government, specifically on malnourished deaths in the district of Kalahandi, citing some of the English newspapers headlines on it, he said, "But the fact of the matter is that during the last five years under the Patnaik, the State has slid deeper into the quagmire of poverty and backwardness, of course, the State Government can and does manufacture statistics to paint a picture of enormous stride taken under the dynamic Chief Minister. While it may be true that the Chief Minister represents the mainstream of Odisha's feudal political ethos, and that his opponents in and outside the ruling party are no more enlightened, the Central leadership can hardly afford to turn a Nelson's eye on the pockets of human misery in Patnaik's Odisha" (*OLA Debates*, 31.7.1985; 100-1).

Suggesting for better governance to the State Government, he said, "I enjoin upon this Government to correct itself. According to your own statistics, 1.5 crores of people are still below poverty line. Whatever assistance you can give them within the time that you are in Government, give them wholesale and on top of that have a proper monitoring device and accountability and the money that we have only yesterday sanctioned to the Finance Minister, over 2000 crores, let us hope it will go for the use for the use of the people and not misappropriated as has been happening over the last few years" (*OLA Debates*, 31.7.1985; 103).

On the prospects of the present State Government and suggesting for a dynamic approach for governance, he said, "This Government must be able to acquire confidence of the people. I have said in a letter that you should have a moral standard and do have integrity and enforce it on your own administration. You should have good integrity and discipline and other things for running administration. Then you will have our support because we are all parts of Odisha. You do it and fight with the Government of India and we shall be all together. You see, when Bengal fights with the Centre, their MPs of all parties get together. When other States fight with the Government of India, their MPs of all parties get together. But here neither the MPs nor you want to take the issue with the Government of India. We remain poor. Someday, we will not be able to see, Odisha people will revolt against the Centre and they are bound to do it. Mizoram is a small land of five lakhs of people. They revolted for 20 years to have State power. Ultimately Sri Lal Denga became the Chief Minister. The youngsters of Assam did the same thing and ultimately formed the Government in Assam. Why are you so weak? What has happened to you? It is only just for a job-Minister or Chief Minister. What is sacrosanct to be a Minister or Chief Minister? If you cannot do good to the people, what is sacrosanct? What is this administration about if it is not meant for the people" (*OLA Debates*, 11.9.1986; 128).

On the issue of misutilisation of central funds sanctioned to meet exigencies of natural calamities like flood, cyclone, etc., he said, "During the five years, 1980-81 to 1984-85, a staggering sum of ₹320 crores were given to the State Government to meet the exigencies of flood havoc for natural calamities, especially floods and cyclones. I remember, Sir, I personally along with all the Opposition parties of the State went up to Delhi and met Smt. Indira Gandhi and requested her to release a large amount of funds. Mr. Pranab Mukherjee, the then Finance Minister and other officers were summoned and at that time ₹320 crores were released. What is the accountability of this expenditure? According to sources, this Government goes scot-free with all its unpardonable crime against the people. The State Government's violation of the stipulations of the utilization of funds has been abated by the Centre for several years. I would like to know why? What is the level of influence? Your Government, Mr. Finance Minister, your department have informed the Centre that the grants were 'fully' utilized. The word 'fully', not 'properly'. But this CAG's report which I have laid on the Table of the House says that the details of expenditure incurred is said upto the ceilings fixed (Nearly ₹320 crores) showing the major heads, minor heads, etc., not been furnished by the State Government even though they were called for. And it goes further to say, 'emergency relief provided in some cases at less than the prescribed rates or quantities. Such relief was also provided in some cases, not affected by any calamity'. ... Altogether, it shows misutilisation of more than ₹35 crores and many things have remained unexpended. This is the part of the Audit report" (*OLA Debates*, 11.9.1986; 123).

On the Paradip Port audit report, he said, "So much was said that crores and crores of rupees have been wasted. My Hon'ble friend from Pallahara who was my colleague, a Cabinet colleague, had said in the House that in a project like this is ten per cent wastage that cannot be considered much. That means in a ₹20 crores project there might be ₹2 crores wastage which would not be abnormal. But what does the Audit Report say? It says that total possible wastage is less than one lakh of rupees only" (*OLA Debates*, Vol. III (6), 29.9.1965; 25-6).

On the performance of the Odisha Government, he said, "The Deputy Chairman of the State Planning Board, has gone on record to say that by the end of the 7th Plan, there will be nearly one thousand megawatt shortage. He says 970 MW. Now on the Power Plant, the Chief Minister has waxed eloquent in the House and outside everyday that Talcher will be definitely done. It will be done a Super Thermal Station. Tender will be done. World Bank will do this and that. What does the Minister for Energy say in the *Lok Sabha*? He said in Parliament let the Odisha Government first perform with what they have. We all know the performance of Odisha Government. As far as Talcher Thermal Station is concerned, its performance is most miserable compared to any Thermal Power House in the country. Tatas operate their power plant. In Bombay, power is supplied by the Tata Electricity Company. Their efficiency amounts to 85-90 per cent. We sometimes fall down to 20% also. We have got the great Electricity Board; great engineers. Whatever it is all, we cannot run a small power plant. And so, the Minister quite rightly said in Delhi that first let the Odisha Government perform with what they have got before they come to us for any proposal" (*OLA Debates*, 11.9.1986; 125).

On misuse of Consolidated Fund of the State, he referred the suggestion given by the then Prime Minister, Shri Gandhi, in the *Conference of the Chairman of Public Accounts Committee (PAC)* on 10 April 1986, that misuse of the Consolidated Fund of the State requires thorough investigation and those responsible needs to be identified. The PAC is trying to catch the culprits, but they are not able to be caught. As understood, there is some wrong in the system. This was the feeling of the then Prime Minister. He also said that under the present management there is unnecessary expenditure.

In this field the State Governments also have a responsibility. He said, "The Public Accounts Committee deals with the utilization and proper protection of the Consolidated Fund of the State" (*OLA Debates*, 11.9.1986; 119-20).

On the Cabinet Government system, he said, "The Chief Minister's order was turned down by the Cabinet-part or whole or whatever it is. He ordered something and in the memorandum to the Cabinet explaining the whole thing what was decided, on which there was a Government order in the Department of Forest notification in the Special Gazette of Odisha was issued, under which contracts were also signed, 25th was the date of notification; 29th the contract was signed; on the 1st of this month the dear Cabinet of the Odisha Government sat there and quietly outmaneuvered the Chief Minister for whatever they did. They rejected this. Sir Ivor Jennings, who is an authority on Cabinet form of Government, clearly lays down-because we follow the West Minster pattern of Government-if a Chief Minister or a Prime Minister, both of whom have the authority to declare policies in anticipation of Cabinet approval and if they find that they in the Cabinet cannot get it approved, it is clearly laid down, the Cabinet shall lose the Prime Minister, and in this case the Cabinet should lose the Chief Minister, howsoever we may try to hide it. It goes to show that the Chief Minister has no longer control of the Cabinet; the Chief Minister has no control of his party. The dissidents are growing. The party's performance is reflected in the Cabinet. My friend, Cabinet is not a party, if you do not know this much, you are fit to be lawyer. Therefore, you must also try to read Constitutional law as framed by the mother Parliament of the democracies" (*OLA Debates*, 11.9.1986; 121-2).

On Non-Congress Government, he said, "How the non-Congress States are profiting. They are literally fighting with Central Government. How do they get best out of the Government of India? Whether it is Mr. Hegde, whether it is MGR, whether it is NTR, whether it is Sri Jyoti Basu, whether it is Mr. Barnala of Punjab. How are they getting?" (*OLA Debates*, 11.9.1986; 127).

On the question of giving suggestions to the Government, rather than criticizing, by the then Finance Minster, he said, "Sir, we did criticize the weakness that is inherent in this Government. If I may recommend, what should I recommend? If there are a bunch of thieves, *Alibaba and 40 thieves*, they are still with us in these days. I have to suggest all the remedies. Does it not strike to their minds? There is total corruption at the top level. It should be stopped at the top level. I am sure if this is done, crores of rupees will be saved, which can be utilized for the betterment of the poor men. This is the suggestion I make. I hope that the Government will accept it and carry on like that" (*OLA Debates*, 31.3.1986; 113).

On the issue of re-appointment, he said, "The question was whether so and so is going to be appointed as a Special Officer or an Adviser which means re-employment of an officer who has retired from service since long, precisely on which the Chief Minister said, 'beyond my imagination'. The intention is quite clear. What is the harm if a public servant who is doing public service offers some of his time for public work? So, the question of appointing a Special Officer or an adviser does not arise. Tomorrow if Shri N. K. Choudhury (former Chief Minister) expresses his willingness to act as Adviser to Government, whether Shri Banka Behari Das will oppose it or somebody will say because he has retired many years ago, who is nearer the grave, he should not be appointed. Supposing tomorrow Smt. Rama Devi offers to do some work for Government, will he say she is old and incapable of doing work? Then, Sir, he will raise another question that the defeated Members of the Assembly should not be put in the post. May I remind Shri Das that defeated candidates have not only been re-appointed but re-assigned for the posts like Cabinet Minister in the Central Government. There are ample instances. Therefore, I said 'much can be said on both sides. You know, Sir, as all know Shri V. Sitaramya, an able social worker belongs to the ruling Congress camp. So, there is no intention behind these honorary appointments. The Chief Minister said 'this is beyond my imagination'. This is quite correct to say that he had not any information of any of these people being re-appointed. He has certainly the right and it is the Governments inalienable right to give appointment to any person to advise them in any manner in any department of Government" (*OLA Debates*, Vol. III (33), 6.4.1972; 10).

On this deteriorating law and order situation, during the moving of an adjournment motion, he said, "If the highest executive of the State, whoever he may be, he may be the Chief Minister or may be Home Minister or the IG of Police or Home Secretary, whoever, if they can make light comments on very serious lapses of administration, particularly on law and order, it is bound to encourage all kinds of lawless elements that remain hidden in the society. It is always there. It is nothing new. It is happening all over the nation. It was happening 40 years back and it is now also happening. It was happening before independence and it is also happening after independence. Sir, if a woman is raped and the Chief Executive of the State says this is a small matter. Sir, you can imagine the fallout of this State. He may, in his mind minimize mischief, say, but it will have maximum effect on the unsocial elements of the State. They will think that they are free to do any kind of mischief they want because the Chief Executive of the State says that this is a small matter. If the Chief Executive will say that Opposition is nothing, Opposition people are impotent, if Chief Minister will say such, then what will be the effect on the society, especially on the unsocial elements who commit murders, etc. If you give protection to murderer under the wing or party man, who is of the ruling group, the Police Department stands demoralized because it knows that these people have direct connection with the ruling party" (*OLA Debates*, 19.3.1986; 86-7).

On the deteriorating law and order situation in Odisha and throwing of hand-bomb on the car of Dr. Radhanath Rath, Editor of Odia daily, *The Samaja*, Sri Gangadhar Paikaray, Ex-MLA, and others, leading to ineffectiveness of Government, he said, "This Government has forfeited its right to govern. The elementary duty of Government is to keep thelaw and order situation intact, to protect life and property of the citizens. This Government has been totally unable to do that. This is my sadness. It is shameful that even after forty years of independence, in this State, life and property is not safe and the protagonists of free and fearless journalism are not safe. It is the concern of the law and order machinery. It would appear that the Government is protecting all the misconduct of the machinery. The machinery that would have been controlled by Government has gone out of hand" (*OLA Debates*, 19.3.1986; 66).

On the pressing problem of starvation deaths in Kalahandi district and how to pressurize the Union Government, he suggested to the State Government by saying, "We must make a thrust to Government of India; even though there is some delay, doesn't matter. You must pressurize the Government much more than these 150 crores and ensure to spend properly whatever money comes; for and on behalf of the people, so that there is no pocketing of money. For this, I am proposing for an all-party meeting in every Panchayat under the Chairmanship of the Governor. They will be watch-dog to see whatever money and food comes is properly distributed, as our Public Distribution System is not functioning in Odisha" (VI (2), 10.9.1987; 13). In this context, he had said, "How State will deal with the Centre. I want to know whether you will deal with the Centre out of your weakness or on your strength.... Delhi should be warned by this House. We cannot remain poor any more" (V (2), 24.2.1987; 80).

On the issue of Relief Code, he said, "This Relief Code, perhaps you are aware, was framed by the British Government, not by this Government. This Government has many officials, but they have no brain. Here many IAS officers are enjoying their life. The Relief Code says that the Collector must have to provide work to every able-bodied person. You learnt about the famine, where lakhs of people died. There was no Relief Code at that time. After that Relief Code was framed throughout India. Inspite of Relief Code in 1942, lakhs of people died in Bengal of starvation. According to Government calculation it was 25 lakhs. Some people died in Balasore also. Was there no rice? There was plenty of rice stock in Calcutta. But the people had no money to buy. The same situation is arising now here. Here two little farmers' properties were attached when they have no crop. It has been done in hundreds of cases. As the Agriculture Minister said, there must be huge collection whether they can pay or cannot pay. This is what is called an unpredictable approach by a Government. The Government is supposed of the people, by the people, etc. But it has failed totally and miserably" (*OLA Debates*, Vol. IX (31), 6.4.1989; 82).

On the issue of good Government, he said, "One youth stabbed the ADM at Angul because that Officer demanded ₹20,000 for a job. It is not a sign of running a good Government –good democratic Government. That is all I ask you to do as Chief Minister. It is a bad tradition-it is a wrong tradition. It was a bad tradition set up for you and any Government whoever comes - it is a wrong tradition. If some young men want to throw stones on us, let them throw. How many times my car glasses have been broken? I do not take a bullet proof car with me. It is repugnant to me. Mrs. Gandhi was killed-sorry-your Government could not protect her life.... You take my words as an experienced person. It is my advice to you" (*OLA Debates*, Vol. IX (2), 22.2.1989; 100).

On the question of delivering a stable Government, he said, "This State belongs to 25 lakhs of farmers, 25 lakhs of homeless workers, adivasis and harijans, etc. It belongs to them. We should take care of them. If you cannot do that you cannot have the Government for a long time. You have seen dictatorial Governments have not run for a long time. Stability is of two kinds, (i) stability of immense progress, and (ii) stability of the grave. Odisha is suffering from stability of a Government which is already dead. Sooner you go, it is better for the State. Sooner the Congress Government is thrown out, the better. Any change will be better. In this little State, you are not Chief Minister. You are a mere Subedar of Shri Rajiv Gandhi" (*OLA Debates*, Vol. IX (2), 22.2.1989; 101).

On the dysfunction of the previous Government, he said, "I would like to remind this House that from time to time, the Government which came during the last 10 years or even before has tampered with the administration, so severely that all my doggedness is finding it difficult to correct the situation..... The lady interferes (referring to Nandini Satapathy); I think she has proceeded too much. If I would like to reopen and say that she began all the criminal actions during emergency time to a great deal, all the high personnel were sent to jail? So we will not go into it. But the fact of the matter is that the entire administration has been so vitiated from the time of Indira Gandhi, when she was Prime Minister till her son took it over that they wanted to have everyone at their beck and call. Whether it is the Chief Secretary or the LG or the Secretaries or even the Judiciary, she wanted that all should be committed to her. Judiciary committed to whom? Judiciary committed to her. Here also they committed to Smt. Nandini Satapathy and Shri J. B. Patnaik, who were the Chief Ministers from the Congress Party. This was a standard practice. This has to be corrected" (*OLA Debates*, Vol. III (8), 17.10.1990; 79). On the correctives that his Government took, he said, "The correctives that this Government is trying to take in the Police administration, which I must admit is far from what is required to maintain discipline in the State to make the people feel that the Police are their friends, not their enemies and let the ordinary persons and the poor people feel that Police is not meant for rich, but also for the poor, which was not the standard practice of the previous Government. I am trying to break that. It will take little more time" (III (8), 17.10.1990; 80). He further said, "To err is human and all errors are to be corrected every now and then. If I mention about the previous Chief Minister, I carefully point out not merely the rights or wrongs and the opinions. The errors could have been corrected, if proper attention would have been given before taking any drastic step" (*OLA Debates*, Vol. III (8), 17.10.1990; 81).

On the Government performance, he said, "A Government can only function, not on the basis of its successes, but it functions better when it takes cognizance of the criticisms which means its failures at different levels of operation. Some of the criticisms are indeed valid, come of them are personal, which I take no notice of. But I come to the State Policy of raising the status of the social order of the State. Let me share, Mr. Speaker, that this Government will not compromise where the poor are concerned. There will be no case of compromise, where the illiterates are concerned" (*OLA Debates*, Vol. IV (3); 21.2.1991; 168). Due to the cyclone and flood in Ganjam district, many Members complained of food problem and other relief work in the district. Biju Patnaik, in response to that said, "We had hoped that the Government of India would come to our rescue as the flood and cyclone was of rare severity. While committees after committees came from Delhi, including the World Bank, I must admit that we have not yet received the assistance which was promised to us. I know that the Government of India's finances are also bad" (*OLA Debates*, Vol. IV (3); 21.2.1991; 169).

On Government performance, he said, "If in 45 years of a type of administration...you have left with 50 crores of people below the poverty line, then there is something wrong in the system. Any Party, any Prime Minister or Chief Minister or the Opposition, the way we proceed the system just failed because the system under 1935 Act was the colonial system and we enjoy the colonial system. So, 50 crores of people, still after 45 years, are rotting below the poverty line. Obviously, the administrative system of the Government and the manner it is running is responsible. The Government has failed somewhere. So, it needs a close look and detailed examination" (*OLA Debates*, Vol. V (8), 20.9.1991; 195).

On Government, he said, "No Government is flawless including the Congress Government in Delhi or in some other States or even In Inidra Gandhi's Government or Rajiv Ganndhi's Government. All had distinct flaws which led to different situations which has caused concern to the Nation" (*OLA Debates*, Vol. X (3), 22.2.1993; 127). He also said the whole purpose of Government is, "You must have confidence to serve the poorest. You are here because of the vote of the poorest, not from the rich. Have you ever bothered to find out the means to help the poorest of the State" (*OLA Debates*, Vol. IX (2), 22.2.1989; 100)?

On the governance issue, he said, "No Government can be dislodged if you are appointing judicial enquiry. I am appointing so many judicial enquire, Government is not dislodged. There has been no student indiscipline in this State. Labour situation is normal. Extremist activities and naxalite movement confined in traditional areas and only they are engaging themselves in the package of development measures launched by the Government. Therefore, I take pride in saying that I am the first naxalite in this country. Excepting that they should not indulge in any violence. Beyond that they are really carrying out the task which I have enunciated and which the unsocial elements are trying to defeat. Now for example there was a movement which wanted to break up this State. Whether it is Koshal or Jhadakhanda, whatever you call it, you will appreciate that the whole thing has just squat and sown and there has been no fall out, because of this movement. Therefore, I can say with some amount of joy that my State continues to remain intact. It will not be divided. For major crimes, murders, dacoits and rapes, kidnapping, dowry death, etc., I do not take pride is saying that Odisha's figure is much less than all India average and also less than that of the neighbouring States like Bihar, Madhya Pradesh, and Andhra Pradesh for every one lakh of people involved" (*OLA Debates*, Vol. XVI (4), 21.9.1994; 70).

Biju Patnaik became highly prophetic in his last Assembly term and said, "I do not know whether this would be my last attendance on a Budget Session of this House; probably it will be and in that context I want to go back a few years of life in this Assembly. The first Assembly of Odisha province was mooted when all the States, native States had become part of Odisha after the independence movement. When the first Assembly session was on, Shri Lal Mohan Patnaik was the Speaker. There were subsequent Speakers, eminent persons like Pandit Nilakantha Das and of that order were there. Sir, I was elected from Cuttack City Constituency when there was no contest. I was uncontested because we had come from the British prison having spent thousand days and thousand nights in chains and shackles. People held us with great respect and fondness and so there was no contest in Cuttack City. Subsequently, Governments came and Governments went: Mahatab was Chief Minister; Nabakrushna Choudhury was Chief Minister, and so on. There was a coalition Government between Mahatab's Congress and the *Ganatantra Parishad*. I cannot see them, but they were here. Unfortunately, I was also instrumental in making that coalition and for the first time in Odisha, a Congress Government was adorned under my leadership. That is way back in 1961. We are now in 1995. Many Governments I formed and in Kamraj Plan, I left the Government. Probably, that was a misfortune for the State of Odisha, but anyhow, I left and others came. Biren Mitra, NilamaniRoutray and so on and later on Nandini Satapathy and so on" (*OLA Debates*, Vol. II (3), 3.7. 1995; 128).

On different Governments, Biju Patnaik said, "Government come and Government go in a democratic set-up. Nobody need be very proud of it. Nobody should feel humble about it. The function of the State, as long as it is there, the State is making progress and visible progress; not merely wishful thinking but really visible progress in all spheres which will make this backward State into a prosperous State. There lies the secret of Government and management by the Government as well as by the Opposition, as well as by the people" (II (3), 1995; 128). He also cautioned the present State Government and said, "But, the way this Government is conducting itself, it would make it difficult for this Government and its Party to continue for very long because of the ill-feeling it has created all round, both for the consumer and the merchants of the side, and total neglect of the poor on the other side. I will tell you why? It does not give any joy to see a Government floundering. I wish the Government to succeed in actual ground situation. Take the case of the increase in Sales Tax, which to my mind is a great error of judgment. You had known that my Government did not raise the Sales Tax. What made you to do that, what made your officers to suggest that, I do not wish to know that, but the same officers insisted you to raise the Sales Tax in your time. Now Sir, we took the Government in 1990 when the Sales Tax revenue was only ₹200 crores. We did not raise the Sales Tax. But at the end of 1994, the Sales Tax revenue was ₹600 crores. It is a pity that this Finance Minister of the Chief Minister did not have the time to deal into it. There is no secret about it. We reduced the tax, but we had a wider net that is why ₹200 crores could become ₹600 crores in a form of direct revenue to the State" (*OLA Debates*, Vol. II (3), 3.7.1995; 128-9).

On the Calling Attention, Biju Patanik made a submission about a Government pamphlet received by him and circulated by the Assembly, and said, "I have never seen such a worthless document. The heading given, *Odisha's New Chapter*, by Public Relations Department. This reveals Nandini's eight months work. Nandini's photograph where a bus line opens, where musical instrument distribution. These are small things. This is so disgusting of all these cases put together, there is not even one per cent of Hirakud, not even half a per cent of Rourkela, not one per cent of Paradeep, not even one per cent of Balimela and not even one per cent of Capital. No Chief Minister ever produced this kind of photographand circulated here" (*OLA Debates*, Vol. III (13), 26.12.74; 6).

Expressing anguish over the foundation stone lying by the previous Government and more particularly with the hopes and aspirations of the people, Biju Patnaik said, "Foundation-stones were laid with great fan-fare but no Planning Commission approval, no budgetary provision and so on were obtained. Apart from the State Ministers, many foundation-stones were laid by the ex-Prime Minister. There was one ₹240 crores fertilizer plant at Paradip. Lakhs of rupees were spent for the foundation-stone laying ceremony. The sea in its anguish has washed away the foundation-stones. If I may say so, I am sorry about the wanton behavior of the people in power. They raised hopes in the minds of the people. I may say, great hopes, because a steel plant means great development in the area. If you have a steel plant of 2 million or 3 million capacity that means a great city is born out of it. Tens of thousands of people are involved directly and many more are indirectly involved. To play with the hopes and aspirations of the people in this cavalier fashion, I submit, is not a decent thing to do by any Government in power. But having raised these hopes, it has fallen to my lot to see and to ensure how this could be brought into action" (*Lok Sabha Debates*, 28 June 1977; 289).

On the issue of food and starvation death, Biju Patnaik said, "I would say that food is not politics. We, on this part of the House, are not interested in politics on food. The people of Odisha are far more important than the 147 people sitting in this House. Their lives are far more important than the whole House put together. So I say, we can jointly put the question, is the Nandini Government competent to get the necessary funds,. to do the necessary work and necessary food to distribute among the thousands of people? If the Chief Minister is unable to do it, she must get out of the position she holds. She has no business to stick to it. No Chief Minister can stand the situation as it is now. Any Chief Minister whoever he or she may be should stake the State and go to the Centre. Unless it is done, I do not feel, we are competent to be here. We are living in a federal country where the Central Government has got all the resources and the State Government is given meager resources. Therefore, if you need 30 crores of rupees you get only 3 crores and here in the House we are knocking each other. If the Central Government does not give adequate funds, what the State can do? The Food Minister should feel ashamed for the failure of his food policy and getting only 50,000 tonnes. This is not what we are shouting about it. It is not enough. Our attitude is – *Indira Gandhi ki jai, let people die*. Government should take its position to the Central Government and threaten to resign unless the Centre meets our requirements. The job is not important in comparison to the lives of thousands of people. We should have proper public spirit and function publicly. Do not try to put politics in the present problem" (*OLA Debates*, Vol. IV (31), 9.4.1975; 75-6).

On the irrigation issue, Biju Patnaik said, "Earlier Sambalpur was a barren area. Amidst lot of hardship and due to the efforts of Mahatab Babu, the area has been developed by Hirakud reservoir. Confusion will be there if any area is hampered. This is natural battle between the people who want to create and the people who want to have the status-quo. Is this Government prepared to battle for its own people?" (*OLA Debates*, Vol. I (2), 25.3.1974; 44).

Discussing on the food crisis in Odisha, he said, "I have no slightest doubt that during the coming March and April, the price of rice will be

₹5 to ₹6 and may not be available. This will be the problem. The Central government will not be able to help. Ramji says at Delhi that they have not got enough stock of food. The World Bank also does not have it. The Hon'ble Minster knew that instead of one thousand million tones, they have got 600 thousand tones. The present agreement of Government of India with USA is only for 3 thousand tones instead of 100 million tones. Canada must have been booked for China; Australia must have been booked for China or Russia. There is no surplus food available. How are you going to solve this?" (*OLA Debates*, Vol. III (6), 16.12.74; 95).

Criticizing the system of levy introduced by the Government of Odisha, he said, "it possess serious problem since there is deficiency on nomenclature. There is no method of fixing the target from which land as to how much is produced and what. All these things have to be investigated so that you can know 4 acres or 5 acres or 10 acres will produce so much and he will give so much as levy which is an arithmetic exercise. I would like the Minister to tell us what other methods he has in mind. We are prepared to assist. Government should arrive at some conclusion.... As I have said earlier that the present levy system should go because this is against their own policy of procurement" (*OLA Debates*, Vol. III (6), 16.12.74; 96-7).

Administrative Issues

On the administrative mechanism and administration during his Chief Minister period, he said, "I hope, Sir, that within these 28 months that I was in the helm of affairs, there might be here and there certain deviations from the declared policy of mine. But by and large, the Members of the Opposition would agree that this Government has indeed tried to be fair. Therefore, when some Members of Opposition say that there is great deal of squandering of money in some places, it is possible. I have not yet been able to find out or evolve a method by which administrative efficiency and administrative correctness at all levels can reach perfection of the administrative machinery is a perpetual study and it is indeed again the business of every Member of this House to engage himself or herself in this perpetual study" (OLA Debates, Vol. V (18), 25.9.1963; 33).

He questioned on the administrative apparatus efficiency to cater the needs of the socialistic economy, and said, "I would like to attract the attention of the Deputy Leader of the House who has presented his budget to recast his views, and while he prepares some projects in future to devote only to one point, i.e., is our administrative apparatus so geared up as to bring about the direct increase of the socialistic economic objective? Does this pattern of finance, does this pattern of administration suit the requirements of the country as I have said a few minutes ago? Because, if the country has to prosper, the largest section of the country must prosper. I do not care if a class of men has a few palaces. I am not interested in a few acres of lands which they might enjoy of course for social justice they must get out-I am not interested if they get a few lakhs of rupees. But I am interested in training of people's mind through our budget, through our publicity, to reach our social objective. Even in a socialistic country like Sweden, Sir, there are some Dukes, there are some landlords who have their palaces, who have to pay income-tax; but that does not stop the achievement of the socialistic economy and better the lot of the peasants, the largest unit of the country. So, Sir, the largest unit of the country must get the tools to finish the job" (*OLA Debates*, Vol. IV (5), 23.2.60; 25).

On the administration mechanism and its requirements, he said, "There are many things regarding farmers, regarding loans, regarding money-lenders, lack of facilities, lack of purpose and many such things which we agree. But creating is one matter and implementing it to our own satisfaction is quite a different matter. We have to consider various things-the administration, it capacity, its direction, its motive force, the legacy that we have taken over from the British days, our own capacity to change, to alter and redesign it, collective capacity not only of the Congress benches but also of the Opposition, the totality of our intellectual acumen to change this apparatus to suit the need of the modern times. Sir, in this context you may remember perhaps that when Kamraj Plan was first ushered in the Congress Party, a paper was prepared called *The Kamraj Plan* and you will permit me to read a few paragraphs which relate not only to the opinion of the Opposition benches but also of the Congress benches" (*OLA Debates*, Vol. VII (25), 31.3.1965; 33).

> On administrative machine, we feel that with the declaration of independence, the administration had to face diverse new tasks demanded by a sovereign Nation. Sovereignty by itself brought in complex responsibilities. Internal consolidation against disruptive forces like caste, creed, religion, language and regionalism presented a formidable challenge. Closer relationship with the rest of the world demanded of free India, leadership of thought for the freedom struggle for the rest of the colonies. Even highly industrialized nations began toying with the possibilities of mass annihilation by the splitting of the atoms, came to look upon India to provide a base for maintenance of basic human sanity. Further responsibility as placed on the administration, the people of India, gave ourselves democratic Constitution, with separate judiciary and audit system, and also proceeded to turn the nation into a welfare State. We have also declared that the development of the masses in this welfare State would be achieved through the instrument of socialist economy within the scope of a democratic Constitution. We have given ourselves a planned framework through which socialist economic systems would be forged. Very recently we decided that India must rapidly develop her military strength with all the complexities of research, production, construction and development of men and material to enable her to meet any foreign aggression.

He said, "In retrospect, we need to consider the quality of the apparatus that the British left us which we face these new responsibilities and greater burdens in years to come. We also need to consider whether the Congress Party has done any really serious, consolidated thinking to reorganize the administrative apparatus to enable it to discharge these responsibilities. Briefly speaking, the administrative machine which free India inherited from the British was designed for their specific purposes. This system was meant to be lofty and secluded from the masses. It was meant to be the rulers' ego and the people were meant to stand in awe of it. The machine was designed to have a halo around it so that no Indian could ever question its efficiency or directives. It was meant to hold a large mass of people in subjugation. The machine itself provided the will and purpose, and the people were debarred from thinking. The machine became the master and the people its slaves. As a colonial apparatus, it was based on mistrust and the institutional growth of this machine depended on the will and policies of the British rulers in London. Thousands of checks and balances, audits and accounts, were perpetrated in this colonial administrative system, which sought to hold its own by creating divisions and mistrust at all levels. Obviously, such a machine cannot be expected to stand the test of present day needs of an expanding economy of a sovereign nation" (*OLA Debates*, Vol. VII (25), 31.3.1965; 33).

"Whereas there are large number of men and women in various fields of our administration who individually would be able to hold their own against their counterparts in highly progressive administration of the world, the colonial administrative system which we have adopted and not redesigned so far, stands as a greater barrier against legitimate utilization of their individual and collective capacity. If a bulldozer cannot do the work of a crane or pump, it is not the fault of the bulldozer. It is the fault of the designers. The designer in this context is the Congress Party, who, having ushered in a new independent India, has not yet rigorously applied itself to this arduous task of redesigning the administrative apparatus. Consequently, when we find that this machine cannot implement the task, which constantly changing urges and policies of the people demand of it, we feel exasperated and smugly state that administrative machine is inefficient or corrupt; that it is weak and holds up all progress" (*OLA Debates*, Vol. VII (25), 31.3.1965; 33-4). The *Kamraj Plan* stated:

> It, therefore, becomes the duty of the Congress, as the ruling party of India, to take upon itself, with the assistance of whatever talent is available in the country to probe deep into every facet of administration and bring about revolutionary changes in the methods, rules and laws which would permit the administrative machine to ably discharge new types of responsibilities and far greater loads. It may be remembered that while we design this new apparatus and put it to test, we should

> constantly watch the flaws found in its operation and continuously attempt improvement. No machine is ever perfect and yet the designer always seeks perfection. Very considerable knowledge, energy and skill of a large band of dedicated and capable men would be required to design a suitable administrative apparatus to uplift 450 million people within a measurable period of time. All this, however, remains completely the responsibility of the Congress Party. While the Congress has to accept this responsibility and get on with the task, we have also to take into account the limitations of our national ability. We should be logical and pragmatic and not be swayed by mere lofty idealist announcement. At any rate, as workmen, we should cease to quarrel with our tools.

Speaking on the crux of administration, he said, "I visited a village where labouers only live. I met an old lady who told me many things, out of which one is, she is purchasing rice at ₹4 per kilo. She told she is eating starch water, and other things. I asked her if you were made the Chief Minister, what you will do. She told me that she will immediately do three works. First, bring down rice from ₹4 to ₹2 per kilo; make arrangements how our people will get work and income every day; and minimum wage to increase to ₹20 from ₹10-12 This is the crux of administration. We are not running the administration for this mass of people. That is 85 % of the total population of the State. We are running administration for the Commissioner, Secretaries, Chief Engineers, Executive Engineers, Collectors and the like. The entire machinery of this Legislature is involved. This must be cut Sir, lakhs of people are unemployed" (*OLA Debates*, Vol. IX (27), 31.3.1989; 82).

On the issue of migration due to no work opportunities in villages in Odisha, he said, "There are same thing in Koraput and Kalahandi districts, which should have been done. Continuously 10 years is a long term for a Government but nothing has been touched. This is unfortunate; if you want a remedy for longer period you should have touched this. Now my main question is this, when the Relief Code provides, Mr. Revenue Minister, that the Collectors shall provide works in the drought affected areas to able-bodied person. May I know, why lakhs of people are leaving Padampur and Bolangir and going outside? Question is this, people are starving. Collectors business is to provide work. I want to know what has been done for them. Nothing has been done. Lakhs of people are starving and they are going to other States because we cannot provide work for them. Why? What the RDC, Commissioner, Collectors, etc., are doing, what developmental work they are doing, why the migration is happening? I would say the Treasury Bench should migrate, if 5 lakhs people are migrating, why are you not migrating? Just to say that people generally migrate is not only an insult to the Government, it is also an insult to the people.. When I had been to Jhadban area, which is a border area, there in the block head-quarter houses no men were seen. When I asked where the men folk are there,

I knew that they have gone to Raipur for work opportunities. I have travelled throughout Odisha. You may not have heard the name of Jhadban. Many women attended my meeting. They were all crying and weeping. You are unable to understand this much. Why the Collectors have failed to provide work for them? Had the Collector been taken to task? Had the Commissioner been taken to task? Had the Minister been taken to task? Then, if not, why? I know, they cannot do it. Result, lakhs of people leave their homes. Lakhs of people are working in Vizag Steel Plant from Kalahandi and Koraput" (*OLA Debates*, Vol. IX (31), 6.4.1989; 83-4).

On the IAS structure and bureaucratic hurdles, he said, "Nothing moves in Delhi. The IAS people those who get promotions and move to Delhi mans the Delhi administration and you have a bureau which sought waste projects. So, I told the Prime Minister, it takes time and the bureau should be disbanded forth with and the projects should be cleared up by different Ministries by coordinating each other. Restrictions I said, in a rapidly changing economic structure of the world need to be put to do away with bureaucratic fetters and various stigmas because the Indian industries live only on tariff loan. There is a big wall on the economic front of India. It rises from customs duties to export duties" (*OLA Debates*, Vol. II (22), 6.7.1990; 64-5).

On the disaster management due to severe flood, he said, "I would like to inform the House that Navy, Air Force and Army have done yeoman service to our State. The House would do well to thank them for all the work they have done. We should unanimously thank them. They are still at the job. They are taking care of our people in areas where it is dangerous to low level. I have been with them for three four days. I know a little bit of flying. I can tell you they are taking great personal risk so that our people can get some relief. The boats sent by Army, Navy, and Paradip Port Trust are also engaged fully. Sir, the problem is we are trying to recover there from this shock of this flash flood that is still continuing" (*OLA Debates*, Vol. XV (2), 21.7.1994; 56). He further continued, "Sir, all I want to say is that seven days relief have been ordered and I have further ordered wherever the Collector feel it necessary, he will extend it further. Relief is a matter which must reach the people, it is not a matter of relief code and what is necessary to the people has been ordered for. The entrance of students to the colleges, etc., and all that care has been taken. The main problem is repair of bridges and embankments of river Subarnarekha. That is a very serious problem" (*ibid*; 61). On the issue of getting funds from the Central Government, he said, "We have given the total estimate to Government of India as on date. One Minister is coming here. The Indian Prime Minister is good enough to send Ministers to the flood affected States and Mr. Antoni is coming here this afternoon. We will give him the white paper and then a Memorandum today or tomorrow. I don't feel he will do help very much because it has happened previously. When Aska flood was there we have spent more than sixty crores only for rehabilitation only for rehabilitation without the bridge. Bridges have to go to the World Bank which has taken three years to clear it. The works have been started now. I have a doubt whether the work will be finished within three months or not. But, once World Bank have taken it up it will be finished. Fifty and odd crores of rupees this Government has spent, but not a single penny promised by Government of India has come to the coffers of this Government. I am very sorry to say this is Government of India? I have told and written to all the MPs irrespective of party affiliation, to fight with Government of India if you at all want to save all these things. Nothing happened" (*ibid*; 62). Expressing his helplessness, he said, "I said, I am begging and for the people of this State, if I am to beg, I would not hesitate to do that.... The Central Government pose their own problems. Inspite of that, they are able to build the underground Railway line in Calcutta, costs 2,500 crore of rupees. They can build new harbor in Bombay, another 3,000 crore of rupees. They can put gas-line to Andhra Pradesh.... These are the problems for which I must take the House into confidence irrespective of party affiliations. This House has to decide this side or that side" (*ibid*; 62-3).

On land acquisition for development purpose, Biju Patnaik said that they are now trying to acquire a bit of land for the past two years, but due to objections, over-rulings, going to courts, etc., it is lingering. He said, "I readily agree with the Hon. Members assertion that the Government servants were not very efficient. That is a fact which remains. If that is so, how could you expect Government to carry on the multifarious work like the Hirakud, Dumduma, etc. The fact remains we are not very efficient people. Therefore we have got to have some rough and ready method. Therefore while we acquiesce in humanitarian principles, all our major work will stop unless land is acquired" (*OLA Debates*, 11 12.1948; 200).

Alleging bureaucracy for the non-progress of Government Corporations and Departments, he said, "It is due to the bureaucracy. Bureaucracy is the inertia which has to be destroyed. This bureaucratic force has to be destroyed. Bureaucratic inertia is too deep in our administration which retards every progressive movement. It is a reactionary force which has to be destroyed. It should be borne in mind whether we be this side of the House or the other. It is our Prime Minister who is also fighting this bureaucracy. She keeps us telling that it throttles our administration. Therefore remember this. Departments after Departments are doing this ding-dong for the last 6 months about the formation of this corporation" (*OLA* Debates, Vol. III (2), 4.1.1972; 44).

On the bureaucracy, he said, "I would like to say as an MLA, I have a right to examine the work done by the Officers, OAS or IAS. Whosoever he may be. If I find he is at fault, it is my business to bring it to the notice of the people of the House and the Government. I do not know whether he is OAS or IAS, or whether after all he is a servant of the Government, servant of the people. When the people representatives want to do something, they are trying to thwart their duties. How do you say democracy in this country exists?" (*OLA* Debates, VII (3), 26.2.1988; 100).

Biju Paper giving the reference of the starting of Paradeep port, and said, "When we wanted to start Paradeep there was no Planning Commission sanction. Here, the opposition at that time was asking where from we will get money. I said, do not ask that question. Money will come in time in the budget. But the question asked to me by the Prime Minister, Pandit Nehru at that time was that do you have the administrative capacity to implement it? I said, *yes*. At that time our administrative services were weaker. Engineering services were weaker. We had to import engineers, doctors, and almost everything from outside at that time. But yet through that administration by the necessary leadership and all that this, Paradeep was possible, say in course of three years. So, it is not enough. When we should demand it, we should also deserve it. The administrative machineryhas to be geared to pick efficiency because Odisha needs its administration must be at peak efficiency. What we find is that inefficient rule is the order of the day! For that should we blame the administration or should we blame the political machinery which was much better in 1961 than in 1975? There is something wrong in the political system which covers the whole House. We must have more investment much more than was envisaged. Our administrative machinery must be more efficient and be able to develop it further. If we do not do it, Odisha will be nowhere. We cannot go on taking doles for everything every time and making our people beggars for all time. Therefore, it is necessary for the government to fine ways and means to have much better investment, possible as it is exhibited now by the Governor's address. As I said before, I do not think it in terms of politics that Odisha's development is concerned. But if the ruling party, which is in existence today, restricts itself to conduct its affairs only with its limited capacity, then they have to stand on the bar of the history of Odisha's development" (*OLA Debates*, Vol. IV (2), 19.2.75; 102). This shows the necessity and significance of a strong administrative structure for the development of a state in India.

On the issue of Judiciary intervention in the administration for one reason or another, during the Judges (Conditions of Service) Amendment Bill, 1996, Biju Patnaik said, "In 1961, when I was the Chief Minister of my State, the matter, whether the judiciary should be separated from the executive or not, came up before the National Development Council. Panditji was all in favour of separation of the judiciary from the executive and equally a powerful man like Dr. Vedante was equally against it. He kept on saying-it was his fear-that if you separate the judiciary, then the judiciary will ultimately land up into an arena of determining who is going to be the Chief Minister. He tried to point to the extreme case. But, ultimately we won and the judiciary was separated. From that time to till now, it is amusing to note that the judiciary is slowly encroaching upon the authority of the executive, which means, the authority of Parliament" (OLA; 178). He cited how the Apex Court directed the CBI to 'have another look. Go into more details and come back to us. Review the situation and come back to us'."They could have admonished the Government and got the report through the Government again and they could have admonished it again if they were not satisfied.... This is a matter on which, I think, Parliament should form a body and both the body constituted by Parliament and the judiciary body should sit together and find a way, whereby nobody impinges on the other. There are three wings of the nation's administration- Parliament, the executive and the judiciary. All must function independently. When somebody wants to impinge on other's authority, the trouble begins" (OLA; 179).

Police Administration

On the Police functioning, he said, "The British left this country and we have just got the apparatus, but the mind has not changed. During the time of British, the police force was an oppressive force. Because their business was to oppress using harass words and abusing every citizen. This needs to be very substantially changed. They have to behave properly like a civilized officer right from constable to S.P., I.G. and D.G. and so on. They have to undergo considerable mental change. I do not want that the Police misbehave the ordinary people, which would reflect badly on administration and that is also not encouraged" (*OLA Debates*, Vol. II (6), 7.6.1990; 194).

On interference in Police administration, he said, "What is the maintenance of the law and order. As a Government or as political machinery, if you interfere with the administration of the Police, then law and order automatically gets eroded. The day the Chief Minister himself interferes in the promotion, posting or transfers of Police officers, I say in this House for something of future Government that the State Government law and order machinery has stood eroded with that" (X (3), 11.9.1989; 138). He also said, "As an elderly person, I may put it--that please note whichever party may be in Government, interference with Police administration will result in the Police resorting to revolt. In our times we were able to manage it, but you are not able to manage it.... The interference in the Police administration, if this could be eliminated by the Chief Minister who happens to be the Home Minister, I can assure the Police administration can take care of all the dacoits, all the murders/killers, all the rapists, all the thieves, etc. They are not able to do that because they are employed by the politicians. Some day will come in this country when the Police administration will be like the CAG, away from the interference of the Government. They will administer the Police administration themselves. It will be a good thing for the nation" (X (3), 11.9.1989; 139).

While encouraging the then Director General of Police in the State, he said, "On words of defense for him, I would like to say that he is a very upright person; he is not frightened by anybody, whether he is a Janata man or anybody. He is not frightened. He has got his weakness like all of us have, like prejudices, likes or dislikes, intense likes and dislikes. On the question of firing, mu instructions were quite clear that no firing should take place except in cases of self-defense and whether on self-defense, these 3-4 firings took place, it is a matter for Commission of Enquiry to judge. I will not give any opinion on that subject at all" (*OLA Debates*, Vol. III (8), 17.10.1990; 80). He also refereed, "Then there is a talk about IG and DG. I know a DG under certain Chief Minister reign said, 'rape is not a crime, and it is no crime'. He (then Chief Minister) did not change him. Because of that, there was discussion countrywide over the issue. The Member from Tirtol who is nodding, he is of the same opinion as it seems to me. There was countrywide agitation on how such a statement made by some very high official and I am sure the person has corrected himself for any wrong ideas about it" (*OLA Debates*, Vol. III (8), 17.10.1990; 81).

On Police reformation, he said, "I have said three things, that there should be improvement in jails, there should be improvement in the Police administration, there should be improvement in the behavior of the Police vis-à-vis public. All these improvements are necessary. But sincewe have not yet forgotten the colonial badge that is in our heads, we have not brought the administration to the people together. We can bring some day democracy a successful democracy. Till that time, we have to struggle. Whether it is the judiciary or whether it is the administration, whoever it is. We will have to fight as the representatives of the people" (*OLA Debates*, Vol. IV (6), 14.3.1991; 94).

On the Police force, he said, "They have politicized the Police force. I expect my Police force, my bureaucracies to be neutral. But you have your Congress party and your people in the last 10 to 15 years, you have politicized them. Smt. Indira Gandhi, erstwhile Prime Minister said, I want them to be committed, Judiciary to be committed. Bureaucracy to be committed. Everybody started being committed. Bureaucracy and bureaucrats include Police. Judiciary includes Judges. Anyhow, these are the travesty of time and travesty of situation" (*OLA Debates*, Vol. VII (23), 26.3.1992; 101).

On the Police performance, he said, "My instructions to the Police are clear that theywill do justice and you will not yield to any pressure from anyone, including the Chief Minister. You must do justice. This is my written order to the Police Force. They are instructed to act impartially and according to law. I said, nobody, including the Chief Minister is above law. But whatever the instruments of law deserve this kind of confidence in my view it is quite another matter. This should be made to deserve confidence if the Government impose on them.... One thing I must say in deference to my Police force. I am proud of them, the House is also proud of them. They have been able to maintain continuously peace and harmony in our society, particularly communal peace and harmony. Maintaining this peace and harmony is something for which the State must be proud of" (*OLA Debates*, Vol. XII (6), 8.11.1993; 155).

On giving more powers to the Police, he said, "The British Constable and our Constable are two different characters, only because the training is different. The British Constable can arrest a Cabinet Minister without batting an eyelid. Mr. Minister, you have broken the law, you are arrested. The British Constable can say it. But here, the SP is to think of arresting a Minister. Why? Because, the training is different. I have tried to change it. I have told my Police force that you will do whatever is just and you will have the protection of the Government. You will not be swayed down by any political considerations. Bit it takes time. Ten years, twenty-five years of political interference with this force has contaminated their minds. They are afraid. If they really do it, they may not get the support of the Government. This is taking little time. I hope, I should be able to slowly detach them and will make them an independent Police force for the good of the people" (*OLA Debates*, Vol. XIV (13), 16.3.1994; 118).

On the Police force becoming more people-friendly, he said, "How to convert our Police force into a friendly force, friendly to the people. People should have confidence in them. But I am sorry to say. I do admit that such is not the case in my State, nor any other State of India. It is unfortunate.... Our Police force has become slack. Physical fitness and training are two essential things for any Policeman. I am ashamed when I see an Inspector with a big belly. He should be sacked. What he will inspect? No, let us not laugh on this matter. A force must be a force. You cannot be a force, if you are unable to walk" (*OLA Debates*, Vol. X(22), 23.3.1993; 128).

With regard to strengthening the Police Stations and equipping them with arms and ammunition, he said, "*Thanas* have to be strengthened. There is no doubt that the constabulary has to be strengthened. Better equipment has to be given to the *Thanas*. Better fire power and training on fire power has to be done to deal with unsocial elements. All these involves a great deal of money. We are working out the cost the other day with the DG and officials concerned and it came to something nearly 500 crores. Sir, if I mention certain things which the House should know and what steps has this Government taken to bring the administration to the people, especially police administration. Therefore, we started an open

House discussion between Police and public every month since January 1994" (*OLA Debates*, Vol. XVI (4), 21.9.1994; 70-1).

On the Police force, Biju Patnaik referred to the incident at Dalli-Rajhara iron-ore mine near Bhillai, and said, "It is most unfortunate that firing should have been resorted to by the Police. Ten persons were killed on the spot and one died in the hospital. Besides, some persons were wounded also. It is my view that this could have been avoided. I am rather surprised that even after the change of the Government; the Police at places continue to be trigger-happy. This Government does not appreciate continuance of this attitude of our Police force in India. The Prime Minister has said time and again that the Police must use minimum force in situations like this" (*Lok Sabha Debates*, 28 June 1977; 284-5).

Participating on this discussion, Biju Patnaik spoke on how the Police force is being politicized by the ruling party and also the problems of the Police administration. He said, "Has the Police administration failed or the Minister-in-Charge of Police administration failed or the Treasury benches have failed or the party in power has failed but there has been a single failure at this facet. We know it for a fact that the Police administration either with the connivance of the political party in power, either with the connivance of the Minister-in-Charge or with collective connivance and collective inaction the Police administration has failed badly which has led to apart from other things a new phenomenon of political violence leading to political murders. This I believe is something new in this state atleast in this country though I am not yet sure whether the Treasury benches wish it. For the time being they are in the Treasury benches, it may give them some luxurious pleasure of reaping political benefits....whether the Treasury benches are in fact at all willing to prevent the growth of political violence leading to political murder in the state. Police administration has also become weak because of various *ad hoc* changes and arbitrary changes made at the senior level or at other levels and not linking them properly in the rank and file. If you want to keep a Police force especially a police force which is supposed to maintain law and order, which is supposed to stand behind the depressed and poor people against the richer and powerful, then the Police force at your disposal must be taken care of in a better and satisfactory way than what is being done today. Dissatisfaction and discontentment is manifest in the Police force because minimum living condition is not assured to then and any government worth the name must try to rectify it as far as possible. Today if you go round the state it is not that this government is able to upheld the rule of law, but it will appear that this government is opposed to the rule of law. This si very unsatisfactory state of affairs and in fact that thing reflects also inside this House. In certain matters at the slightest provocation or the slightest opposition there are Members of the Treasury bench who usually stand-up and show like this – come, let us fight – which you must have seen here in the last two weeks.... So I would like very much for the Department and the Minister-in-Charge of Police administration to review the entire thing to make it efficient and not to make it what is called the politicization of the Police force or to be a party to taking side between factions in Police force at any level just to suit your own political requirements. The day it done, there is an end to this democratic rule in this country, security force and the armed forces. This form of democracy and this sort of administration should go" (*OLA Debates*, Vol. III (11), 20.12.74; 74-5).

On the Demand for Grant for Police and speaking on the impartial and neutrality of the police force, Biju Patnaik said, "There is no doubt that like all the departments of Government, Police department also has to be not only strengthened quantitatively but also qualitatively because we have one of the major colonial apparatus that we have inherited in this country, i.e. police apparatus. Therefore, this colonial and feudal system will have to be changed and police is not exception to that. Nevertheless, various police reforms have been introduced in this country from time to time after independence, but without much tangible result yet. To say that, police would be the protector of the poor is still a dream and is yet to come over in our country. But what I suggest is that, efforts should be made in that direction for the training and if necessary, for this particular purpose, social justice. The fear is now misuse of force, whether it is police force or other force of law for political end or political gain, that's what is exercising in the mind of the people.... The whole thing is justice must not only be done but it must appear to be done. Similarly, any democratic Government styles exposed to this view that what the Government does must appear to be fair and above board.... But what is required is that whoever be in the Government, if our democracy is to be progressive rationally there must be a feeling in everybody's mind that no force of law of a State is to be used against an individual if he is in the political opposition. If that feeling grows, democracy would continue. I do not know how the Home Minister overnight will be able to change it because there are forces within a political party which want this thing be done and that thing be done to their advantage and I know several promises are made. But promises must not be made under any condition where justice is likely to be denied. The more promises are made the more degenerating forces of democracy are there because democracy can only function on fairness to the opposition by the party in power. The moment you cow down the opposition, you have suppressed democracy to that extent. Therefore, it is not a one-way traffic. Everybody should be alert to see that the feeling of injustice, especially, any political persecution is not engineered by any action of the Government..... It is not enough to say just leave them alone; the law will take its own course. The British also used to say that. If you say this, I think, we have only exchange the black-men in place of white-men" (*OLA Debates*, Vol. III (7), 17.12.74; 119-20).

Speaking on the public and political demands for transfers of police personnel on some political grounds, Biju Patnaik said, "I had cautioned the Chief Minister that if you do things like that, no Police Officer will have independence. If things are done like this, how do you think administration can function and how do you expect the people to get justice under these circumstances... When there is conflict of interest, when there is difference in attitude, attack and counter attack, trust and mistrust, there is a clear case of judicial enquiry in the highest level i.e. by a High Court Judge" (*OLA Debates*, Vol. III (8), 18.12.74; 101-02).

On the Demand of Grants for Police, Biju Patnaik said, "There is no gainsaying the fact that the Police have to be modernized. We are still living in a feudal system not only in Odisha, but all over the country as well. The society is based on feudal consideration; the literature is on feudal thinking. We cannot have a story without *Rajas* and *Ranis*. This is our historical background. So, the Police of the Government, what we have today are largely convenient for the feudal system. We have not been able to effectively change the administrative system of Government, much less the police administration. The Police Code and Police Manual had been enacted at the time of the colonial rule. It does need considerably change in thinking, in attitude and management" (*OLA Debates*, Vol. II (15), 27.6.74; 107). Comparing the Odisha Police with US Police and the technological innovations, he said, "If an Odisha Police Force is sent to serve in the City of Chicago, that Police Force will be murdered in 24 hours. This is how the technology of crime and the technology of modern criminals are moving. We have no modern or very little of modern technology" (*OLA Debates*, Vol. II (15), 27.6.74; 108).

Federalism

On the subject of infrastructural development in the context of federalism, he said, "We are not an isolated State. We are part of a federal structure. There are competing States. If we do not do it in Mahanadi, then Narmada will do it. If Narmada does not do it, Harbhanga will do it. It should be the combined effort, combined desire, combined incentive of all of us in this House to take over certain profitable, workable projects for irrigation, for power, for industrial development, for modern agriculture, for efficient transport system and technical education and the like, which alone can change and transform this poor State to a rich modern State. This is the crux of the problem. In the process of implementation, if there are lapses, legitimate charges of inefficiency, these should be reviewed, verified and corrected. It is certainly the business of the Opposition to point out these to the Government. It is certainly the business of Members of the Treasury Benches also to point out such defects. Progress of the State is indivisible and the collective responsibility of all" (*OLA Debates*, Vol. IX (3), 23.2.1966; 14-5).

To this Hon'ble Member Prasanna Kumar Dash commented, "We have said many times, where are the tile-roof houses and piped water?" Biju Patnaik replied, "I agree with the Hon'ble Member from Khunta that this is a legitimate charge. I welcome this charge. Why the Government, when they made a plan, could not fulfill it? That is a legitimate charge. But to say, that crores of rupees were wasted in Paradip, etc., when there is no evidence of such waste, is an improper and illegitimate charge. That is all what I wish to convey the House and I am sure Hon'ble Members would agree with me" (*OLA Debates*, Vol. IX (3), 23.2.1966; 14).

On a legal clarification the Leader of Opposition Rajendra Narayan Singhdeo asked to Biju Patnaik, "Why was the issue of Jawaharlal Nehru laying the Foundation Stone for Paradip port raised. Why was Nehru brought to lay the Foundation Stone of Taikarparaproject? When it was not approved? On these different facts cropped in, the Central Government said one thing, the State Government said another thing. Shall I ask now or at the end of this speech?" (*OLA Debates*, Vol. IX (3), 23.2.1966; 16). To this Biju Patnaik replied, "The question that has been posed by the Hon'ble Leader of Opposition is how can these works be taken up without the so-called administrative approval? The Hon'ble Leader of Opposition, a formerly princely, is a product of the past and I claim to be a product of the future. Administrative approval, administrative set-up, rules and the regulations, all these are of a colonial set-up under which he functioned, lived and thrived" (*OLA Debates*, Vol. IX (3), 23.2.1966; 16). To this, Hon'ble Member Prasanna Kumar Dash said, "He is a princely product, but the Hon'ble Member is a capitalist product". However, Biju Patnaik then continued and said, "The Leader of Opposition has got in his blood a system of colonial administration under which he flourished. We demolished colonialism to set-up a new administrative machinery where achievement becomes the motive. Any colonial rules and regulations that stand on the way must be pushed aside; new rules must be substituted so that the targets can be achieved. Therefore, if the Prime Minister comes and lays the Foundation of Paradip while there is no administrative approval, no Planning Commission approval, no colonial regulation approval, I would say that between the Prime Minister of India and the Government of Odisha of that time, if they decided that Paradip must be built the decision became final. The rules, the regulations, the *status-quo*, the officials, the inert minds, all had to abide by this decision. On similar basis, Foundation Stone was laid on Tikarpara. Tikarpara has been delayed. Well, I have no doubts about the future of Odisha. I say, Tikarpara should be the vanguard of the future prosperity of Odisha. The Governor has made a pointed reference to this. We have it at page 27 of his address, as follows,

> We have to streamline our administration and equip the cadres effectively to undertake responsibilities to meet the changing and multiplying

> requirements of a developing Welfare State. Integrity, expedition, and economy have to be their watchward. They have strictly to adhere to the code of ethics and follow the accepted rules.... (*"He says the* accepted rules, *not the present rules"*) .... But the deadwood which hampers progress and causes delays must be removed. We have to remember that rules and regulations are a means to an end and that that end is achievement *(*OLA Debates, *Vol. IX (3), 23.2.1966; 16-7).*

He then continued to say, "This is what the Governor has said, which the Hon'ble Leader of the Opposition, if he ever wants to run or lead a Government of a progressive State, would do well to remember that sticking to the inadequate colonial rules would hamper the progress of a free and progressive State. Therefore, I say that if Members of the Opposition today, wish to be the Government of tomorrow, I enjoin on them, I plead with them, I emphasise that their sights must be set higher, their attention must be on the future, their criticisms-whether politically based or for temporary use must not cloud their vision of the future. Let them not criticize for demolishing a Government by short-sighted means, because in a democratic set-up, no Government is sacrosanct, no party is sacrosanct; only the purpose is important. The Governor has drawn pointed attention of this House and of the people at large when he says, '*We must, therefore, be prepared to amend or scrap any rules and regulations, which howsoever useful they may have been in the past....*' He means the colonial administrative set-up of which the Hon'ble Leader of Opposition insists on continuing as an integral part. The Governor stated, '*The present challenge of Odisha is a transition from stagnation to dynamic self-sustaining growth. The gap between intention and action, and between promise and performance has to be bridged*'. The Hon'ble Member from Khunta said, 'We, the PSP intended, preached'. The Leader of the Opposition said, 'We the Swantra Party preached and promised'. I say, the Congress Party, the Congress Government bridged that gap between the promise and the performance. I have no quarrel with their intention. Their intention was good. We performed. Do not blame us for the performance. The Congress Party and the Congress Government will go on performing and as more facts come to the light, more would the Congress gather strength and the number of the Opposition will suffer progressive reduction. It is their own work that makes it so. It is not what I desire. It is their canard that makes the people revolt against them. I do not desire that. What I have to say is that if you wish to remain as a responsible Opposition, which the Congress party hopes and desires for smooth running of the democracy, I have no doubt that your criticisms should be such as would assist this House collectively to take this State forward and not remain as dead wood or a matter of the past. The people will not forgive us" (*OLA Debates*, Vol. IX (3), 23.2.1966; 17-8).

On the issue of finance through loans, he said, "The State Government cannot float loans unless it has the concurrence or approval of the Central

Government because ultimately all debts, whether they belong to the State or Centre form part of the national debt and that the guarantee capacity rests only with the Federal or the Central Government. Therefore, when we get some sanction for loan, it is know that the loan would be raised from assured market of the Central agencies financing the loan, such as LIC or State Bank. So, what is effect has taken place in the seal of approval of the Centre to our work, to our achievements and a bright future to which this House can legitimately lay claim" (*OLA Debates*, Vol. VI (2), 18.2.1964; 43).

On the resolution of changing the name of the State Odisha to Kalinga or Utkal, he opined to create a modern State of Odisha as a part of modern India and said that in this regard we are not against any "analogical thinking or reactionary thinking", but it should not be imposed upon others. He said, "We may think of everything but we may discard many. There is provision for freedom of thinking, freedom to speak, freedom of association, etc.' in the Constitution, which are normal provisions in the democratic Constitution of India. If at the pan-India level the different little sentiment will start saying on the basis of his language, Odia, Bengali, Tamil etc., and for this Pandit Nehru said that India is a 'Unitary State'. India has been constituted by taking various languages and areas. This is a great country. The geographical identity has been created since Asoka period. We have the entire instrument to create our modern India. These are Central Government and State Government, Central Parliament and State Legislature, Central Planning Commission and State Planning Board. India has not been able to stand straight even after having plan and development for the last twenty-five years. One reason for this is that there is no people's involvement in plan and development work. Planning is done in Delhi and in Secretariat of New Capital and so is disjointed from people. National plan and State plan are being imposed upon people. These plans have no thinking about the people. For this even after 25 years, 70 per cent of people are in the stat of poverty, whereas smashed Germany and Japan could reconstruct after a period of twenty years. We must very seriously examine this point. Why this happened? The thinking of Hitler destroyed Germany, but still then it established as a superior nation, due to patriotism. So, without imposing our thinking upon others, we should restore the nation. We want to be one with others. Even after twenty-five years of independence we have not reached even the minimum of our requirements. Why? This is a matter of argument. This broader patriotism is totally lacking in the political floor of India. The Indian political floor is imposing something on the people. The Central Government is called the central machine; the Planning Commission is called the house of arithmetic and the State Secretariat is another machine. It is all a combination of machines and figures. There is no vitality, there is no energy, and there is no people's enthusiasm for treating it as a part of the national adventure. It is not there. Twenty-five years of experience has shown us that everyday there is experiment-Experiment in respect of villages, in respect of constituency. It shows people and the administration, people and the Government, whether of the State or of the Centre or of the national level, are just non-existent. How do we reverse it? If we cannot reverse it, I may tell you that this country called India or State called Odisha will not reach, I repeat, will not reach the state of affluence even in thousand years, even if hundred Indira Gandhi, hundred Nandini Satapathy or thousand Biju Patnaik say so, unless the mass plan and begin to dedicate themselves, sacrifice, can work for 12 hours for 6 hours wages to enable this six hours for enriching the nation. Mere slogans, mere bickering with each other, mere fighting against ourselves in a stage like Assembly or elsewhere cannot lead us to affluence. For the last 25 years, we have collectively failed. What then is the machine? The machine in the whole national fibre is the patriotism which in turn will allow several persons to dedicate himself or herself and offer the sacrifice which the national would demand from him (*OLA Debates*, Vol. V (10), 23.2.1973; 28-9).

In the context of Federal structure giving adequate powers to the States, he said, "Because if everything fails, then only we should take to extreme methods as happened elsewhere. For example, as has happened in Karnataka and Tamil Nadu over distribution of Cauvery water. There is trouble all over the place. The same thing happened in Assam by ULFA activists. Everything is created because of this situation because they have been neglected. I have raised this question in totality in terms of the Federal structure to give adequate power to the States to mind their own business on their own resources. It is obvious that in many cases it should be diverted from the Centre and given to the States. The royalty, cess, etc., is one of them where the State Government will have wisdom to take correct judgment which will not affect the State and at the same time it will not affect the movement of the Nation" (*OLA Debates*, Vol. VI (5), 20.12.1991; 96). He also gave examples of other items, like, Consignment Tax, non-renewable assets, from which the Odisha Government is not getting its appropriate share. He said, "This matter can only be sorted out if the Centre-State relationships are reviewed honestly and properly. Had it been done properly, I am confident, Punjab situation would not have arisen" (*OLA Debates*, Vol. VI (5), 20.12.1991; 96). He continued to say, "What really we are to do is to execute the Centre-State relationship, where the State will have the necessary authority to take care of itself. We do not want Defense Ministry. We do not bother about foreign relationship. But the foreign relation should be defined by the people of India through their Chief Ministers collectively" (*OLA Debates*, Vol. VI (5), 20.12.1991; 97).

Advancing the above arguments for his demand for Fiscal Autonomy for States, he said, "I hope in this struggle this House, continuously at least for net 50 years, whoever is in Government, whoever in Opposition, should collectively try to ensure (a) the population is maintained if not reduced; (b) our resources should be mobilized that is why, Sir, I had asked for fiscal autonomy. The Prime Minister said yes, that is a very good idea. But that is where it stopped. No one wants to surrender his little power. If I have fiscal autonomy, I need not go to Government of India for guarantee to raise loan. I would only talk to the Foreign Banks for that. But they say you are not a sovereign guarantor. Only your Government of India is a sovereign guarantor. So, I wanted fiscal autonomy, so that any State can become its own guarantee for the loan. So, we are within this. I keep on raising it every time in the NDC. All Chief Ministers say, 'Yes', but nothing happens. They have no idea, no confidence in themselves, in their people and on the nation. This is the problem that we have been facing" (X (7), 26.2.1993; 117-8). On further elaboration, he clarified, "The main hurdle is when the State Government guarantees the repayment of foreign loan in dollars and the dollar price goes crumbling, who will give guarantee for differences. This is real bone of contention which is going on with the Government of India. How can a foreigner make his supplies in dollars, suppose ₹30 per dollar, if it drops to ₹50 per dollar, who make up the differences? This is the problem in a country like ours, when the structure crumbles down, no Government can deal with it. Therefore, how can you expect a foreign supplier to supply us equipments? I sympathise with the Finance Minister of India. This is a great problem for him. I sympathise with the foreign companies, without such a guarantee for the differential make-up, how can they supply even if they wish to supply, even if they take equity, what good is that equity, if they do not get the balance of payment. These are the problems that are facing the balance structure. This is true. I have talked to Dr. Manmohan Singh after he presented the budget. We have to take some rough steps to find out the way. The Prime Minister says, you must have two steel plants, five steel plants. But how? If you do not remove these bottlenecks? And you remove these bottlenecks; can you give guarantee that the dollar price and the rupee price will remain constant? That is why every finance house is going to China and India is being scouted because they guarantee everything. Their State can give guarantee, but we are afraid of giving guarantee. One Secretary says, how we can guarantee, if it will be for so much then what will be our position. This kind of two minds are always hostile for any development" (X (7), 26.2.1993; 118). On the question of political instability being not conducive for fiscal autonomy, posed by Sri Umesh Swain, Hon. MLA Balikuda, he replied, "Political instability is not the question. Indira Gandhi was stable. She did not do steel plants. Mr. Rajiv Gandhi was stable with maximum number, he could not do anything. This is the mind, this is the power of decision to the point where you match development with possible losses. That is what we have to decide. But that decision is not with us because we are not a sovereign State, that lies with the Government of India, who is sovereign" (X (7), 26.2.1993; 118). He also said, "I asked Delhi to give the States the fiscal power to develop their own lots. But they will not do it. They have got little power under the Constitution of India, and they must stick to it. They do not want to part with it" (*OLA Debates*, Vol. X (3), 22.2.1993; 128).

On the State's autonomy, he said, "Central Government authority are run by officials and they are making central policy on central subject, and not the Ministers. The State does not have any initiative in it. The State does not have power to make slight changes. Therefore, I say 'to beg' I am ashamed of. I refuse to beg. I want to beg 'master' in my own house, however poor my own house may be. Nobody can object. I do not want to be dictated by anybody. I do not say I am going for war.... It should be a national effect treating the State effect with national effect i.e., the Ministry concerning the Centre and the Chief Minister in the State jointly make a treaty, desist war or peace or no peace. These are the major points for discussion. Autonomy of the State is nothing new. Federalism cum State autonomy was part of our manifesto of the Janata Dal" (*OLA Debates*, Vol. V (8), 20.9.1991; 194-5).

On decentralization, Biju Patnaik said, "We have two cement factories but we are not getting cement from these factories. Sir, you will be surprised to know that the cements that the two factories of Odisha produce are exported to Delhi and some other Andhra cements come to Odisha. This is Government of India's distribution policy. We have got a sugar mill at Aska but these are sent to other places outside Odisha and sugars from outside is coming to Odisha. This is the reason why I suggested decentralization of power. For various reasons this kind of policy is being followed by the Centre. But States like ours find it great difficulty to get more quota as the power of lobbying of our Government is poor inside and outside of Parliament at Delhi" (Vol. II(10), 1974; 130-1).

On the issue of inter-State border conflict, Biju Patnaik said, "I would like to bring to the notice of this Government about the encroachment on to the border areas of Odisha. Whether it is called Adibasi Movement or Jharkhand Movement. I have seen the Jharkhand map. Seven other districts are added to that map. Bisal Jharkhand area, whatever you call it. As I was joking with the leaders of Jharkhand, I said why don't you make it whole of north Bihar and Odisha as Jhaarkhand, then there will no problem. Apart from this joking Sir, it is necessary to be cautious about the future encroachment by various sections of people who have decided not to or want not to remain in Odisha or whatever they want to do, it may take Rourkela, it may take part of Sambalpur. So, I would suggest the Government to plan accordingly in such a manner that in the coming years these things are settled once for all (V (2), 1996; 110). He also said, "Why Jhadakhanda movement was started in the previous Government's time?

The only reason is they suppressed it. That increased the movement. Only because, I have not taken notice of it, the thing has subsided. Odisha is a part of Jahdakhanda. If we want development of backward people, then we should assist them. If backward people want to develop themselves, then we should assist them. This message has gone to the people of Mayurbhanj, Sundargarh, Keonjhar, where this Jhadakhanda movement wanted to rise. I am to inform this House, it is no longer an acute problem of this State. So the division of the Stateis for the time being at least stayed" (*OLA Debates*, Vol. XIV (13), 16.3.1994; 120).

During a discussion on drought in Odisha on 28th November 1996, Biju Ptanaik raised the issue of fiscal federalism, which he was strongly arguing during his Chief Ministership in 1990-95. He wanted the states to have more autonomy in financial matters. He said in the House, "Could I have a separate financial independence so that your Central Government does not swindle all my resources and leave me high and dry? The taxes that Narasimha Rao ji and this present Government of India has taking from Orissa's resources amount to ₹700 crore a year, and what do they get from the Prime Minister it is niggardly ₹50 crore". Biju Patnaik also reminded former Prime Minister Narasimha Rao that he wrote a distressing letter to him, during his Chief Minister days, "asking for only ₹125 crore and I wrote at the end, for my people, to beg I am not ashamed — I have not yet received a reply from Shri Narasimha Rao till today—and they draw ₹500 crore to ₹700 crore from my resources of say everything coal, bauxite or whatever it is. Don't you?" Biju Patnaik also said that as Opposition party in Odisha state, they cautioned the state government about an imminent drought. However, the state government did not pay any heed to their caution. He said in the *Lok Sabha*, "The Chief Minister and the state Ministers have gone to Japan. I had pointed it out that this was not the time to go and flirt around and sightseeing in different countries, you would get nothing out of those countries. Japan is not yesterday's baby. But they go to Tokyo, Korea, Hong Kong, Singapore for a nice long jaunt and here the people are running away from the state..... Today, in the Assembly the Chief Minister is saying, it is a national calamity. Was he sleeping all this time"? This was Biju Patnaik's concern and commitment for his state of Odisha that he often compared with the ancient days of Kalinga under Emperor Kharavella rule. Biju Patnaik further expressed his concern for the system-failure in India. He was very broad-minded in his approach, for which he never blamed a particular person, but tried to address the problem in a 'holistic' manner, where the 'top' person managing the whole affair has to enthuse upon the system. He cited the example of Railway lines, where the British laid 58,000 miles of lines, while India has added only 8,000 miles. He also gave the example of steel production where India, per annum, produces 15 million tons, while China produces 110 million tons. He said that, "A Government is a continuous affair, Shri Narasimha Rao was the Prime Minister or somebody else may be the Prime Minister today and some third person will be the Prime Minister tomorrow. That is not the point. But the point is that the Government machinery has to function and that machinery can function only with the urging of the top people, whether it is the Prime Minister or the Chief Minister or whoever it is. Now that is not happening. Is it not sad? I do not wish to decry any person. It is not a person that I am interested and it is the system. The system is not working".

It was during this drought discussion in Lok Sabha when Narasimha Rao said, "The industrialization programme in Orissa has not yet taken off in spite of two 'Patnaiks' struggling with it". Biju Patnaik immediately rebuffed, "One Patnaik is struggling, the other is not". The other 'Patnaik' was in reference to Janaki Ballav Patnaik, the former Chief Minister of Odisha and former Union Minister.

On the State autonomy, Biju Patnaik said, "Laying foundation-stones is a primitive method; it is a feudal method, it is a waste, it is a national waste and intellectual dishonesty, a total fraud. All over the world, Russians have not laid any foundation-stone; Americans landed in the moon; they did not lay any foundation-stone. What is the method of laying foundation-stones? We call ourselves socialists. We still believe in total feudalism. Why our industries are going to be delayed by two years.... Our Ministers should know that in a federal structure there are unitary Government. Our State has a status-quo Constitution. We do not want to have any patronage from anybody. Why should our Ministers run after the Central Ministers? Is Odisha begging? Therefore, State autonomy is required so that we can plan our line of action. Why should we depend on the leap of a Minister at Delhi? We have enough of iron-ore; we can have three more steel plants. But everything is stumped. Therefore, I raise this political question" (*OLA Debates*, Vol. IV (23), 24.3.1975; 63-4).

Panchayati Raj

On the Panchayati Raj implementation, he said, "After the introduction of Panchayati Raj in the State, Gram Panchayats have become the main agency for execution of all development works under different programmes. In order to enable the Gram Panchayats to efficiently discharge their functions, it is necessary that there should be improvement in their financial and administrative set-up.... Though this decentralized system of administration is still in its infancy and it is too early to indicate about the consequential changes the systems would bring about I would like to sound a note of warning that unless the representatives of the people at various levels, realize their own responsibility to the electorate and forget about their own personal interests or party pressures, we are not likely to make much headway in this direction" (*OLA Debates*, Vol. IV (4), 1.3.1963;

12). On another significant issue of Panchayat industries, he said, "With a view to utilize local raw materials fully, improve skills and cater to the consumers' demand in rural areas, we have started Panchayat Samiti industries with the idea to set up small-scale industries in rural areas and thereby breaking the concentration of these industries in towns. Panchayat Samitis will have an abiding interest in it by share capital participation as well as participation in its management. The organization is intended to be cooperative, with workers or cultivators as members. To integrate this development of industries in Panchayat areas, our programme is to set up rural industrial estates and for this purpose, the Budget of the year 1963-64 provides ₹19.67 lakhs" (*OLA Debates*, Vol. IV (4), 1.3.1963; 15).

On the panchayat functioning, Biju Patnaik said, "Behind this whole Panchayati Raj idea, the great thought was that Government must belong to the people and begin with the people, from which emanated this Panchayati Raj system. Since then, we the Members of the Legislature, Members of Parliament, over the decades had been the real culprits who have taken away their powers. You may recollect, Mr. Deputy Speaker, that when 14 years ago we gave real powers to the Panchayats, we gave real powers to the Panchayat Samitis, we gave real powers to the Zilla Parishads, the compliant came from the Members of this House that powers have been taken away from them. Nobody are now caring for the MLA. This is where the sickness lies. If we want that people should do Panchayati Raj system, then we must have faith upon people. If Panchayats commit mistakes, then there is corrective machine; but if Ministers, MLAs commit mistakes then there is no corrective machine. How are we better that them? I had earlier told that each Sarpanch is a Chief Minister. Just as a Chief Minister functions taking the advice of all, similarly a Sarpanch functions. For this Panchyat Raj started. I am in favour of decentralization of power. Centre is now taking away all powers from the States and making it a municipality. This should also be decentralized. Decentralisation should be made in such a way that it is possible to get funds from Consolidated Fund. There should be Constitutional protection for it. Earlier, I gave power to the Chairman of Panchayat Samiti will write the Character Role of the BDO; now situation has come where the BOD is writing the Character Role of the Chairman of the Panchayat Samiti. These things have to be corrected. It is sad that the then leaders in Government said it is administrative failure. Administrative failure is an excuse. There should be safe-guards in it. If we want to have democratic system, then we must have faith upon people. Government that has come in the name of the people, has no faith upon people. Hence, when the Minister is taking corrective steps, I would request to form a House Committee to consider all things so as to bring a comprehensive bill. The House should recommend the Central Government to do Constitution amendment. Constitutional protection should be given to all the. There must be three-tiers of Government, only then there will be welfare of the State and the country, and a new chapter can be written in the history of India" (Vol II (9), 1974; 105-6).

On the delay in holding the Panchayat elections, he said, "I am not convinced why year after year you are delaying the election to the local bodies. What is the difficulty? Your Assembly election has since been over. In the meantime, you have consumed five years. It is immaterial who wins or who loses. It is a democratic process. It must be maintained. You are going to extend it year after year. It is not good for the democracy or for the democratic practice. That is why I plead. Why you do not definitely mention a date" (OLA Debates, Vol. I (6), 21.3.1985; 43-4).

Speaking on the perspective of the Panchayat Raj, he said, "Wisdom or capacity of brain is nobody's monopoly. We have collective wisdom; five heads are better than one of our wise-man through ages. Let us put our heads together and make it functioning, make it competitive, make it a matter of joy for our people to work and ones for all let us treat and enable our Sarpanches to really behave like Chief Minister with wisdom with sense of justice and great deal of integrity. This is for the august House to explain it to our brothers and sisters at Panchayat level. Sir, this is an experiment which now needs to be finally shaped in motion and I am sure that by the end of next year this House would feel proud of this Panchayati Raj" (I (5), 22.3.1990; 31). He also said, "Panchayat will be a crucial experiment and we will see that various factors of that Panchayat are motivated. If one Panchayat can be developed, then more Panchayats can be developed in the same method" (*OLA Debates*, Vol. II (21), 5.7.1990; 66).

On the question of giving power to the Panchayats, he said, "I would draw the attention of the House o consider the following. We shall give power to the Panchayats, not the type of 'Rajiv Gandhi power' but real authority. We will call them Chief Ministers of Panchayats. We will give them a Secretariat like I have a Secretariat as Chief Minister of the State. But what is still missing is motivation for the people" (*OLA Debates*, Vol. II (21), 5.7.1990; 65).

On Panchayat issue, he said, "We have decided in a National Front, that Panchayat Raj should be on direct election at all the three levels, i.e., Sarpanch, Panchayat Samiti, and Zilla Parishad. Three boxes will be placed and each voter shall vote in three boxes for three offices. We have also said to raise the level of women of the country. We have to give reserved seats for women, minimum 30 per cent to start with. We have done in Andhra Pradesh and in Karnataka also and it has yielded tremendous result and tremendous focus on women. The Sarpanches or the Chairman of the Panchayat Samitis should be treated with dignity and prestige. I will call each Sarpanch a Chief Minister in his own area, not put the MLA on top of their head" (*OLA Debates*, Vol. IX (2), 22.2.1989; 99).

On Panchayat system and people's power, he said, "When we talk of power to the people, it is an idea and it is also a concept. Now we being elected have come here and with the majority formed the Government. We have an Assembly. Has any power delivered to the people? It is a moot point. What is the real meaning of power to the people? I experimented 1961 on what motives the people have voted. Only motivation of the people in all over the world is competition. We are here as MLAs. We have defeated somebody; the Opposition was defeated by somebody because of competition. This motivation was introduced by me in 1961. This was discussed by me at length with Pandit Nehru. I asked him some question regarding what makes the people to compete. Sir, if you recollect at that time all the Sarpanches were here for a conference. We have set-up a competition between Panchayat and Panchayat. Production, birth control, education, health and other items. If one Panchayat in a block becomes No. 1, he gets ₹1 lakh as prize to do what the Panchayat likes and if in a division a Panchayat Samiti becomes first he gets ₹1 crore. The idea was to start Small-scale Industries to provide employment in rural areas. ₹1 lakh subsidy money should attract a loan of ₹10 lakhs from the financing houses. At that time, Sir, I remember I had produced all the OAS boys. I picked up and trained them. I taught them how to keep accounts, how to progress the industry, how to collect raw materials and also about marketing. I had to take days and days for training them. Things are never permanent. Chinese war came, I left Odisha to help Pandit Nehru to force back the Chinese. Pandit Nehru died, and the edifice of Panchayat Raj collapsed" (*OLA Debates*, Vol. I (5), 22.3.1990; 29-30).

On the reasons of the collapse of Panchayat, he said, "Today we have no Panchayat Raj. We have only skeletons. There is no motivation; there is nothing to look forward. The entire thing is in chaos. All the money was misspent. Nobody felt concerned. We should be concerned. Therefore, Sir, Panchayat Raj is to be fully established with proper motivation, with proper financing, with proper competition and budgetary provisions. I have decided to bring about a certain remedial alteration to see that the work goes on and money is spent properly. Therefore, Sir, instructions have gone out to all the Collectors that an executive committee should be constituted in each Assembly constituency and at block levels. The Committee shall finalise the action plan and prepare projects under *Jawahar Rozgar Yajana*, after consulting the *Grama Sabha*" (*OLA Debates*, Vol. I (5), 22.3.1990; 30).

He further explained the role of the Executive Committee, and said, "This Executive Committee is not only supervisory or advisory body, it is an executive body that I have formed, to supervise and execute through newly constituted Gram Panchayats, Gram Sabhas and ensure proper utilization of resources, take steps for prevention of misutilization, malpractices by enquiring into the same and recommendation" (*OLA Debates*, Vol. I (5),

22.3.1990; 30). He also included the role of people in it and said, "It is not that a district administration runs it when the whole motivation force becomes operative. The nation has to be put to work; the people have to be put to work and there should be accountability. There are conditions on which the administration runs. The people's administration needs more supervision, more control by the people who are more able.... We have taken it ourselves with the Government of India in New Delhi to introduce and correct the weaknesses in the structure" (*OLA Debates*, Vol. I (5), 22.3.1990; 30).

On the future prospect of Panchayat Raj, he said, "Nevertheless, we have decided to bring ladies into the field of administration and such a thing will give impetus to the entire Panchayat Raj system. I look forward to the day when none of us would like to go to Panchayat, Zilla Parishad, Panchayat Samitis, and so on. To my great satisfaction I found boys who have passed M.A., M.Sc., are standing for Sarpanches. It is gratifying to say that they have decided to serve the people. I have not lost hopes. In fact, I am encouraged by these phenomena and I am sure we will go a long way by collective thinking and collective wisdom" (*OLA Debates*, Vol. I (5), 22.3.1990; 31).

On the question of completing the Gram Panchayat and Municipality elections within the Constitutional time-limit i.e., within six months of dissolution of these bodies, he said, "The time limit is going to pass because the State Election will need six weeks to complete the election process and even till today (26.12.1995) no notification has been placed in this House and time limit given to this Government is 2 February 1996. This construes a total failure of the Government to meet the demand of the Constitutional responsibility. Therefore, I would like to know whether this Government has Constitutional right to remain in Office or not. This matter is such a serious matter that the resolution as has been brought by Hon. Members of this House" (*OLA Debates*, Vol. IV (1), 26.12.1995; 94). On the next day, 27.12.1995, he referred to the statement given by Dr. B. R. Ambedkar in the Constituent Assembly on 14 October1949, "Every Constitution rests on the tacit assumption that the people who run the Constitution will not want only to wreck it. Ambedkar said this is important for us to know and to record I have not anywhere found in any Constitution a provision saying that the Executive shall obey the Legislature" (*OLA Debates*, Vol. IV (2), 27.12.1995; 110). He again said, "Here the Executive and the Legislature are one. Legislature passes one Act and Executive refuses to follow it, is not that the case? It is generally understood that the provisions of the Constitution are binding upon the different organs of the State, i.e., the Parliament, Judiciary and the Executives" (*OLA Debates*, Vol. IV (2), 27.12.1995; 110).

In this context, Biju Patnaik gave his own illustration on 1961 and said, "As early as in 1961, long before this House assembled as the Congress

Chief Minister, following the dictates of Pandit ji, I had got people elected right from the lowest level to highest level. Eight thousand elected members assembled in Bhubaneswar and the Minister in-Charge came to address it. It was a joy for anybody to see that the people's power had gone back to the people. *Sarpanches* were elected, *Panchayat Samities* were elected and *Zilla Parishads* were also elected. Then on top of that, power was given to the women for *adalati panchayats* to hold courts and punish anybody. To give justice and punish this kind of powers were given and the people of this State were proud of it" (IV (2), 1995; 111). He also said, "What has happened is that democracy at the lowest level stands murdered by an act of this House" (*OLA Debates*, Vol. IV (2), 27.12.1995; 110).

On the issues of growth and development, Biju Patnaik said, "Points of growth is the theory of Government. The points of growth do not depend on the districts; these depend right from the Panchayats. Hence, in my time I tried to make plans that every Panchayat and every block must have certain industrial input so that a large number of Panchayat factories will be established. Take for instance Calcutta. There was no Calcutta 200 years ago. But, today Calcutta provides employment to half of the population of Odisha state just because there is point of growth. I hope that this would pursue that policy. Rourkela could have been a point of growth. But there is no sufficient Government pressure to ensure point of growth. But Durgapur is a point of growth. It all depends on the capacity of Government to pursue the policy.... Odisha Government can think of projected development subject to national limitations or subject to national guidelines. It is question of initiative for the State. The State could create projects. The State could negotiate subject to Government of India's limitations. Only recently you have noticed that the Industries Minister of Tamil Nadu has entered into an agreement with European firms. It must have been subject to the Government of India's concurrence. Within that concurrence, within that limitation, what prevents you for projecting your areas for industrial development?" (*OLA Debates*, Vol. II (24), 10.7.1974; 155-6).

Political Party

On the different political parties' ideology and attitude, he said, "While the Swatantra party chooses to pursue a policy of unfettered free enterprise, this Congress Government must try to demolish this policy by introduction of controlled socialism. While the Communist party would want to follow principles of totalitarianism, we must necessarily come in violent clash with their policy by declaring the essence of democracy as enshrined in the Constitution. Therefore, Sir, when one party clash with a certain issue, another party clash with certain other issues. But these are issue of policies which are vital for us as indeed it must be vital for other parties. Therefore, these are clash of policies. These are clashes in administering the people based on certain policies. On such issues, as I announced the other day, we shall not compromise. But when it comes to administration, between man and man, Government stands firm and it becomes like a fair judge and thinks that all men are the same" (*OLA Debates*, Vol. V (18), 25.9.1963; 33).

On the issue of political party, and Opposition, Biju Patnaik while responding to the discussion on Motion of No-Confidence, said, "You have said that the Opposition will be united; but your Opposition is still very divided, as it should be, between some persons and sycophants. It is divided between some who worship sycophants and some who worship sanity. (*Interruptions*) This is the first time in many years-I know it because I have been in the Congress. I have known Nehru's style of functioning; and I have known Indira's style of functioning. This is the first time that this country has the most democratic Cabinet, during the last 30 years...We have party problems-less than what you have. You, gentlemen, from one party you divided into ten parties. We have brought 10 parties together into a united party. For the first time in the history of India, instead of dividing the forces, we have combined the forces. It will take time for us to fuse into powerful entity. You have divided, you will sub-divide and sub-divide, again and again. But this party will unify more and more, as it goes on in time.... When some Hon. Member from my party attacks the Government and says that the Minister should resign, do you think that he means that he should resign? If you think so, then you must have lost your sense of balance. Our party consists of new blood, hundreds of new people.... They will take time to learn. We have not learnt it in one day; we have also learnt by our mistakes, corrections and everything. We have still to learn. If we have a new person as Minister or Chief Minister and if he cannot run the Government, let him be corrected. If there are some omissions, should not the democratic institutions of the country give him some time for correction and give some advice?" (*Lok Sabha Debates*, 10 May 1978; 389-91). He again said, "But, as long as you are a sycophant of a psychopath, your party shall never in the resurgent India become a Government of the nation. This is the time when we talk of the second independence of India. Remember this, the people are wide awake, people are conscious of their power. When they threw out a dictatorial and authoritarian Government, they can also say- infact, they have said it in bits and pieces-if the Janata Government does not behave, it will also be thrown out. It can throw out the Janata Government. This is the greatest insurance for democracy in India" (*Lok Sabha Debates*, 10 May 1978; 393).

On the issue of politics, Biju Patnaik said, "We have our politics and you have your politics. Who are you to point out our problems. It is our business, within us and the people of India.... That is why you are there and you will remain there for the next 30 years. We are here as the trustees of the people of India.... (*Interruptions*) It is true they want to see one face, they want to see a united face and they want to see a powerful face. If we do not show that, they punish us, as they did punish us in one, two or three places. But we are not bothered of a few losses in a few places" (*Lok Sabha Debates*, 10 May 1978; 391).

On development of the State and political party, Biju Patnaik said, "I have said earlier that for the development of the country there should be no politics. The development of the State should be the business of the whole House. If you do concern, I am sure better ways can be found out for administration. In democracy, majority party has right to carry on its policy. But while implementation, Government should seek the help of other parties. That is why the Assembly, that is why the Committees are there. It should be done by consultation. But in all critical points you have gone in your own way. Therefore, you must take responsibility for yourself..... So let us combine for the development of the State, for the development of railways. The whole House can devote for this national cause. When it concerns State, let us not have any politics, let us take some action......Let us rise ourselves and come forward and do something in the interest of the State. If we cannot, we will go down in the history as bunch of people who were sitting in the Assembly combined together spreading disaster in the country" (*OLA Debates*, Vol. IV(25), 26.3.1975; 43-5).

On democracy and party responsibility, Biju Patnaik said, "In democracy, it is political commitments, i.e. democratically elected people or their party make commitments to the people and people therefore vote a party or the individual to power. I have pointed out in other cases that, the Congress Party in Odisha has totally failed in keeping their political commitments which they announced during the last general election..... What is the Government today? It is partisan; a satellite of the Communist Party of India, undemocratic and fascist. They want to demolish democracy. It is only the Opposition that can save the country, save democracy from the House top. That is the only way. It is only Nandini Satpathy who can be fascist" *OLA Debates*, Vol. IV (23), 24.3.75, 65).

On a matter of coalitional tactics by the party supporting the Government, Biju Patnaik said, "I would like to draw the attention of the Chief Minister, through you Sir, that a matter which happened outside the House, affects the prestige of this House. The Leader of the Party of the House, and one of the leaders of the CPI Party from Delhi is reportedly advising the Leader of the House to withdraw a Bill regarding the Essential Services Act. This, sir, is a direct interference in the conduct of this House. I would strongly object to any person, however worthy he may be, to direct the Leader of this House not to bring a Bill on pain of withdrawing their support from the Government. This is a blackmail of the worst order and I am tempted to say on this occasion that if the Chief Minister makes up her mind to bring that

Bill with slight democratic modification, we will entirely support that Bill. I do not like that the Government should be blackmailed. If there is anything wrong in the policy we should attack it. We do not want to blackmail the Government" (*OLA Debates*, Vol. II (15), 27.6.74; 108). On the time of holding **election**, he said, "Election, whatever it may be general election or bye-election, should be conducted with prior concurrence of the State Government to conduct the election. That is the normal practice" (*OLA Debates*, Vol. II (15), 27.6.74, 110).

Opposition Politics

On a tradition of cooperative thinking and logical criticism by the Opposition, he said, "I would like the Hon'ble Leaders of the Opposition parties to cooperate in a manner that would establish democratic traditions. When I say 'operate', I do not mean, and I repeat that I do not mean, they will accept what the Government says. On the contrary, they should as Members of the Opposition, not only focus attention on matters which need to be looked in by the Government and rectified, but also here the views in terms of public opinion as they consider fit. Only here in this case they should ensure that the best democratic traditions are maintained. Sir, time has come when this State like all other States and indeed the whole nation must set itself to hard work. We have so many difficulties; we have got powerful traditions of castes, sect and religion which are deterrent to modern industrialized society's concept. We have other traditions of tribes which have so far refused to associate themselves in the current of modern civilization in India. Therefore, Sir, taking the entire background together, we find that we have great hurdles to cross before we can proceed on our way to a society of mechanized affluence. Many factors in our past are against us. We have to ride over them, we have to subject them and create new conceptions of thought and development. We have given ourselves to democracy; we have given ourselves to various administrative methods. But whatever we give ourselves in terms of Government or democracy it must be remembered that the Legislative Assembly is the supreme House created by the will of the people to frame the laws and remain as watch-dog of people's destiny. Another thing, Sir, which I wish the Members to consider, is that in democracy we have to face elections, and it has been determined by ourselves, once in five years. It is legitimate that a few months before the elections the parties must take positions, must be able to find fault with each other in terms of substance or even in terms of propaganda. Before the Assembly is dissolved all the party Members go to the fields to seek confidence of the people. But, Sir, if the air, thoughts and procedure of elections continue to permeate the proceedings of the House for the rest of the period then, to my mind no purpose is served by this August Assembly in terms of people's development. Sir, we must build a tradition by common wisdom in a fashion that immediately after the elections so that as soon as the House gets down to its business, personal acrimony must cease with the election; policies and problems, targets and achievements, savings and increasing of asserts must alone remain the business of the Members of this August Assembly. In this new Assembly, Sir, we have merely gone through fifteen months and while going through the records of the debates in the Assembly, I, as the Leader of the House can assure that you on my own behalf and on behalf of the House that I feel ashamed. The blame must be lie largely with me, as the Leader of the House, because obviously I have failed. But I am glad to assure you, Sir, that the Leaders of Opposition parties as well as myself have now decided to consult, pull ourselves together and create a tradition which would be the best in the country-a tradition of cooperation thinking and logical criticism with only one purpose-to progress and push ahead the people of our State. But as it would be proper and legitimate in democracy, perhaps 3 or 4 months before the net election, as we joined in the mid-term elections, all parties must take their separate positions, must mount attack against each other in terms of party platforms to get the confidence of the people in general and the newspapers, which again would be in keeping with the best democratic tradition. Another thing, we have decided Sir that politics will cease with the elections and will change over to the only concern of development of our State. Sir, it must be understood that whereas through our present democratic practice the administration is left in the hands of the Government the responsibility of the development of this State lies entirely on this House as a whole" (*OLA Debates*, Vol. III (11), 5.9.62; 40-2).

On the practical scene of the State and the Opposition in it, he said, "What do we find in this State? Personal attacks, based on deliberate misrepresentation; sabotaging facts, misleading the House, the newspapers and the public by completely wrong presumptions, wrong arguments and wrong methods; by falsification of facts with which only they seem to be conversant. Such cannot be the qualities of Members of a responsible Opposition party. They may indulge in it for a little while now and then as everyone in the House can and may have a right for bantering for the party. But throughout the months that the House sits, the only thing that we hear from the responsible leaders of these groups is pure, personal vilification without facts. They say that I am a tyrant; they say I destroy the very foundation of democracy. I will now proceed to bring you facts which will show how tolerant this Government has been, how extremely more tolerant it has been when it concerns the Members of the Opposition. The so-called charges that they have leveled against some Members of this Government, for the apparent timidity to level charges against the Members of this Government (*OLA Debates*, Vol. V (13), 18.9.63; 41).

On the issue of Opposition behavior, he said, "Apart from blindly supporting the objections of the Members of the Opposition, one can very easily say that there is no responsible thinking of the future from that side. Sir, we build technical institutions so that technical personnel can come out of it. We want to utilize them in various projects in the State so that the skilled man-power and the raw materials available in the State put together can produce surpluses which we can distribute to create a new and proper social order" (*OLA Debates*, Vol. IX (3), 23.2.1966; 12-3). To this Hon'ble Member Rajbajjav Mishra commented, "Engineers are sitting idle". To this Biju Patnaik said, "Why are Engineers sitting idle. Is it not the business of the Hon'ble Member to ask the Government or demand why so many new projects have not been taken up and utilize Engineers to construct and complete them so that the State can get surpluses? I have till today not known one single demand made by the Opposition Benches to the Government on this account. Sir, they said, we shall not have Tikarpara. That is their political slogan. We shall not build Paradip that is their political progarmme. Why? Because the Congress Party will be popular if these are built. Is this the way to look at national interests? Is this the way to look at the interests of the future generations?" (*OLA Debates*, Vol. IX (3), 23.2.1966; 13).

On a Motion to remove the Deputy Speaker of the Odisha Assembly, he said, "It appears to me from the introductory speeches of the movers of this Motion that the Deputy Speaker of this House is merely being used as a bait to chastise the Government....... I am afraid, because he belongs to the Congress party, he suffers from a complex when he sits on the August Chair and if at all he over-reaches himself, it is all the time in favour of the Opposition Members, most of the time to the great anxiety and depression of the Members of the Treasury Benches. In other Houses, Sir, when Members form the Opposition Benches have misbehaved as they often do here, the hair has ordered removal of such Members from the House or they have been suspended from the House. In fact, one Member in the Bombay Legislature has been removed by the Speaker for the whole session by a Resolution of the House. Similar things have happened here. Similar threats are offered by no less a person than the Leader of Opposition himself and Leaders of other Opposition groups and the Deputy Speaker merely looks on and he tolerates as he desires that he should tolerate then because he belongs to the Treasury Bench. One almost feels sometimes that perhaps if the Deputy Speaker belonged to the Opposition Party, they might have shown him more honour, they might have given him due dignity that the Chair deserves and perhaps might have even behaved with greater decorum and greater decency........ Various points have been raised by the Leader of Opposition, by the Leader of the PSP group and others in support of my contention. I stand corrected, Sir, they changed their Party name to SSP.

They have continuously stated that they are afraid of the Treasury Benches inside the House because of the oppression of the Treasury Benches on the poor Members of the Opposition. The Chair has seen that the Members of the Treasury Benches wait patiently till all the histrionics in the Opposition Benches are exhausted" (*OLA Debates*, Vol. VI (55), 22.9.1964; 37-8). Hon'ble Member Harihar Patel remarked, "A;; combined will be less than your". On the activities of the Opposition Members inside the House, he continued to say, "There great shouts of interruption, songs, exclamations and facial expressions are seen only on the left side of your Chair. Nevertheless, not only the Members of the Treasury Benches look on, but the Deputy Speaker keeps on smiling as is he is bound to give protection, because he has given them latitude and shown kindness, they have brought a no-confidence against him. It is an irony of fate. But coming back to the main theme this is only a bit to chastise the Government" (*OLA Debates*, Vol. VI (55), 22.9.1964; 38). He stated how the Members of the present Opposition parties are bringing allegations of corruption against the present Congress Government and also when he was the Leader of the House, and even prior to that, but conveniently by-pass the period during which these Opposition Members were in the then Congress Government and Congress party. "Sir, you will be astonished that several Members belonging to the Opposition parties here in this House along with their counterparts in New Delhi belonging to Parliament have sent a memorandum to the President of India making certain charges and requesting him to appoint a Commission of Enquiry. I only pity the Members of Opposition that the same charges were given to the Leader of the Opposition to be the Jury and Executor by then Chief Minister and Leader of the House. He accepted the brief and later rejected it. Then it was given to the Public Accounts Committee.... They have now gone to Delhi for redress; the Leader of the Opposition, the Leader of the PSP or what they call it now the SSP and others are in Delhi. Pleading, as I said yesterday, on their knees to my Party Leader of who I am proud, the Prime Minister of India, the Home Minister of India, the Ministers of the Congress Party with charges against Ministers of same Congress Party in another sphere. I can assure you we welcome this. We know in this House, and the Members who have signed the charges also know that the charges are not worth the paper they have written on, the charges are spurious, they are politically motivated, they are a pack of lies, that they have no foundation, no facts.... Now that they have requested for a Commission, they have pleaded for a Commission, they have approached the Leaders of my Party for a Commission. I am proud of it. I would like to make a very simple request, a very polite and humble request to all such Members of this House and the MPs of the Parliament including now I find in the newspaper, great and revered Acharya Kripalini, our great friend Mr. A. D. Mani and other Members who have now taken up the cause of the

Hon'ble Members of this House in trying to insist on a Commission" (*OLA Debates*, Vol. VI (55), 22.9.1964; 39-40). Discussing on the issue he openly challenged the Opposition Leaders for disenfranchisement for six years, if the charges are not proved, and said, "...all these Hon'ble Members should swear a guarantee or affidavit in the Court of law, before the Prime Minister of India and before the Home Minister of India that they will stand disenfranchised for six years" (*OLA Debates*, Vol. VI (55), 22.9.1964; 41). To this Hon'ble Member Rajendra Narayan Singhdeo said, "Why for six years? We accept for ever to be disqualified" (*ibid*).

On the issue of Opposition giving cooperation to the Government, he said, "The Chief Minister has courage enough to say that the Opposition should assist him in reconstructing the State. That should be the aim of every politician to remove poverty. We all know that. There is no doubt that the Opposition will give fullest cooperation in this matter.... I had asked specifically in all these new industries, what is the total employment opportunity you have generated. You did not answer to that. How many families have gone above the poverty line and how much have remained below the poverty line. I am putting it to you that on this basis, the smallest fraction is .001 per cent of 50 lakh population, i.e., only 50,000 may have gone over the poverty line. This is the state of affairs of the people of this State.... We would assist the Chief Minister and his Government fully, but the figures about removal of poverty is a farce. I am sorry, if this will be the position, this Opposition cannot assist him, if he will go on bluffing us like this. I say, Mr. Chief Minister, 500 years will pass at this rate, development will not increase, but decrease" (*OLA Debates* Vol. I (3), 18.3.1985; 54).

On Opposition assistance on the matter of Chasnala accident where a few engineers and workers were killed underground "when water poured down like an avalanche", Biju Patnaik said, "Very soon I will request my colleague, the Labour Minister, to make a formal request to the Leader of Opposition who, with his colleagues, can go into these things and advise us. We do not want our officers to get demoralized" (*Lok Sabha Debates*, 28 June 1977; 286).

Explaining the role of opposition in the agitation of the people that is also a "right in the democracy", he said, "the leaders of the opposition are always accused; their movements are shadowed and marked; they are very often targets to the vindictive attitude of the government.... It gives an impression that they have something inherently in the Congress government and their method of administration. If an MLA of Opposition criticizes, put him under MISA; if JP fights for something good, accuse him; if Biju Patnaik says something raid his houses and so on.... Therefore, I say lack of education breeds undemocratic methods" (*OLA Debates*, Vol. III (11), 20.12.74; 77).

He mentioned that whether it is the Treasury or Opposition benches, "we are all colleagues for the development of Odisha" (*OLA Debates*,

Vol. III (11), 20.12.74; 78). Speaking for the development of Odisha and the role of the government and opposition parties in it, he said, "This House has the supreme responsibility to ensure that Odisha comes at par with any other developed state in the country. We have huge natural resources in our state and as such our state should be number one state in the country. I told this government – if you are prepared to achieve this objective, we will be putting you back in every election till you become the hero of the people. We are not anxious to sit on the other side. We want you to function so that you could be proud of yourself; the state could be proud of yourself; and we all could be proud of our state" (*OLA Debates*, Vol. III (11), 20.12.74; 78-9).

Congress Party

On his resignation from Chief Minister and on the Congress party and Opposition, he said, "The statement that I wish to make as to why I am leaving office is hardly necessary because the reason for which I from this House and several other colleagues of ours in other States are leaving, are well known. We have left together with some hopes and some desires to engage ourselves in more intense activities of reconstructing India through the agency of its great servant, viz: the Indian National Congress. We have seen that the history of this country is the history of the Congress party. We have seen that if the Congress party is strong, the nation is strong; if the Congress party weakens the nation weakens. We have also seen that the Opposition parties which we wish to nourish and develop have not made adequate headway to fulfill their destiny in Parliamentary democracy; at least not yet. Therefore, we considered in the summit of our great Organisation of AICC that it is necessary for some of us to go out of the seats of office and try and reconstruct the Congress organization and strengthen it in manner which will fulfill its obligation to the Nation. Sir, I have said on one occasion before that if in this country of ours we have a responsible Opposition party which could reasonably be expected to take over the Government after defeating the Government at the polls, perhaps it would not be so necessary or incumbent upon the Congress party to reconstruct or revitalize itself. The fact that we will do so is that we have fulfilled the historic responsibility. That is, if the Congress disintegrates, the nation disintegrates. So, in our collective wisdom, we found that the weaknesses which are around the country are strengthened and that can only be strengthened if our own party is strengthened, our own House is put in order. We have no intention to interfere with the arrangements of the Opposition parties. We have brought in democracy in our country, we wish the Opposition parties well. We wish that they should develop in economic horizons, in social horizons based on certain fixities which will give them strength in time to come and bring them into the Treasury Benches. But we do not see any signs of it now or the possibility in the near future. Therefore, as I said earlier, they have not yet fulfilled the role allotted to them in parliamentary democracy. Sir, coming back to this State, we find the same story, i.e. the inadequate Opposition, the divided Opposition, the unprepared Opposition, who could never within a foreseeable future thin in terms of a unified party to take over and run the administration. Therefore, in this State it has become necessary to set our own House in order, to progress the interests of the State, to progress its future by strengthening the Congress party. It is no threat to the Opposition, if I may say so, because as I have said before, we wish the Opposition well and we wish to leave them to enjoy. But if in this process of our strengthening a divided and demoralized Opposition crumbles, then the Opposition Members and not to blame the Congress party" (*OLA Debates*, Vol. V (22), 1.10.63; 37-8). To this, Hon'ble Member Prasanna Kumar Dash objected and said, "Sir, he is making a controversial statement. He accuses the Opposition as demoralized Opposition. This has to be refuted" (*Ibid*). Biju Patnaik then continued and said, "Sir, I do not say demoralized people or demoralized people. I said, if the Opposition, in the process, gets demoralized and crumbles, then they should not blame the Congress party. I wish them luck. I wish them fulfillment of the democratic role required of the Opposition. But since we find no signs of it, now or in the foreseeable future, the only alternative for maintenance of democracy or a strong party lies in the strength of the Congress. If the Congress by its strength creates such an effect that the Opposition gets disunited as you see today...... (*Voice: Your Party*).... Don't bring in Congress party because that is not our intention. I will also hope that while I will be outside the Governmental authority, I will try to strengthen the various public institutions, revitalize the popular institutions and party institution. The Opposition may also perhaps consider strengthening themselves, because it is only by strength, the joint and common strength, if I may say so, of the democratic institutions that democracy survives. If the Opposition does not or is incapable of strengthening itself in a combined way and remains little groups.... (*Voice: What is that to you*). The only thing to me and to us is that virtually party dictatorship would come to the country in the name of the Congress. (*Voice: It is the desire of the Congress party*).... It is not our desire. What I am trying to say is that the Hon'ble Members of the Opposition should not forget that they have also a historic role to play provided they are responsible Opposition. But if they are irresponsible, they find themselves demolished or divided then they should not blame us. If the Hon'ble Member from Khunta or others continuously say *what is our business*, then I would say that it is everybody's business in the House. Therefore, if in the process of their weaknesses, and, of our processing and strengthening ourselves, we find that in the net elections the Congress gets 110 seats or 120 seats, it is no joy to us. Because to me at least the Opposition in Parliamentary democracy is the spice of democratic life. Because I do believe in democracy and I do believe-although I do not agree with one word, I will lay down my life to defend the interest of democracy. Therefore, I wish the Opposition well. But I am rather suspicious that with my going out for rearranging or strengthening our party, they may not stand the test of the risk of competition, competition in work, competition in effect, competition in creating wealth for the nation, competition in making the little men to keep to their little sizes and when I finish these little men if they no stature to grow, I humbly request in the name of God, that let the little men vanish and big men grow in their place. Let a strong Opposition come, let towering Opposition come and destroy and demolish the dictatorship in any form for all times from our country. I have nothing more to add. When I leave the seats of authority, I assure the House that they may hear of me in this House and outside much more and more than they have heard of me before because at that time I can also assume the role of somewhat irresponsible manners. And just before I close my speech, I would say once again that as the Leader of the House I have enjoyed these 27 months of fighting squads of legislators shouting, counter-shouting, no-confidence, confidence, leaving the House and all that goes into our Parliamentary life. One thing, however, I would request that we may still attempt and continue to attempt to raise the level of debars. It needs of us much more and greater, deeper study. It is not in the way of aspersion, I should say, because it applies to all of us that if we have to raise our State, we have to have to study more, supervise, bring our facts, search lights in fact, not any political weapons but facts which may create greater standards in our own minds, in the minds of the public and in the administration itself. Because it is only by this combined operation of the Members of the House and their representative Government and the whole lot of people engaged in the administration; it is by the combined effort of all of us that we can hope, to raise the State. Why? As we combine in social and economic growth of our State, the status of all of us will proportionately improve and increase. If the millions of our country people become stronger, more healthy, get more employment, and raise their heads and don't have to crawl within the power of the castes or class, then the representatives of the people can raise their heads slightly and can say that we live in a healthy country, we live in a wealthy country. Then they have something to be proud of. But now we are proud because we belong to superior class or caste. We are proud because we have more wealth than the net man and expect low caste or low class men and non-wealthy men to crawl before us, to bow down before us. If we do so, we should hang our head in shame. Man has a right to live as man with others. He wants to be free from poverty, illiteracy. But if we do not provide adequate employment, provided by modern technology and science, if we do not destroy the very foundation of caste and class which makes the man crawl, crumble and whimper out, then we have not done anything, we have not served the political purpose enjoined on us by our Constitution; be it in the Opposition, be it in the Treasury Bench. At the end, as the Leader of the House, I am grateful for the way this House has dealt with me and I wish them luck and prosperity (*OLA Debates*, Vol. V (22), 1.10.63; 38-40).

On the Congress system, he said, "Of course, I was in Congress and that Congress and this Congress is far different. Those who are now coming in the name of Congress have no base and background. They have already forgotten the value system of Congress and your totality is corruption. Corruption is so rampant that I would like to flow the river Mahanadi to clear it up. This is our administration" (*OLA Debates*, Vol. I (4), 21.3.1990; 51).

On the prospects of the Congress Party, he said, "You are going to face a Parliament election. About the prospects of your Party, I am sorry to say my friends in the Congress Party that it is gloomy. It is opinion of anybody and everybody and never mind it, I am not in your Party. I was there" (*OLA Debates*, Vol. II (12), 14.7.1995; 100).

Speaking on the majority numbers in the House and the representation system, Biju Patnaik said, "I would say this Government as has been installed and foisted on the people of Odisha is not only a minority number in this August House but with a minority poll in spite of all their efforts. They received only 37 per cent, whereas the *Pragati Party* received more than 37 per cent, i.e., 38.5 per cent. If we take the other members of the opposition who are with us, altogether it must be much more than the votes secured by Congress and others who are with them. The joining of the Communist Party of India with the Congress is not a happy situation, which the people of Odisha should enjoy. Therefore, I say this Government is borne out of fraud, out of blackmail. The methods used by them were breach of all Constitutional proprieties, all the legal reasons fraud and purchases of votes. Tampering of ballot boxes was not uncommon. The Prime Minister of India made speeches where she mentioned, 'If you do not vote for Congress, central help in the shape of money will be refused'. This is nothing but blackmailing. So fraud, blackmailing and such other things of this type on which the Congress party rests. They call themselves progressive; I will come to this later on. Accordingly, to my judgment, the methods adopted by the Congress cuts the very root of democracy. Of course, by this method some of you are installed as Ministers for some time to come but it will destroy the whole vitality, zeal and forces and of the people of Odisha. I know you have no capacity to meet the situation. There is slightest difference in the method and working of your party with that of Hitler's *National Socialism*. The method is the same, the process is the same. Intimidation, threat, purchase of vote and blackmailing all these are methods adopted by the Hitler and the Congress Party of India adopts the same method. Now the Congress party is saying that we enjoy the full support of the people. I do not understand how they enjoy the full support of the people. They say so due to lack of knowledge in arithmetic. By receiving 37 per cent votes and they say they represent the people of Odisha. Like this by securing 28 per cent votes in UP, the Congress represent the people of UP. If it would have been proportional representation, it would have been otherwise. But we have a Constitution, we have a methodology. This should be destroyed. That is a separate question" (*OLA Debates*, Vol. I (2), 25.3.1974; 39-40).

With regard to the Congress slogan of *Garibi Hatao* (Remove Poverty), Biju Patnaik said, "During the last election they did not use that slogan. Then they said that poverty cannot be removed in a day, but it will take years. The words spoken in the year of 1970, was withdrawn in the year 1974 and the poor became poorer, and were told, 'take note, give vote'. There is no more shameless thing than this. In this manner they have committed greatest crime in human dignity. You have purchased votes. But we want to raise people's dignity. We are supposed to be the greatest democracy in the world. But the Congress party is taking advantage of the poverty of the people. They purchased votes from the people and thereby murdered the democracy and destroyed the human dignity. Not only myself, but the educated public of Dodisha deeply suspect what benefit this Government has done to the 2 crores 30 lakhs poor people. The Governor said that Odisha has seen cyclone, flood and drought all the time, and for this the poor people are not benefitted. There is no shameless argument than this" (*OLA Debates*, Vol. I (2), 25.3.1974; 42).

Indira Gandhi

On Indira Gandhi, he said, "Your Indira Gandhi laid the foundation stone of the Vizag Steel Plant. People told me to remove it, but I did not remove the foundation stone after I became the Union Steel Minister, but said, Indira Gandhi was my friend. Let her failure foundation stone be there. I sanctioned ₹3000 crores in 1979, but our Government failed unfortunately" (*OLA Debates*, Vol. I (4), 21.3.1990; 51). In reply to a criticism of not able to make second Steel Plant in Odisha during his tenure as Union Steel Minister, he said, "I want to remind that Her Majesty, The Queen of India, Indira Gandhi, had put a foundation stone at Vishakhapatnam with great fanfare just prior to election and she had requested me to take it up when I became Minister. So, I promised to do for her" (*OLA Debates*, Vol. VII (26), 30.3.1992; 86). He also said, "Long time back when the previous Government (in Odisha) was in position, I myself took a team of MLAs/MPs and had gone to Smt. Indira Gandhi, when she was Prime Minister. It was during flood season. She sanctioned ₹2 crores. Mr. Pranab Mukherjee was then Finance Minister. She told Mr. Mukherjee over telephone before me, 'whatever Biju wants you give him" (*OLA Debates*, Vol. X (13), 11.3.1993; 47). When J. B. Patnaik, the then Chief Minister alleged him, "You have put Indira Gandhi to imprisonment" (*OLA Debates*, Vol. X (3), 11.9.1989; 135), Biju Patnaik replied, "Jayaprakash Narayan cremation, we were at Patna. I asked Indira Gandhi, we spent 18 months imprisonment, you will not remain for 4 days. This is all personal matter between two friends. I do not want to discuss here" (*ibid*).

Showing respect to the Prime Minister of India, Biju Patnaik, said, "We have greatest respect for the Prime Minister of India. Prime Minister is not your property. She is the jewel of all the citizens of India. Few motivated Members of this House should understand this" (*OLA* Debates, Vol. III (2), 4.1.1972; 43). Speaking on election propaganda where it is said that the keys are with Indira, all the butter and honey will flow – our *xyz projects* will be done, he sarcastically said, "Even I was confused leaving alone the voters. I also thought, let the state prosper. What does it matter who is in the government" (*OLA Debates*, Vol. III (11), 20.12.74; 81).

On the emergency period, Biju Patnaik said, "In the case of the Congress Government established during the emergency, there was no *Ma-Baap* of anybody. Only one *Ma* and one young *Baap*. Beyond that there was nothing" (OLA; 48).

On the second Steel Plant and equation with Nehru and Indira Gandhi, he said, "About the first Steel Plant at Rourkela, I was instrumental to bring it from Pandit Nehru some 45 years back. Now I thought that we should have a second Steel Plant and I worked for it. I could have done it earlier when I was Steel Minister. But I gave it to Vizag. You will be glad to know only because of the request of Indira Gandhi at that time, I gave it to Vizag. She said, Biju, you do something for me because I have laid foundation, although for political purpose. So I gave it to Andhra Pradesh, which I could have easily diverted to Odisha as a Minister. I have got trust with Pandit Nehru's daughter and a friend of mine, who although booked me in jail for more than 19 months that is her privilege as a woman. This is a different thing altogether" (*OLA Debates*, Vol. XIV (3), 25.2.1994; 86).

On the killings and violence after Indira Gandhi's assassination, he said, "After Indira Gandhi's death, you (Congress I) murdered 3,000 sikhs and raped 5,000 women. I do not say this; Justice R. N. Mishra says this, who pointed fingers just like other judges at Mr. Dhawan. Your Government displaced State Governments saying that they are inefficient. People are getting killed. What Rajiv Gandhi and Buta Singh are doing? Everyday 20/30/40 people are being killed in Punjab" (*OLA Debates*, Vol. X (3), 11.9.1989; 135). On the security system in India after Prime Minister Indira Gandhi's assassination in her house by her own body-guards, he said, "The day it happened in the Prime Minister's residence, it must be admitted that total security system of India has failed. If the Prime Minister's own bodyguards could fire and assassinate her, then there is total security system failure. On the same day all those who were in the house must be cross-examined, let it be Rajiv Gandhi's wife or R. K. Dhawan. The nation has the right to know everything that the Prime Minister cannot be slaughtered by her own guards. In the Parliament, every item is discussed and much alarming information is coming out. The needle of suspicion is moving towards Dhawan and it may move towards various persons, may be members of the *Darwar*. The nation should know the entire truth, so that these things will not happen again" (*OLA Debates*, Vol. IX (27), 31.3.1989; 80).

Communal Politics

On the communal disturbances in Rourkela, and his subsequent visit to the town on 21st March 1964, he described how the Hindu community group, armed with *lathis* and daggers were congregated in the town and how he discussed and pacified the group. He said, "The story that they gave out was that they have been told that the Muslims of Rourkela were coming to kill them. They told me that there were four to five thousand Muslims packed up by the authorities and located in a cinema house who attempted to come out and kill them. Of course, I had some prior knowledge as to how things happen in Bengal, Assam and other areas. But here was a body of men, young and educated, in an excited State where there was no balance of mind or capacity to receive reasonable advice. There were two or three youngsters with red marks, *Sindoor* (vermilion), on their heads trying to excite others to go and attack the minority community. I pointed at one of them and asked how much money he has been paid for this propaganda by the Pakistan agent and believe me, Sir, very quickly he turned out and fled from that place. Anyway, I told the people not to believe the propaganda and they dispersed. The same morning, I went to some other troubled spots in the town and then I went to the control-room where the District Magistrate had established his headquarters, just opposite the cinema house where a large number of Muslim men, women, and children were given protection by the Police. From that place I went round without any Police protection. I went to the Regional Engineering College (renamed as National Institute of Technology) where I found that students and staff have given protection to 35 Muslim families and they were under continuous attack by the angry mob on one side and by the *Adibasis* on the other. The House would be glad to know that road blocks were made by the College NCC to give protection to themselves and other people and they took care of their protégés in a manner for which the House will be proud......In the afternoon, when I went round to another place in a jeep with the District Magistrate and the DIG, Police, with the intention of inspecting the outskirts of the town, we found that an angry mob of about four thousand *Adibasis* had killed many people and set two villages on fire. These villages were looted and altogether it was a bad show. I probed deep into the causes and I would like to state from what I saw and what I observed. I am convinced and I have no doubt that the House will be convinced when I finish that there is a deep-laid conspiracy by our enemies and I found that at all key points, the enemies' agents were at work. The fact of the matter is that from a refugee train one person came out and spread the story that the train was carrying women with breasts cut-off. In fact, there was no truth in it. You can well imagine, Sir, had it been so, these women could not have travelled so far from East Pakistan. How could they be alive and on top of it display their breasts for public gaze? Next some persons came to give food to these refugees at Rurkela Railway Station. Some people spread the news that poisonous food has been given to them by the Muslims. Such diabolical false propaganda was spread. In the evening, every home, every officer, who had a Muslim servant, a driver or who gave protection to some Muslims were told on telephone that unless they throw out the Muslims, their houses are going to be mobbed. Telephone calls were received several times in the Ispat Hospital and the Director of the Hospital was told that unless the Muslim patients who had received the injuries are thrown out of the hospital, they are going to mob the hospital" (*OLA Debates*, Vol. VI (26), 23.3.1964; 4-5).

With regard to the building of rumour and communal strife, he said, "There was a well prepared plan of conspiracy and the methods have either killed a Hindu or burnt a Hindu shop or poisoned Hindus, etc. The second step is-that the Muslims are fully prepared with guns, ammunition and bombs and are going to attack the Hindus. The third step is-that when mob hysteria begins, set one or two shops on fire or stab one or two people. All these set-in motion a chain reaction and mass mob violence begins. These are undesirable elements in our society. They have been tempted by Pakistani agents to work for them. There are certain sections of people in the Indian society who are also working with them. They create all these tensions. These are people in the society who are counterparts of RSS and Jan Sangh, who advertently or inadvertently, are playing as the tools of Pakistan and are implementing Pakistani agent's propaganda. They are continuously financed to carry out this propaganda. These agents want that Muslims should be killed in India. So they spread the propaganda that Muslims are going to attack the Hindus. Can you imagine that a handful of Muslims can ever dare to attack large number of Hindus, But such a situation has been created that wherever I went, I found that a psychosis of fear has been created that the Muslims are going to attack. Further, when I probed into the matter, I found that a plan has been in operation by the Pakistan agents, by which large-scale chaotic conditions is to be created in major industrial centres and in the main lines of communications with a view to reduce production of critical industries. To reduce the production at Rourkela, this commotion has been created" (*OLA Debates*, Vol. VI (26), 23.3.1964; 5-6). He also said in this context, "Today they (Pakistani Army) are out to create mischief if not direct invasion. It appears they are trying to create troubles in the heart of our country in terms of exciting our people, with the result that all the anti-social elements, *goondas*, and fanatics are benefitted through looting and arson and murder. I have seen all these things. It is indeed a matter of deep regret that such a thing should have happened in our State which was free from communalism. The statement of the Leader of the House, Leader of the Opposition and other groups jointly issued for maintaining peace was scoffed at by these *agents provocateurs* and hot-headed youngsters of the RSS. They did not have an iota of sense of awe or prestige for the statement issued by this highest House of the State. They are determined to throw the Constitution to the wind. They wanted to create a situation by which the thousands of citizens of India should live in fear. The whole thing is pathetic and the entire story is disgusting. At this moment when the Government will have to consider and implement several drastic actions and ruthless measures to ensure that such vandalism is ended once for all so that the citizens can live without fear and in peace (*OLA Debates*, Vol. VI (26), 23.3.1964; 6).

On the mood of the people and what will sway them, he said, "Whatever sways them they have trust and reliance on the leadership that he is trying... Sir, smart political speeches does not sway a people. It can be a cut across. If we cut across the political line-ups and tried to sway the people. What destroys the people is divisions., whether by caste or by religion. Whatever it may be, if you divide it, destroy it, then you destroy the motivation of the people" (*OLA Debates*, Vol. XIV (3), 25.2.1994; 84).

On the Babri Masjid demolition, Biju Patnaik said, "This is all game of votes. But is is destructive game. Suppose you get a chance to form the Government, will you throw 14 crores Muslims outside India. Now you are sponsoring a movement. Congress divided the country into three parts. You divide the country into ten parts. This is the only thing the BJP can do. One thing has to be clear. I do not say anybody is untouchable. What you are saying about this, first thing is so many mistakes which are committed by leaders of Congress Party. I was at New York at that time. When I came back, I met the Prime Minister. Since this Babri Masjid structure, whatever it is, was demolished, both Vajpayee and Advani and other leaders said that this is a great error. I know what RSS is. They are making orders that RSS should be banned. What are they saying now? They are hanging their heads in shame because they knew it is a ghastly deed and cowardish. No religious structure is demolished by another religion. Tolerance is real Hinduism -- *Sarba dharma Samanwayah*, all Dharma is equal, is the essence of Hinduism. My dear friends do not try to destroy it. Do not say something which is far beyond this Nation's historical growth" (*OLA Debates*, Vol. X(3), 22.2.1993; 129-30).

On the *Ram janmabhoomi* dispute, he said, "When Jayaprakash wanted a movement arising out of unemployment and so on and so forth, the order was to start arresting en-mass which was called emergency. Today, on Mandal Commission Report there are agitations. Then Ram *janmabhoomi* is steering us on the face. If one step there shows the caste consideration, it will split the country. The Ram *janmabhoomi* may split the entire country on the basis of Hindu and Muslim cult. This is a dangerous trend that we are facing. If they succeed and they go on, there will be holocaust in the entire country which we must not have ever seen. They may lead to massacre and our every attempt should be to prevent it. I say, no one should be permitted to bring this nation to such a situation on religious grounds. In fact the nation is proud of itself when Mahatma Gandhi says, *Ishwar Allah Tere Naam, Sabko Samnati De Bhagaban*. If we forget that, we forget our own pedigree. So, neither the country should be divided on caste basis nor on religion basis. There should be extreme tolerance in the country socially and economically and others point of view should be taken into account to adjust ourselves as far as possible. We should combine to correct the situation whatsoever by joint consultation whenever it is necessary" (*OLA Debates*, Vol. III (8), 17.10.1990; 81).

On the issue of secularism, on 27th May 1996 during the Motion of Confidence in favour of Atal Behari Vajpayee government, Biju Patnaik remarked during discussion that Mr. Prime Minister started so well in his line of persuasion that many of us thought to go and join you, "but in the meantime you touched on points that dissuaded us from joining. When you talk of secularism and non-secularism, you are propagating the voice of non-secularism, and why? That was not your intention. Why have you done it ...". He also said, "I want that all of you should abandon Hinduism and join hands for the sake of the country". This shows his commitment to the principle of secularism and his aversion to the role of religion in politics.

Rashtriya Swayamsevak Sangh (RSS)

On the RSS, he said, "RSS is a disciplined organization. I know about RSS more than you. I know their bias. It is a disciplined body. Why did you breed this kind of things in everybody's mind, it is not understood? These things have to be given good-bye if you really tend towards building up a nation. You cannot build up a nation by cutting the feathers of the same nation. (*Interruptions*) Please do not make it more intolerable. Don't try to defend. Because you have no badge you become BJP. Everybody has lot of hopes that this is a discipline organization and do not build up something for the Nation, do fight for the cause of the Nation and bring discipline. But what have they done? They have broken the whole secrecy of the Nation, destroyed the very facet of the civilization. For me, it is a sad thing. A damn lot demagogue, styled as Sadhu with *chittas* (sandalwood paste) and all that talk of Ramachandra and do you call them as your leader?" (*OLA Debates*, Vol. X(3), 22.2.1993; 131-2).

International Relations and Politics

On the international politics, he said, "I may tell that in the year 1942, when Japan occupied most of China, your present father-land, I used to supply ammunitions" (*OLA Debates*, Vol. VII (25), 31.3.1965; 45). To this Hon'ble Member Ram Chandra Ram remarked, "A regular bluff". To this, Biju Patnaik replied, "You ask your Zhou-en-Lai. You write to him, you will get an answer" (*OLA Debates*, Vol. VII (25), 31.3.1965; 45).

Speaking about the starvation deaths and socialistic countries attitude, he said, "I would like to tell that when Stalin took over the Russian Government, he said the first generation must starve and die, second generation must be the slaves and the third generation can think of some convenience. You know Sir, the first generation really starved and 5 million Russians died of starvation. They were not bothered, the Government and their party were not bothered.... Have you ever heard during the last two or three years millions have died in Odisha for starvation as they were made to die in their countries? Only the socialistic countries that plan their programmes in a dictatorial way and try to achieve their ends within a reasonable time can do so. If we cannot do like them, we shall take a longer time, we shall have to take bigger trials, we shall not go by death due to starvation but continuous under feeding, if we wish to run a welfare State, welfare society by democratic process" (*OLA Debates*, Vol. VII (25), 31.3.1965; 37).

On the Russia and China system, he said, "I want to make the difference between two fatherlands, Russia and China. I do hold Russia as a socialist country in the world, its policies being Socialist at home and abroad. China is obviously different. China's policy is communism at home and imperialism abroad. These are vastly different concepts in their relationship with the communities of the world. The conflict comes out of this concept. In China Sir, you must know what their education system is today? Millions of students in schools and colleges have been shown maps of areas which were presumed to have been taken away by the imperialists, Tsars, the British and so on, some three hundred, five hundred, thousand years ago. All these millions of children are taught a type of sovereignty in terms of imperialism lost long ago for the reconquest of these areas in the coming generation. That is the threat of China. This is their mind through which millions are being taught for the reconquest. It is this mind which has to be curbed and those people who live in India and are India citizens do not understand this simple fact and are swayed either by blind idealism or blind ignorance to call the Chinese as the liberation army for India. I then only say Sir, that they are the most dangerous people that India can ever afford to hear of. Therefore, when you see the threats of China spreading out to different countries, yet we have men in India to say that we support China. You may support China, you may love China, you may know nothing of China but do not support their policies which are obviously dangerous to human beings, which is obviously dangerous for the simple reason because this policy may bring about a nuclear warfare in the world. China does not need land masses. It occupies more land masses than India. Why does she want to be more than what she is? She has quite many problems inside the country. It is only this sub-conscious imperialism in China, which lives there from the time of Chengiz Khan. China has lived thousands of years, it does not live today and it is this mind which refuses to accept any modernity as the Russians have done. It is this mind which wishes to go back thousands of years back and think in terms of greatest emperors, greatest rulers of the world. It is this mind which is the greatest danger to international peace. Therefore, I entreat on my friends, even though who blindly follow the Chinese jigsaw of puzzles without understanding these puzzles, I enjoin on them to reconsider what they are supporting. They are supporting nothing but misled men and women who form the fifth column of this country apt to sabotage the integrity of this country. Sir, they should take note that when a country is faced with problems of her sovereignty, it will be equally the same in China and Russia facing such problems in their own countries there can be no mercy but only liquidation" (*OLA Debates*, Vol. VII (25), 31.3.1965; 38-9).

On Pakistan, he said, "I had gone to Pakistan and had a meeting with Zia-ul-Haq, though he was junior to me in the army he was my friend. He said to send our Generals to check installations. Sri Venkatraman, this fellow now President of India said, 'why should we send anybody'. I told then make up your mind there is no attack from Pakistan" (*OLA Debates*, Vol. X (3), 11.9.1989; 136). Sri Gangadhar Mohapatra objected to the word 'this fellow' as unparliamentary for the President. Biju Patnaik replied, "I said this because he was then a Minister. A poor Brahmin boy from Madras could he be a Defense Minister" (*ibid*).

On the issue of how leadership of great leaders building up a strong economy and a strong state, Biju Patnaik referred about Germany, and said, "When Germany was down under earth and the League of Nations put Germany totally under their thumb, German Industries were virtually closed. Hundreds and thousands of Germans were without jobs. Dr. Swat, Hitler's Finance Minister, who was not indicted on what they had at that time as criminals in 1946, was having a small Bank under his name in a

Hotel where I was staying. I had the privilege of inviting him to breakfast or lunch, I do not remember exactly and he was good enough to come. And I asked him, Dr. Swat you recovered, not only recovered, but revamped entirely the economy of Germany to the extent that you could think of conquering the whole world. How did you do it? He said, Finance is not a matter of figures of Science. Finance is a matter of Art. If you know how much finance depends on the people, if you know how much the people can sacrifice and how many of us can work with half wages, your nation's finance get built. This is the moot point. We can build a leadership, this Government, next Government anybody or everybody build a leadership which will make our people work? We all know that we work half the time. We all know that we waste the time. But, he said we were looking out for a leader who could make German nation work for full time or overtime with half the wages and we found that in a leader like Hitler. Hitler was a much hated man in Western democracy-a much feared man. But, this is what Dr. Swat told me that they were looking after a leader and Hitler produced the leadership. He made German people work for 12 hours with 6 hours wage. After devastation of Germany, I used to go there twice a year because I had to build some factories and get some machines and so on and I could see in my eyes, hotels are coming up, number of bridges are built up. Germany got rebuilt and the whole nation was at work. Do you know Sir, Germans work so hard and were so indoctrinated to discipline that when somebody went there to his factory, he had to click his heels, bow his head and stand for the nation. This is discipline inculcated there by Hitler. And, he has said that we are rebuilding the State" (*OLA Debates*, Vol. II (3), 3.7.1995; 129).

On the East Pakistan crisis, Biju Patnaik cited the reference of twenty-five years earlier of Nehru's help to Indonesia, then India under British rule, and said, "When the question came to Indonesia, which was the internal affair of the Dutch, a Jawaharlal Nehru then thundered-the country was not yet technically free-that India shall not tolerate domination of the Dutch over the people of Indonesia. A mission from the Dutch insurgents was maintained here at the cost of the Government of India. A sum of ₹10 crores allotted to their Mission in Delhi and further sums were allotted to them in Washington, in London, in Moscow, in Australia and in other countries and the matter was taken up by the then Prime Minister in the Security Council and the issue was forced. Similarly, when it came to the question of Ranas in Nepal, arms were rushed to the Koirala people, the so-called Nepali Congress at that time, and the Ranas were thrown out. That was in 1951. These are matters of recorded history of the operations of this country" (OLA; 3). He also said that the people managing the Policy Divisions of the State Department of the United States are mostly Rhodes Scholars, and as such, these Rhodes scholars have their first allegiance to their spiritually other country, England. "It is the British policy, the British thinking that is followed by the Americans although the Americans in their gayer moments call England as their offshore island. Nevertheless, it is the British who divided the country; it is the British who decided to maintain this division and therefore, it is the dictates of the British policy which the Americans usually follow in this area, as they have done right through beginning with Kashmir, Pakistan war, and now the Chinese war. Therefore, to expect that conditions will be created to stop further influx of refugees and ensure their early return, Madam Prime Minister, a lot of wishful thinking must have gone into it" (OLA; 4).

Expressing deep concern for India's international prestige and its submissiveness to international politics, he said, "The Prime Minister knows that India's image, compared to what it was 25 years ago-and I mentioned the question of Indonesia-when India could stand for the liberation of all the subject people of the world and enjoyed her rightful prestige in the world has sharply declined. Today even the African countries, the Asian countries, the South East Asian countries and the Middle East countries do not hold us with any great respect, and this decline is in direct proportion to our submissiveness. The Prime Minister takes pains to say that 'for twenty-three years India has never tried to interfere with internal affairs of Pakistan even though they had not exercised similar restrain. Even now we would not seek to interfere in any way'. No one ever said that India was a belligerent country. In fact, the image outside is that we are beyond redemption as a submissive country. We are a country which does not know even to stand up for its own right, stand up for its own prestige. That is the kind of image that we project today. When China attacked us, we did not use our Air Force to blast behind their line. Why? Because we were afraid, shivering in our boots that the Chinese bombs may drop on Calcutta, DVC, or Nangal. That was the thought behind. This country has never been a theatre of war. The only time when it ever went to war and conquered was Lanka, which we celebrate with a great deal of gusto as *Ramlila*, which is a crying shame. That is all that this country has ever done. This country has not gone into a state of war; this country has not gone into a state of new creative energy in terms of war. We take delight in saying that we are a peace-loving people. May I suggest with all humility, let us not try to couch our weakness in extraordinary words?" (OLA; 5-6).

While supporting the motion that India should be the first country to recognize the Government of Bangladesh, he elaborated what does recognition really mean? He questioned, does recognition mean going to war with Pakistan or its allies both in West and in the East? In this context, he said, "China has recognized the Hanoi Government. America is fighting in Vietnam. But America and China are not at war. The same is the question with Isreal. Different Governments are supplying arms, ammunition, heavy equipment, bombers, and fighters to different countries. But they are not at war with each other. Here is a question before us that by this inaction of ours we are going to be saddled with a further expenditure equivalent to the expenditure for our Defense Forces. If at this rate of persecution by Gen. Yahya Khan and his allies in Peking, ten million refugees are thrown out, and they could be easily thrown out-then we would be saddled with an expenditure of over a thousand crores. Right! That finishes our economy; all the hopes of our development, as the Prime Minister rightly put in her speech, gone. So, this action of Pakistan in East Bengal or Bangladesh or whatever you call it, has ceased to be an internal affair of Pakistan-it has become really an internal affair of India" (OLA; 6-7). He also said that the logic of not recognizing the Bangladesh Government, is "only to save ourselves, in our interests, we have no other option, but to recognize Bangladesh and give it all the material help with what we produce in our own country, a fraction of which would be more than enough for these to treat freedom fighters of Bangladesh" (OLA; 7).

Acknowledging the role of erstwhile Soviet Union during the formation of Bangladesh in 1971, Biju Patnaik said, "An amendment to the (Governor's) address which if you all like can come as an official amendment later that we are thankful to the Soviet Union for the deep understanding of the problem in the Indian sub-continent and standing for the cause of India and Bangladesh. I think, Government should accept this amendment because this is vital for Bangladesh and also vital for the humanity. The role of the Soviet Union in this context cannot be under estimated" (*OLA* Debates, Vol. III (2), 4.1.1972; 42).

On the wishes of the people of Sikkim for strengthening Indo-Sikkim cooperation and inert-relationship, Biju Patnaik said, "I want to make it clear that Sikkim is not annexed to India. Sikkim people do not want to become Indian citizen and they are the citizens of Sikkim. The people of Sikkim wanted two representatives to the Parliament – one to the Lok Sabha and one to Rajya Sabha. I am afraid our big neighbor on the other side of the border may think it otherwise. It may be our neighbours like Nepal and Bhutan may feel wild and it is just possible. Therefore, in this situation, it cannot be said that it is free from all difficulties" (*OLA Debates*, Vol. III (11), 20.12.74; 120-1).

Biju Patnaik was elected to the Rajya Sabha on 13 May 1971 and resigned 6 Otober 1971. In the Rajya Sabha on 25 May 1971, during a *Short Duration Discussion*, Biju Patnaik, while giving prime importance to people's cause, articulately spoke for immediate recognition of Bangladesh by India. He cited the instance which India extended to Indonesia in July 1947 by Nehru, even though India was not a free nation, and went against the Dutch colonialists in their internal matter. He enthused upon Prime Minister Indira Gandhi that she herself being a freedom fighter should not delay the recognition of Bangladesh and uphold the objective of India's legacy of defending human rights in any part of the world. He said, "I am pained to say that this country had greater power of perception or greater sense of adventure when it came to human rights twenty-five years ago". That 'sense of adventure' for human rights which guided him in 1947 to rescue Sukarno and uphold supremacy of Indonesian people over Dutch colonialism guided him in May 1971 to demand immediate recognition of Bangladesh by Government of India" (m.dailyhunt.in).

In a *Calling Attention Notice* in the Rajya Sabha on 23 July 1971, on the reported intrusion of two Pakistani Mirage aircraft into Kashmir, Biju Patnaik narrated how he saved Indian naval bases from the lethal submarine launched attack from Pakistan during 1965 war. During that period, Indonesian President Sukarno had a mutual defense agreement with Zhou En-Lai of China and Ayub Khan of Pakistan, and as per it, was to supply three submarines to Pakistan, which already was at war with India. The then Prime Minister Lal Bahadur Shashtri requested Biju Patnaik to visit Jakarta and persuade President Sukarno and desist him from this supply. The then Foreign Minister Swaran Singh facilitated the urgent mission of Biju Patnaik, and finally President Sukarno honoured his request and the submarines were stopped from being sent to Pakistan. Biju Patnaik said, "We had no defense in our ports at that time, no defense at all. Imagine the situation, if the three submarines had bombed simultaneously Vizag, Madras and Cochin, what would have been the position?" The then Defense Minister Jagjivan Ram, in reply admitted neither having the adventure nor knowledge as Biju Patnaik has and said, "it is first-hand information from first-hand knowledge".

On international arms sale tactics, Biju Patnaik spoke about an observation made by him on the answer given by the then British Prime Minister while leaving Mumbai when she said, that If Pakistanis are acquiring arms for their own national security, India has also been doing so and why can't they do more. The suggestion of the British Government who are, as Napoleon said-a nation of shopkeepers and merchants, is clear-push off to one side some arms and try to sell arms to the other side by creating a fear psychosis. While desisting from such arms-race, he said, "I wonder if the Minister would assure the House that we are not going to be taken in by this kind of thing and ruin our finances by running into an arms-race" (OLA, Oral Answer 29.4.81; 162).

On a national power grid for India and the international demand for aluminum rising due to its low weight, American Government contemplated to bring in legislation where the car manufacturers will use aluminum instead of steel for better mileage due to increasing oil prices in the international market. "Today the world wants aluminum. The Arab countries, Iran and other countries where they get cheap gas, can produce cheap power. For Alumina, power is the largest raw material and one who could get raw material cheap, can also produce aluminium at a cheaper cost". In order to have a robust power supply for alumina production, "the House should perhaps think whether the time has come now for a national power grid so that the whole thing can be planned properly and not left to the whims and fancies of individual state power boards. We have not got the national power grid yet, a national power grid which can be controlled by Parliament. That is why I have brought this matter" (*Lok Sabha Debates*, 28 June 1977; 298-9).

War Issue

On the issue of China war of 1962, he said, "Here is a challenge of a powerful aggressor against, if I may so, the greatest democracy in the world. During the last few days the world has discovered that Communist China has merely made a show of friendship towards India, whereas in reality it is bidding for world power. Communist China, with its twisted thinking, out-heroing the hero, is trying to introduce what it calls communism, by force of arms over the whole of Asia. In their twisted insanity they tried this in Malaya, in Vietnam, in Cambodia, in Indo-China, in Indonesia, in Burma and now in India. They took a long time for this preparation while professing friendship. In the history of the world such a deception was not known. It is a mass deception that can only be practiced by an insane Government, which is now present in Communist China. This Government with their leaders felt that the greatest Socialist Democratic Republic of India, making tremendously headway towards a welfare State is out to discredit a regime based on regimentation of the lowest order. A regimented nation, with bayonets pushing, goading every citizen of their nation to build up a war machine to frighten and destroy the world. The great Socialist Republic of India has accepted that challenge. In the last few days, Sir, we have seen with great joy and pride that this nation under the personality of our great leader, Pandit Nehru, has created an effort in all parts of the country unequalled in the history of democracy. Here, there is no question of bayonets, communes or Governmental machinery. But it is the people, the millions of people, the peasants, the workers, students, the clerks-everyone has reacted in a manner for which this nation must be proud. There is no question of fear. It is told that the Chinese army or their war machine is a very powerful force. The nation scoffs at it. It is told that the Chinese Air Force is a mighty one. The nation laughs at it. We are not afraid of death. We have been taught by the Father of this Nation to fight the mightiest empire known in the world's history with nothing but our hands. We have been taught to die and to sacrifice. Such a nation as this under the leadership of the disciple of Gandhiji scoffs and laughs at the Chinese aggression. In this context of life against life, vitality against vitality, we, a peace-loving nation, should do our utmost for the reconstruction of this country. We must understand and deeply understand the necessities of defense and all that it represents. The defense of a country is not merely a few guns, ammunition, air-craft, and missiles and a few fighting men. The defense of a country is based on its entire economic and production power. If a country like ours does not wish to tighten its belt, as indeed all of us should; if everyone in every Legislature, in Parliament, in every village have not done so till today; if the entire nation wishes to feed itself by buying millions of tons of food from outside; if we cannot prepare ourselves for smallest sacrifices, how can such a nation prepare for war? If we always demand all over the nation that every bit of comfort must come first, how can such a nation prepare for hardship, privation and sacrifice for binding the will of this nation to prepare for the war machine. To the extent that we train our engineers, to the extent we have to maintain various technical institutions, to the extent that our research laboratories work to the full capacity to the extent that all this combined technological intellect of our nation has been developed to produce all those specialized items which can be converted into a war machine, would be a measure of our real power for resisting the aggressors. A great democracy like ours quite rightly hoped that there would be no aggression on India because India has no designs on any one. If we do not have any designs, why in the modern world, another nation should have designs on us. We have a right to expect an answer. But that right, that inalienable right of a free man to live according to his conscience through the process of democracy have been dashed to the ground. Therefore, this tremendous will of ours have to be harnessed into the greatest war machine. It is not a question of few ministers to prepare the nation for war. In a democracy, it shall be only the will of the people that would voluntarily offer every sacrifice so that an efficient apparatus can be built to protect the nation. It is not the chastisement of a Krishna Menon or ten replacements of Krishna Menons that is going to prepare this nation for war. The only remedy for unpreparedness is preparation. Our leader has called the nation to prepare in every field of resistance activity; to stop all kinds of wastage; to conserve all the time; so that the surplus from all sides can go into production of highest priority requirements, for training of our men in vast numbers to defend, our women to go to hospitals for nursing, and hundred other things which the exigencies of war would demand of the nation. Before I proceed to inform the House the elementary outline of what we wish to do in this State, I would like to bring some other matters to their notice, only as a measure of warning of how even inadvertently, we can rain the cause of our nation. I also warn the treacherous fifth column in our country. I am constrained to say before this House that there are still in the Communist Party of India, a large number of men, who think in terms of international communism by force. I say with cold consideration and without any anger, let them remember that this great democratic nation of ours which has decided to shoot down the Chinese invaders like mad dogs, will not spare the mad dogs inside the country. Those belonging to any section of the Nation who do not feel like Indians first and Indians last, have forfeited their right to live in India during this time of national emergency.... Today, in a national emergency there are no parties but a nation. There is no flag but the nation's flag. Everything else stands submerged. We have decided to subjugate even our fundamental rights of democracy. I do hope that when this emergency is over and we have thrown out of our land the invading Chinese Communist hordes, we will not see any more flags on this soil of India which reminds us of Communist China. During this struggle, the nation would intensely hate the sight of any flag which is similar to that of Communist China. I would even recommend to my friends of the Communist party to consider this, when this emergency is over, they might think of another flag. We have no doubt that there are many amongst them who feel equally strongly against the Chinese aggressors. But there are many others among them who are willing to greet the Chinese Communists with open arms calling them as Chinese Liberation Army. It is to them that the entire attention of our civil defense forces will be directed. We will protect the rear of our armed forces. I am grateful to note that the newspapers of this State have taken action to mobilize the defense efforts of our people. I am glad to note the enthusiasm of our youth to mobilize the public will and I can assure them that Government will give them every support in continuation of this good work. Coming to our own State, our entire administrative apparatus will undergo a thorough change to be able to reach peak efficiency. Inefficiency and corruption will be treated very severely because in times of emergency when orders are not implemented due to inefficiency it may cause loss of thousands of lives. If during an emergency, a corrupt official twist and delays the order, it may equally cause loss of thousands of lives. Consequently, in times of emergency, inefficiency and corruption are treated as treason. We are contemplating rising a Militia force in terms of civil defense up to one hundred thousand. All towns, districts and sub-divisional head-quarters, centralized industrial areas, important installations like power and transport systems will become key points of training and protection. The details are being worked out so that every village, every man, woman and small children would know what to do when nations demand comes to them. All the youth clubs and *Mahilla Samitis* (Women's associations) of the State would be mobilized to produce such materials as needed for amenities of defense forces. Various factories will be reoriented to produce materials for war. I am grateful for the voluntary will of my workers all over the State that they themselves, without communes, without any bayonet pushing them, have decided to maintain their plants in full production, to give extra time for specialized work and to serve in their own way for the cause of the nation. It is not necessary for me today to ban all kinds of strikes. The will of the people themselves have made it unnecessary for such a law to come to force. I convey to those workers, their associates and management the grateful thanks of the people of Odisha. Our youths in the colleges and schools have demanded compulsory military training. It is not that we need a law to conscript. It is again the will of the youths who demand conscription. We have decided to expand our NCC activities to take in immediately ten thousand boys and girls of the senior institutions and to train and build them to shape, to teach them how to fight and how to die for the cause of the motherland. In the administration, Government is considering heavy curtailment of all leaves and holidays, extending longer hours of work to ensure that all the heavy responsibilities that devolve on the Government, the administration and the officials are discharged with highest efficiency. Finally, Sir, this State of ours also has to mobilize our resources. It has already been started by the will of the Legislators who represent the people of the State to carry out a programme of maximum economy, so that the nation can prepare for throwing out the aggressors. While the greatest socialist republic of the world fights the naked aggression committed upon it by Communist China, let us all remember again and again, that today there is only one nation, only one flag and only one leader to whom the whole nation, this democratic nation, the nation proud of its fundamental rights, has surrendered to the last man all its rights and privileges and has decided to forge itself into a weapon of war-one single deadly weapon and offered it in the hands of our great leader to blast the aggressors out of our motherland. It must be understood and it has been understood by the people throughout the nation that while this aggressor was preparing for years and years by subterfuge, practiced friendliness with us while preparing for war, we must in the initial stages be prepared to suffer certain amount of reverses. It is not anything new that an aggressor commits aggression because he is prepared. This nation of ours which had just begun preparation for war will naturally take some time. But let the Chinese not feel too happy about it. The day of reckoning would come and would come very soon. Let them understand that this sleeping democracy can become the most deadly war weapon they have ever come across. They have woken up the proverbial sleeping lion and slowly by the will of the people it is gathering a momentum which may not stop at the bounds of MacMohan Line between China and India. When this great democracy of India is built up into a war machine, it may not halt at the Himalayas, its traditional boundary. As one of our great leaders, Dr, Rajendra Prasad said, when this great force of ours is mobilized it may even force out the Communist Chinese from other territories under its occupation and cut this Communist Government of China to its proper size, so that it does not raise its head for many centuries against other nations of the world.

Therefore, Sir, as a token of our will, every Member of this House has declared that we will tighten our belts and will divert the surplus funds to the cause of defense and in obedience to that will I have brought this amendment Bill for consideration of this House" (*OLA Debates*, Vol. III (29), 30.10.62; 2-7).

On the question of food self-sufficiency and defense production, he said, "War is the dominating situation in the country today and not a matter of a mere passing reference. As the Prime Minister of India has repeatedly warned and cautioned the country, every other activity of the State and of the people would be subordinated to the first responsibility of the State and the people of India, i.e., the preservation of national integrity. It is true, as the Hon'ble Member from Sundargarh said that people cannot fight or live with empty stomachs. Therefore, the food front becomes the second front in the war, second only to the preservation of territorial and national integrity. Here also we should take certain specific data into consideration.... if this country wishes to be free from the economic domination of other countries, if this nation of ours wishes to hold its head high, to project its own political thoughts and political actions without fear or favour of other countries, it becomes imperative for this nation to do one or two important administrative necessities. These are that we shall not beg for food from other countries; we shall not wait for our defense materials from other countries. These two are the most essential factors for extending the nation's politics and upholding the nation's honour, if we wish to safeguard our national sovereignty in terms of preservation of our national integrity. It is said that war is only an extension of politics. If war has been thrust on us by such an extension of politics in the Asian theatre, if war has been thrust on us by the extension of such politics by those Western powers who for hundreds of years had divided and ruled this country are yet capable of raising the beastly passions of the people and make them fight and bring war to their homes, we do have to get up some day and grow up into our political structure and believe in a fashion which would add courage to the mature politics and extension of political thoughts. We cannot say, we know, that we do not like western interference in the Kashmir affairs and in the affairs of our national integrity. At the same time we will go and say we must have our food, 6 or 7 million tons as we cannot reduce our consumption commensurate with national honour. We cannot have both the things (*OLA Debates*, Vol. III (6), 28.9.1965; 17-8). He continued to say, "I love battles but despise persecution. I would like to say that the problem of the country with regard to food and defense materials is that we should be self-sufficient which will enable us to hold our head high" (*OLA Debates*, Vol. III (6), 28.9.1965; 20).

While illustrating how some of the nations recovered after severe shock, he said, "After the 1945 war, German rose from ashes. All their buildings were smashed. Projects, factories and everything were totally destroyed and year after year they have grown up. How it was possible for that country? Let us know how it was possible. That country was of course a disciplined one under Hitler, a nation who planned to conquer the world must have great deal of discipline. They decided to work for 8 hours for wages, and 4 hours for the nation free. That is nation. We were a nation of that type in the age of Kalinga, when half of the Indian empire was conquered. Java, Sumatra, Burma was in our empire. The wheel of time is running, and we were up during that time. We have to turn the wheel of time in our favour. Can we not collectively push the wheel of time? If we cannot turn the wheel of time, then we can never go up! If anybody is thinking that someone from Delhi or outside will come to lift us, then that is a greatest fallacy of the world. Only we can build our nation through our effort as we did at the age of Kalinga. We have oceans, forests, youths. We are unable to motivate our youths, for which our situation is like this.... After being smashed to the ground, if they can rise, so can we. If we cannot do it, we have no business to sit here and talk here for long time on petty things" (*OLA Debates*, Vol. I (4), 21.3.1990; 53). He suggested to have Consultative Committee for development, and said, "I wish to have Consultative Committee of each Department and you gentleman are part of that Committee. Give your ideas and those ideas will crystallize the shape of policy of Government. Let us see, if we can work together" (*OLA Debates*, Vol. I (4), 21.3.1990; 53).

Legislative Issue

On legislative matter, Biju Patnaik said, "The Speaker in Lok Sabha did not allow the adjournment motion because no Minister is involved, the Government is not involved. But here two Ministers are involved and themselves they have made the statement. Therefore, it becomes a matter of public importance for this House. So you have to consider to allow discussion in the matter on that basis when Ministers are involved" (*OLA Debates*, Vol. IV (16), 13.3.1975; 43-4).

On another legislative matter, Biju Patnaik said, "Yesterday I pointed out that people remain present during discussions on which they are interested. The ruling party is claiming they are progressive. Saying we will do welfare of the labourers. Today there is discussion on labour. Only 7 members of the progressive claiming ruling party are present now. Even the leader and members of the CPI who claim to be more progressive are not present. From this where their interest is known. Their interest is in corruption" (*OLA Debates*, Vol. IV (16), 13.3.1975; 65). He said, "Apart from rules and norms, this House is the sovereign House of the State. The Parliament is also the sovereign in the country. We, the Members, have taken oath in the Treasury Bench and Opposition to offer democratic conditions in the country. Regarding the Adjournment Motion which was ruled out.... When

Government is oppressing, sanctity goes beyond the '*Niyama*' (rule). The Sovereign House has to take some decision in the democratic set-up. I do not want to waste time of the House. When such things are happening, when democratic conditions are thrown out, what shall be the business of the House? We shall be the spectators and after the accident, we will bring it to the House or we should take preventive action?" (*OLA Debates*, Vol. IV (16), 13.3.1975; 56).

Expressing concern for legislative process and Members' presence during passing ofbills, Biju Patnaik, said, "Mr. Chairman Sir, to start with, I am rather surprised because the House has to have fifty per cent of the Members to be present here to pass this Bill. But I see all the seats of the BJP and the Congress are vacant.... It includes my side.... The Left parties are there.... Your party seats are vacant. What is the use of making speeches here? This will not go through at all. You do not have requisite number of Members. How can you go through this?... Shrimati Sushma Swaraj, where are your Members?" He then said, "It only shows that this Bill is not going to be passed today because we do not have the numbers. It is as simple as that. Do we have the 50 per cent of total number of Members who are required to vote present here? They are not" (*Lok Sabha Debates*, 12.9.96; 530-1).

On the question of 'Point of Order' as a legislative procedure, he said, "Rule 219 authorises any Member to raise a point of order at any time. The question therefore, is at any time we can raise a point of order and the Speaker shall-it is mandatory-must listen to it and dispose it up. If some other business is going on, the Speaker should stop that business and deal with the point of order first.... It is strictly a breach of Rules. Point of order must take precedence over anything else. You can dispose it off and then go to any other business.... Point of order is a point of order, it is not a point of privilege. In the Business of the House, a point of order has got preference. This is a very simple thing. Even in the Parliament, when the Prime Minister speaks and a point of order is raised by some Member, then the Speaker asks the Prime Minister to sit down. It is everywhere happening, It is nothing new" (V (13), 13.3.1987; 73-4).

On a serious Constitutional crisis where the Governor made contradictory statements during Budget presented and speech outside the Assembly, he said, "We are passing the Appropriation Bill, giving authority to Government to pass vast sum of money by 31st of this month. All these are under the authority of Governor. The Governor presented an address here in this House, praising the Government-stated that all action of the Government are sound, proper and for the welfare of the people. By giving his assent to the Appropriation Bill, the Governor became as much a party to the passing of the Budget as the two Houses of the Legislature. In this case, these observations amount to such contradictions. The address is presented by the Governor under his signature. The question is Sir, we cannot discuss about the Governor here, but Governor making such statement in different parts of the State virtually contradicts the action of the Government under various Departments. He said that for the last 35 years or 38 years of independence, literacy is at the minimum level in one district i.e. Bolangir district. About another district, he said inspite of noise raised on Kalahandi where he praised the press for bringing out the fair facts, goes in contradiction, what the Ministers, Chief Minister or Revenue Minister have been emphasizing in this House that the press has exaggerated. So, the Constitutional crisis is here, the Governor presented his address, signed the Appropriation Bill, which are debating here in this House; the same Governor now said, on record I am to say, something which is opposite of his own address and presentation of the Appropriation Bill. Therefore, it amounts to a Constitutional crisis, in the sense that, the position must be clarified either the Governor must be corrected by the President of India or the Chief Minister should resign, because Governor is expressing no-confidence on the Government's functioning.... The Hon'ble Law Minister has condemned the Governor by saying that his statement is unfortunate" (OLA *Debates*, 14.3.1986; 71-6). J. B. Patnaik, Chief Minister, replied, "In the Assembly Governor speeches are made justifying the Government policies. But while implementing the policies, if there are certain faults, then I and my Ministers disclose it in the open. When the Governor has given his address, he has mentioned about the policies of the Government. Nowhere, the Governor has said that the Government has failed. The Governor has said about a district that it has not progressed much. It is much low in literacy. I don't understand how the Governor contradicts his presentation. I do not understand how the Governor presentation is discussed here. Whatever it may be, the matter will be discussed once the Governor returns from outside. It is not right to create controversy over the Governor's Budget presentation" (OLA *Debates*, 14.3.1986; 77).

On the Governor's role during President's Rule, Biju Patnaik said, "During the President's Rule, when the Governor governs the State, he did certain acts for which he should be adversely commented. At that time there was no ministry. Governor was responsible for all the acts done at that time.... He was directly in charge of the Government. So, his acts may be commented by all". To this the Speaker cited Rule189 that states, 'A Member while speaking shall not reflect upon the conduct of the President or any Governor or any Court of Law in the exercise of its judicial functions'. To this, Biju Patnaik replied, "We know that. We are concerned as to how he acted during the President's Rule" (*OLA Debates*, Vol. I (3), 26.3.1974; 58).

The Privilege notice was given as Biju Patnaik, Leader of Opposition, had given an open threat in a public meeting at Jajpur that unless the Congress government beg apology to the people, Assembly session scheduled to begin on the coming 9th instant will not be allowed to sit. This has been published in the *Prajatantra* on 3rd December 1974 and *Amrita Bazaar Patrika* on 4th December 1974. In response to this Privilege motion, Biju Patnaik said, "Where is the contempt of the House? It may be contempt of the government in power. That right we possess. If I say that unless certain things are done, if outside I say and insist here which I am saying every day and I have only said yesterday that government business cannot continue. This is parliamentary right to force an issue inside the House. To press a point is our privilege. Any member has got the privilege to do so. So, it is not a question of bringing any contempt of the House. So it is absurd to say that a Member of the House is putting the House to any contempt..... If I said the Assembly session will not be allowed to sit – but the Assembly session has sat and is going on everyday.... So, where is the question...." (*OLA Debates*, Vol. III (10), 20.12.74; 63-4). He again said, "Sir, the manner of bringing this motion of privilege, to my mind, is ridiculous. It appears that the mover of the motion has no idea of the majesty and dignity of the House. It must have come to your notice that many people accuse the Members of the House, many people accuse the House and the government. You must have noticed that no less a person than George Fernandes accused the Treasury Bench in the Parliament as a gang of thieves, touts and brothel... the Mother of Parliaments that is the Indian Parliament itself, there also '*gherao*' is done during deliberations. Fifty thousand people are coming; one lakh people are coming and saying we will paralyse Parliament. Has the Parliament taken any notice of it? Has any Member taken any notice of it? Has the Speaker or Deputy Speaker taken any notice of it? Even what I was mentioning about Parliament, especially it was said for the Treasury Bench, the Congress people, they are gang of thieves, touts – then none from the Treasury Bench rose to oppose, no one brought Privilege Motion. Rather demand came from Opposition, but Treasury Bench, including the Prime Minister refused it. No one brought Privilege Motion. This is Parliamentary precedent. Even if we wish, we cannot waive this precedent. We can at least go by the national Parliamentary precedent" (*OLA Debates*, Vol. III (10), 20.12.74; 74-5). Later, on 23 December during the Appropriation Bill (No. 4) discussion, he said, "George Fernandes had said Parliament is a den of thieves. Piloo Mody and Madhu Limaye brought the Privilege Motion, but Treasury bench refused it" (*OLA Debates*, Vol. III (11), 20.12.74; 104).

Speaking on a matter of high controversy during those days in Odisha, he said, "Sir, there was a Bill which came before the Parliament recently, i.e., in the last session. This is a special legislation-Prohibition of Prostitution (Amendment) Bill. What was the amendment? If any newspaper or magazine or anybody writes about sexual excess or improprieties about a person in high office, first he must be made to resign. This law exists in Pakistan. If a newspaper mention that so and so gone to a brothel or so and so has done sexual excesses, the first thing will be, he must be made to resign. This is the tradition of India. One washer-woman said about Sita and Ram Chandra took an extreme point. In Pakistan, since it came out in newspaper, the Pakistani Minister was removed. Our Prime Minister Shri Rajiv Gandhi had brought a Bill in the Parliament saying that any aspersion on a public leader on this kind of affairs, which here I need not mention, which has been going on and on in the State, brought all our heads down in shame. He must be immediately removed. This is the Bill that has come. Instead of attacking the person on whom allegation has been made for the sexual excesses, the person concerned has used an old law for arresting him, Sri PritishNandy, a top-grade journalist of this country. This law was dead in 1982, but this law has come to life suddenly. Instead of using that Act to arrest himself and remove himself from his *gaddi* (seat), he has used this Act for arresting Sri Pritish Nandy. This is the funniest part of the situation. Such is your Government. Mr. Finance Minister, such is the character of your Government. Such is the standard of your Government. Such is the ineffectiveness of your Government. This has not been proved by me, but by the Auditor General of India and Accountant General of India and Odisha that this Government does not work. So, Odisha is ina bad way" (*OLA Debates*, 11.9.1986; 127).

Commission of Enquiry

On the question of Commission of Inquiry, he said, "Setting of Commission of Inquiry under the Act is prerogative of the Government. I will place it before the House as to whether the House is going to surrender its authority before a third person or will you have to seriously consider it. I have said earlier, if the Government is not satisfied with the findings given by the RDC, it will consider setting up a Commission of Inquiry.... Why are you not going for setting up of a House Committee comprising of all Opposition Members to investigate into it. I have no objection. What I want to say is, do you willingly surrender the authority of this August House to somebody else. This is the question. Sir, the Courts are also sometimes over-stepping their limit. One of the Speakers was directed to present himself before the Supreme Court bur he refused to do so and the matter ended there. So, they have to act. If he does not act, what will he do? The Speaker is not supposed to surrender himself before a Court. Speaker is the authority of the House, authority of the Parliament and authority of the Assembly. So, we must be sure of our own authority. We shall consider it at proper time and do the needful. But, outside party telling the Government they must set-up an enquiry Commission is not understandable by me" (*OLA Debates*, Vol. IX (9), 6.11.1992; 117-8).

On the issue of setting up Commission of Enquiry, he said, "The subject matter which is a part of investigation of Commission of Enquiry, by a sitting

Judge of High Court should not have been discussed here at all. Therefore, I will not go into these matters right or wrong, which are the subject matters of the Court of Enquiry. A Commission of Enquiry has already been started. Therefore, we better leave it to the Commission to give its findings. One thing I would like to mention here that the subject matter which is a part of investigation of Commission of Enquiry, by a sitting Judge of High Court should not have been discussed here at all. A Commission of Enquiry has already been started. Therefore, we better leave it to the Commission to give its findings. On all matters starting from the burning of a driver and the bus at the Vani Vihar campus till the end of firing, right or wrong, whatever it is, I will not go into it, because what was the Government order, how much it has been flouted all that will come into enquiry" (*OLA Debates*, Vol. III (8), 17.10.1990; 79).

With regard to Inquiry Committee, Biju Patnaik had said, "Committee must have adequate legal powers. It cannot have legal powers unless it is constituted under the Commission of Inquiry Act. The Chief Minister says why should there be a High Court Judge; let anybody else. I told her at that time that the Executive have been reduced to such a position in India, people have no confidence in it. Whatever little confidence now remains, it remains with the Judges, good or bad. Therefore, a sitting High Court Judge is a person on whom some credibility can be placed. But some of us can be there, however good he may be, it will not pass public examination" (*OLA Debates*, Vol. III (9), 19.12.74; 134).

On hooch tragedy of Cuttack city, he said, "Once I had said and ordered for an enquiry by the RDC, Central Range. The House can very well consider their report and if it is not satisfied then the House can advise and even direct the Government to set up a Commission of Enquiry. This is the privilege of the House and I have already said I am prepared for that. In this matter, the High Court intervened and directed the State Government to set up a Commission of Enquiry. Well, I said, the High Court has no jurisdiction. High Court is not the last Bible. Last Bible is the Supreme Court. Therefore, we went to Supreme Court to find out whether in fact the High Court has any jurisdiction to direct the State Government to appoint a judicial enquiry or any inquiry because any inquiry conducted is made with knowledge of the Government. So, this is what we have gone through and this is nothing great that is going to be disputed. All we are asking the Supreme Court whether any High Court has any jurisdiction over the Government and direct them for judicial inquiry. In fact the matter was discussed in the last week-end at the *Inter-State Council* meeting. I raised this and the Law Minister who present there said, as a lawyer, I can say the High Court has no jurisdiction. That is why we have gone to the Supreme Court to get it settled because many other States have also pleaded for that. When the Supreme Court directs several other States to implement their orders, this comes as a Constitutional point then. Beyond that I have neither point, neither of the House nor any Member of the House. In fact, none else than Sri Bijay Mohapatra inspired upon judicial enquiry. But, for what? I said if the report that comes from the Commission is not satisfactory, then I will have judicial enquiry. Now, the High Court got unnecessarily involved into this and this has been referred to the Supreme Court which will pass judgment whether the High Court has any jurisdiction or not. If they say-Yes, in the same day judicial enquiry will be ordered. We will order a Judge to have judicial enquiry, there is no problem" (*OLA Debates*, Vol. X (3), 22.2.1993; 132).

Biju Patnaik on the justification of demand for judicial enquiry to political murders, said, "He does not deny to what the Chief Minister said, but what she said that political violence leading to murder nothing like that happened in Odisha, I object to this. There has been some political violence leading to murder and there is tendency which would lead to political murder. We should not judge it lightly. That is why the opposition demanded for judicial enquiry. But the Chief Minister said, she is not prepared to do that. She strongly rejected the idea of judicial enquiry. Hence, she discussed with me to form a high-level committee. Probably, this will not be accepted by the Members of this side of the House. The high power committee, whatever you may call it that will not be acceptable to Members of this side of the House. So let there be a discussion" (*OLA Debates*, Vol. III (15), 28.12.74; 10-1). With regard to the formation of the High Power Committee, he said, "This type of High Power Committee consisting of politicians of the state, appointed by the government by a Press Note, does not give any sanction at all. You say that High Power Committee will probe.... Unfortunately, the Chief Minister, in her preamble, denied any existence of political violence which nullifies the entire question of having a Committee.... I have no doubt, our dear Chief Minister has followed the footsteps of Bengal, where political murders take place, elections have been vitiated, people have been threatened, the opposition parties especially the CPM have been intimidated, to come to the polls.... I would like to know from the Chief Minister before the House considers that will this Committee have any legal sanction? Will this Committee constitute primarily of politicians or other judicial persons? Will this be under certain Act, say Commission of Enquire Act, by which it will have the power to take evidence of officials and non-officials? Let the Chief Minister confirm this or deny" (*OLA Debates*, Vol. III (15), 28.12.74; 51-2).

3

Economic Issues

For any nation, economy is a matter of great concern, and it should be managed very efficiently and with all sincerity. With the economic policies, people's welfare and prosperity depend on a lot, and it also leads to the continuance of a Government in a democratic system. Economic policies are the determining factor in a democracy, for which reason Biju Patnaik was very much concerned for the economic growth of Odisha and with it that of India. He was inclined for the industrial development as it caters to both, the direct and indirect employment opportunities.

Economic Policy

On the budget and economics, Biju Patnaik said, "Even the economists fail to suggest the measures to heck the inflation. If this be the situation of the economy of the country what is the worth of this budget and promises.... I regret to say that this budget does not give us any information which is meant for the development of the country. This budget is only a conglomeration of accounts that is presented but there is no planning there. What we invest is an investment for the economic development of the country. But there is no planned approach to this budget. There is an escalation of prices of various commodities all over the world and that escalation has brought about great escalation in this country which the Government is simply unable to cope with and when I say Government, I mean Government of India and naturally this State is in far greater difficulty in trying to meet the situation commensurate with its problems. We cannot diverse neither politics from economics nor political pressure in a federal structure like India between State and State and achievement of one State compared to that of another State and the achievement of a backward State like Odisha compared to more advance State. We cannot free ourselves from this and if we can do, we will not be practical. In the budget speech or during debates on various demands we have not got a picture that this Government has been able to influence the policy-makers at Delhi to give this State the necessary support that is needed to make the lee-way" (*OLA Debates*, Vol. II (24), 10.7.1974; 106-7).

On the feasibility of Socialism, Biju Patnaik said, "If you want to have any Socialism, two things are essential – discipline of production and cost of production. If you stick to it ruthlessly and bring social error in society, I have no objection. Do not just parade your progressiveness. Let me see in concrete terms what you say, and then I will be satisfied" (*OLA Debates*, Vol. I (2), 25.3.1974; 45).

On the economic system, Biju Patnaik said, "How do you propose to generate a self-generating economy? How do you propose to bring about a discipline in the society which will work for 12 hours a day instead of 5 hours? How do you propose to do this? Examples of Moscow? I say, yes, do it. Example of Peking? I say, yes do it. You want to live in a capitalistic society with all the comforts for yourself, for your children, for your family, and talk of socialistic state. I say, it is dishonest. If you want capitalism, do it and this will lead to a State like America. If you mean socialism you do it, it will take you to your goal of production. But by this method as you say now, this is neither fish nor flesh. How do you propose to do? I want a clear-cut answer, by a mathematical diagram producing a graph by which you can prove how you propose to do it. You must be very clear in your mind" (*OLA Debates*, Vol. I (2), 25.3.1974; 46-7).

On the income-gap and economic scene, he said, "The Government is saying that steps are being taken to set up communist pattern in the country. No one is focusing on the fundamental fact. Everybody is talking of communism. In reality, we are far behind in the economic gap. No steps are taken for the salary of the low paid employees, like the peon, watchman, etc. The salary of the IAS and ICS is about 120 to 150 times more than these low-salaried employees. This type of gap exists only in our country. This is not there in England and other countries. In England, the gap is about 15 to 20 times. In Switzerland the gap is 5 times. If this is asked to the Government, then it say that if we do not pay them such salary then they will not work for us and we will not get such officers. I wonder how the countries that pay much less salary get the officials to work for them. In actuality, if the policy of the Government is communism, then the gap in salary should be reduced. If it can happen in China, then why not here? During the discussion on middle-class share-croppers, it was said that the industrialist class are gradually increasing, but no system has been set up for this yet. The Socialist party have decided that the income gap must be between 1 to 10 times and land should be between 1 to 3 times. Then only we can have all type of facilities, but no one is heeding to it. There is no facility for the tribe and *harijans* of our country. There is no good facility for their education. The fault here is due to the fact of middlemen in between. Several faults arise due to the management by bureaucratic organization. We do not have the interest or the courage to provide them the facilities for their emancipation. For this, we are having the system like this" (*OLA Debates*, Vol. VIII (31), 7.4.56; 63-4).

On the topic of 'socialistic pattern of economy', he said, "Take the case of Odisha. We have here one and a half crores of people. Odisha having the lowest per capita income in the whole country has only 150 rupees a year per capita income, which means also in the reverse 150 rupees a year per capita expenditure. If we multiply 15 millions of people by 150 rupees a year, it comes to 225 crores. Sir, to my mind, that is the budget of the people of Odisha, 225 crores a year of which, the State budget in the form of tax only comes to about 7 per cent, that is, 15 to 18 crores a year in different forms apart from the loans, borrowings, subsidies and other forms of capital which comes into our own budget. Sir, nowhere in the world in the history of economic progress of any nation, it can be held that a Government raises the status of the people. Take the American history which was nothing but tremendous opposition from the inhabitants of the land plus millions of refugees who came from Europe under religious persecution. I may like to draw your attention to the American history, 200 years ago, when 200 million refugees fled from Europe to America under religious persecution only to find out land. Their present economic history can be studied. I can say that their master-mind were really ruthless Communists, but not the Indian Communists. Their economy in 40 to 50 years has gone to such a height not from the Government budget. It is not by the directive of the budget, but by the directive of the people. It is the directive of the party in power that built up such tremendous economy. That is why, Sir, I say today, the Congress party's clear directive is that the society shall be of a pattern of socialistic economy. There is no going back from that because that is the very article of faith. There is no power in India which can retard this thinking and progress whatever be the class adjustments even with the conflict of different political parties in India. Coming to the point, Sir, in Odisha, the people's expenditure, the people's budget is 225 crores, whereas the Government budget is a small quantity of 15 to 20 crores. To accentuate my point or to expand my point, I would ask what is meant by people's expenditure? I would like to bring to your notice, Sir, a simple fact which you must have noticed through your long years that cities after cities have sprung up all over Odisha. People being conscious have built up big buildings in the towns and small houses in the villages and these are our assets. We make error on our part and think that all the remedies of all the ills lie in the Government. Therefore, all our best minds have been focused on the Government. In 13 long years, we now discover that is not the only thing. The expenditure of the people also has been canalized and the efforts of the people has been canalized to certain productive instruments, call it factories, call it associations, call it mines, etc., so that the revenue of the society is assured" (*OLA Debates*, Vol. IV (5), 23.2.60; 22-4). He then said, "Industries are, in modern socialistic economy, the productive units. They are a friend, in modern language, to the socialistic economy and they have to be planned only on one basis, i.e., the greater productive capacity of the largest section of the people of this country. That is the best" (*OLA Debates*, Vol. IV (5), 23.2.60; 25).

Odisha being primarily an agriculturally dominant system, the small cultivators need to be protected and this can be possible by land ceiling. On this significant issue, he said, "The Estate Duty Act was originally passed in the Parliament in 1953. We are merely re-introducing that here in the form of 1953 Act of the Parliament. A support for big land-holders or big agriculturists cannot be considered in the present context. The present context is ceiling and more consideration for the small agriculturists, so that he can use his full time and get the maximum production. The time for considering big farms whether cooperative farm or State-owned farm will come in the wake of industrialization when machines will be used for agricultural purposes by the farms. At that time the quantum of land a farm can keep will be considered. There will be bigger machines and smaller machines and power-tillers. All these things will be taken into account to fix the quantum of land. But that will need another five to seven years. We should always frame our laws to suit the time. Today's requirement is something different than the requirement which was prevailing some ten or fifteen years back. That requirement has become redundant now. Originally, we had in our social structure big and lords owning ten thousand acres and twenty thousand acres of land. Lands were being given on some profit-sharing basis. Some were maintained as farms. There were various classes of land-lords. That was the form of society then. But when we are talking of the present agricultural society, our immediate requirement is maximum output. Therefore, the incentive can only come to a small cultivator because he has got one pair of bullocks and he can only do a certain amount of land. The other argument, as I said, is that the bigger areas of cultivation which are in the form of cooperatives and so on, will come when our nation-building capacity grows in our country, in our State and we can bring machines for the productivity of the land. That will take place when we have developed industries, when men are no longer available. Indeed, they are scarce in some parts of the State. They are no longer available for cultivation for primitive type of cultivation. When more men will go to factories, will go to public works, these big land-holders will not be able to cultivate their land, as indeed some of the big landlords feel the scarcity of man-power. Now man-power is not available at the appropriate time. Therefore, we have to build up a society for the next decade or so where the agriculturists will stick to cultivation and not move on to the industry. The surplus man-power, the landless labour and so on will move on to the field of industries or public works. When machines are built up more men will move on to the factories. So, such will be the change in our social structure from decade to decade and we must be able to catch up the social requirements and our essential requirements from time to time" (*OLA Debates*, Vol. V (16), 23.9.1963; 11-2).

To this Hon'ble Member Harihar Patel commented, "The Hon'ble Chief Minister said that machines will come into play and men will be replaced by machines. Since we have not developed our employment potentialities to that extent to absorb all capable young men, is it desirable to accelerate this process and replace men by machines"? To this comment, Biju Patnaik replied, "In areas where industries have developed, there is tremendous shortage of agricultural labour. With the advent of industrial growth as we are planning now, the availability of labour for agriculture will further diminish. Therefore, what looks odd for the landlords today-I mean the Estate Duty-will be a blessing to them within the next decade. Later on the reverse will take place. You have to have big areas of land brought under cultivation by a single machine. The machine power will determine the quantum of land. Then you may have, farms, State farms, Cooperative farms, whatever you like. In a machine age, the machine will determine the quantum of land. It is the machine's capacity, the machine's scope that will determine the area" (*OLA Debates*, Vol. V (16), 23.9.1963; 12).

Speaking on the basic problems of Odisha, he identified two prominent issues that are, under-utilization of resources and backward techniques of production. He said, "In a large measure. The later is responsible for the former. It should therefore be our endeavour to replace as fast as we can the primitive techniques by modern and more productive ones and stir the rich potential of nature to activity. The modern tools of science and technology have to be carried to every nook and corner of the State so that the slumbering thousands may be awakened to their destiny. In brief, our strategy is as follows: produce more power from water and coal, take it to the village, set up suitable industries at every stage, the village, the group of villages and the region and organize technical schools not in isolation but as integral parts of the industrial fabric, on the one hand and the educational stream on the other. Improvements in transport and communications and other items of economic and social overheads will of course have to be dovetailed into the above patterns. These measures will set in train the process of replacement of the costly human and bullock power and the relaxation of the present unrelenting pressures of population on land" (*OLA Debates*, Vol. IV (4), 1.3.1963; 4).

Critiquing the Swatantra Party on the economic issue and propagating certain misleading information in the House, he said, "The Hon'ble Member from Patna propounded a theory of leveling of incomes. I do not think that is the theory that the Swatantra party propagates. In fact, they are the scions of private sector, of unlimited income and unlimited properties and the rest of it, that one rich man and million poor men is quite in order in their type of social order which they try to expect us to follow and live in. Sir, there is only one class of people in this country left now who are the privileged-they are not the industrialists, they are certainly not the cultivators, they are the e-rulers; they have enormous properties left to them which they can go on selling-I know the Hon'ble Member from Patna is not one of them-which they can go on selling at rising market price and live for ten generations. They have a privy-purse left to them on which there is no Income-Tax. These two privileges alone make them a super class of people.... Apart from the rulers who are privileged by certain treaties which we ourselves have granted to them, the theory of Swatantra party is unlimited income, unlimited property, and it is quite astounding to hear from the Hon'ble Member from Patna that he wants to limit the income to ₹2,000 a month or something like that. Their interpretation and this kind of talk do not go together. When you talk of limiting the income, it is to curb the basic principle of enterprise that has the capacity to create incentive; it curbs the capacity to create wealth. I do not know if the Hon'ble Member from Patna professes his personal view or the view of a senior Member of his party. Similarly, in any field of production there should be incentive. Ceiling on land, because we do not have enough land, is a question of social distribution because the largest portion of our people live on land and we try to provide some social justification for them. But the fact remains that production will not increase unless and until the food prices are subsidized, modern equipments are given. With education, man will not remain in the field with this sort of implements that he has got and with all these work methods that he has got. Unless machines are given to him, unless he gets higher price for his products which will enable him to live in conveniences of urban standard, unless the whole structure of food prices are revolutionalised, as in Japan, the USA and in other highly developed countries, man will not remain as a farmer in the long run. As you know, Sir, when we build modern factory, we build modern house for labourers, electricity, water, sewerage are provided, we provide schools for their children and provide hospitals, dispensaries and various other things. Since as society gets educated, there will be mass exodus from the land to the town, where there are all these facilities. Therefore, Sir, any Government which is planning for the future must also provide for the social overheads in their budget preparation to enable these peasants to get a higher level of wages or returns for their products because without their products the society cannot sustain; so that the urban conditions become the resultant creation of that order and they too can have the conveniences of urban conditions.... I do caution Government that unless we change the entire financial structure of production and properly project the peasantry, we will have more and more difficulties as time goes on; less and less *pro rata* production which in the reverse will defeat the purpose of this great social legislation that we are trying to push through in this House today" (*OLA Debates*, Vol. VII (30), 7.4.1965; 35-6).

On the non-tax revenue earning of the State resources, he said, "I have no doubt that during the currebt year (1965-66) we shall be able to earn substantially higher revenue than the last year. I am sure of it. It is only possible to earn more and more revenue from this, only because the State has introduced a State monopoly system. But the vested interests, collaborators of the Agents, representatives of the Swatantra and *Ganatantra* would be inimical to the interest of the State. Therefore, public exhibition of baser characters or characteristics displayed by the Members of the Swatantra Party and some others do them any particular benefit or credit. Time to time they spread rumours and untruths which have been defeated by facts" (*OLA Debates*, Vol. IX (3), 23.2.1966; 12).

On the privy purse issue, he said, "I have voluntarily made available an amount, a fund which goes virtually to disburse the total privy purse taken by the ex-rulers of the State and yet this party-*teen bhais* (three brothers) as they call it-Maharaja of Patna, Raja Saheb of Dhenkanal, and Maharaja of Kalahandi. They are inter-related having a very happy relationship. (*Voice-Do not bother about them)* I have no desire to enter into that happy relationship. But this leadership takes away 30 to 35 lakhs from the State" (*OLA Debates*, Vol. VII (25), 31.3.1965; 42). To this a Member remarked, "Is it not your party which gives them"? He replied to this, "I agree. Panditji once said, *bachhan de diyahe* (given the word of honour). It is the word of the *bachhan* of the Congress by which 30 lakhs a year are being to the gentleman and their families. It is not that an influential member has profited, it is a Congress Member who mobilizes all the idealism of the Congress, has voluntarily given it away to the State exchequer. The Rajas and the Maharajas should forgo their privy purse" (*OLA Debates*, Vol. VII (25), 31.3.1965; 42).

On the transformation of the economic system from a feudal to industrial system and with it a greater role for the administration, he said, "We are in an age in India and particularly in our State where the basic transformation in taking place from a totally feudal system to an industrial system. Naturally when an established system like feudalism which lasted for centuries is replaced by an industrial system, there would be considerable amount of upheavals at different levels. Whenever you change a system, you will find that it takes long time for the human mind, for the society and the administrative apparatus to adopt themselves to the new system. Let us take the case of our industrial programmes, building up basic industries in the villages; at the Panchayat Samitis and then at the State level and so on, which the State apparatus found in the Corporations. So long for 15 to 16 years, all that the Department did was to issue permits and licenses and there the responsibility ended. Now the Department through these Corporation or Corporations will have to implement themselves, like Industries Corporation, Small-Scale Industries Corporation, Fishery Corporation, Forest Corporation, Construction Corporation, and Mining Corporation and so on, which are all social apparatus of the State to produce maximum benefit to the society as well as maximum profit to the State exchequer. Now all these are new works. Obviously for success of this there would be great change in the rules of the administration, in the codes of the administration, new terms have to be established because the administration on the old term was made with the old apparatus, i.e., to issue licenses or to give sanctions, not for implementing it within their own capacity or ability. Therefore, Sir, we now come to a situation where we are at crossroads. We have decided that maximum social justice and maximum utility in terms of society would have to be generated within the structure of our administration and our society and when we say that, we honestly do believe that it should be done. We have to set up new pattern of administration to administer new ideas. We obviously have to set up a new pattern of education to administer the new ideas. When we cannot do it, i.e., we cannot bring about a new pattern, new system of administration and alter its thousands of rules and regulations to the new notes and that would be the business not only of the Government but of the collective intelligence and leadership of the House and if we cannot collectively do it, it is futile for us, day in and day out, to come out to this House and pick holes and faults and failures of our attempt in administering a new horizon. The question is how to do it and by what instrument of law, by what instrument of administration, by what qualitative establishment that we can achieve these things (*OLA Debates*, Vol. VI (8), 26.2.1964; 16).

On the question of private sector growing in Odisha, he viewed that without State Government initiative and active intervention, the private sector cannot develop. "Even the small industries have to be so sponsored. It is unnecessary for Calcutta, it is unnecessary for Bombay. But it is necessary for Odisha. In Odisha it is imperative. Therefore, Sir, you may imagine how much responsibility delves on this State and its administration. I, therefore plead not only to the Government but also to all the Members and to try to get over this vast gulf in comparison to other States, if we sincerely want greater points of growth in this State. It is not an easy task. But by no means it is insurmountable. If we work together and advice effectively whether from this side of the House or from that side of the House and do it continuously to create points of growth, then our State will prosper. If we shall all be united in our effort, both inside the State and outside the State, then nothing can stand on our way of progress. We shall have to compete with others in several points of growth. Every year we shall have to find out new points of growth. This can be done only with our united effort. Otherwise, if we go on like this our distance will be bigger and our gulf will be widened" (*OLA Debates*, Vol. III (23), 21.3.1972; 50-1).

On the issue of people living under poverty line in Odisha, he said, "In 1977-78, the Planning Commission has said that wherein Odisha only 69% of people are below poverty line in rural area, about 67 % or so in urban area. There is a famous saying of a great scientist, 'there is no adequate defense except stupidity against the impact of a new idea'. I hope you try to understand it. Sir, I am putting here that Odisha Government lastly put a High Power Committee under your own Chief Secretary to find out what really id the position, how many people are living under poverty line. Whatever they produced, the thing is that it is 85%-from 69% they went to 85%. The Chief Minister, at one time in this Assembly or in the last Assembly said it has come down to 32%. Then he raised it to 52%" (*OLA Debates*, Vol. I, 30.7.1985; 60). He gave the instance of the then Prime Minister's visit to some of the villages in Phulbani, "where he found that only ₹300 has reached the people. The subsidy has been kept back. He has discovered 17 cases and he has taken all these 17 cases back to Delhi. If my information is right only ₹300 to ₹350 was received by the person who was supposed to get the aid against ₹3500. The other thing is that he stared at poverty and starvation wherever he had gone in the villages. So where has it reached, this 14 lakhs of loan.... Now this is the problem. Just to say, I have given some kind of loan to 14 lakhs of people they have come over poverty line, this is the most absurd proposal that this House has ever heard.... I am not arguing because I am convinced that 1.5 crores of people of this State were below poverty line according to the Planning Commission in 1979-80. We say it has increased. You say it has decreased. The population has also increased. So, in effect there is no decrease, no real effect. Is it not our combined business to see that whatever you do is monitored, effectively supervised and those who cannot keep up to targets, severely punished" (*OLA Debates*, Vol. I, 30.7.1985; 60-1).

On the functioning of the Government corporations and companies, he said, "We have 62 or something like that of corporations and companies. Now I ask, whether these corporations or companies have submitted their audit reports and balance sheets for the last 16 years to 20 years? Where is the Company Law of Government of India under which these corporations or companies are functioning.... So, I would like to ask the Chief Minister and the Finance Minister what action Government has proposed to take against these Directors or Managers of these corporations and what action has been taken so far? Supreme Court has now decided that Government can take action against any Government official if Government is satisfied that he is not functioning for public good.... Of these 62 corporations are defaulters, and none of them produced the balance sheet up to today. AG has also pointed out year after year failure of these corporations. Apart from that, I question about the competence of this Government to run this corporation efficiently and effectively. Government is a continuous affair. This is the question of life and death of the people of the State. So, the basis of this corporation would get away with anything. Stop the wastage and pilferage" (*OLA Debates*, Vol. I, 30.7.1985; 58-60).

On poverty line in Odisha, he said, "I want to ask the Chief Minister that according to his calculation, there are 50 lakhs families in Odisha living below the poverty line. He has given a calculation where 12 lakhs families have been helped, hence there remains 38 lakhs. In 1983 as per the Planning Commission figure there 79 per cent.... When we define the poverty line, the Planning Commission has said that a minimum income of ₹1,500 a year basing on 1971 price. I want to ask the Government, that the assistance given to the poor families on this basis, how many persons have an annual income of ₹1,500" (*OLA Debates* Vol. I(3), 18.3.1985; 13). The then Chief Minister replied, "It is eight thousand". He then asked the Government what investment has been done to get an annual income of ₹1,500. There is misappropriation on that investment.

On the issue of increase in agricultural production during the last five years in the Governor's address of 1985, he challenged by saying, "I challenge this statement, because your figures do not confirm your statement. What was the production in 1979-80 and what is your production in 1979-80 and what is your production now, what is the increase? How are you telling 'considerable increase' simple by adding little more canal system, little more water system? Secondly, you told about surplus, notable surplus during the five years. I want to know whether the surplus has risen by increase in production or by reducing consumption.... It is written (Governor's address) that *maximum emphasis will be laid on agriculture*. It goes on to say that all the 314 blocks of the State would be covered by crop insurance to protect farmers from natural calamities and to increase fertilizer consumption to 20 kgs per hectare by the end of Seventh Plan.... If you say maximum emphasis should be laid on agriculture, I would say the prime emphasis should be on crop insurance" (*OLA Debates* Vol. I (2), 15.3.1985; 10).

On the subject of poverty amelioration and number of poor in Odisha, he said, "I understand that this 20-Point Programme, whatever this Government has undertaken, or the Central Government has undertaken, during the time of Indira Gandhi, they proposed to have introduced, may be the number of people below poverty line in Odisha in 1961 was 52 lakhs and just now in 1984-85, it is coming to little over 2 crores. So your amelioration has led to rise in the number of people below the poverty line by more than 4 times in 25 years. This is infact the performance of your Government, Mr. Chief Minister" (*OLA Debates* Vol. I(2), 15.3.1985; 9). To the comment that in the mean time the population has increased, he replied, "The population of the poor has not only increased, but the population of every class, rich, etc., has also increased. But here from the Governor's address, I came to know that this Government is for the poor" (*OLA Debates* Vol. I (2), 15.3.1985; 9).

He traced the evolution of the Cooperative movement in India, and said, "Even in this country Sir, after we became free, Panditji and his associates were toying with ideas of forming Communes in India. Later on, it was decided to form and encourage cooperative. Commune is the alternative of cooperatives. Thus, the movement of cooperatives was started in India. It was the purpose of forming these land communes where the machine could replace man and man could go to manufacture machines. This is the standard practice of development of agricultural economy. Sir, there was two major things which the Nation ought to remember and the State which is a part of the Nation ought to remember that when the Communist Government came in USSR, they had to practically and physically liquidate thousands of middle-class cultivators before they could establish their communes. Sir, the same thing happened in China also. Now Russia has 1/6th of the world's land mass. It is ten times of India's land mass. Why they have not produced necessary crops for their population? Their population is 1/3rd of our population. Are they not able to produce enough crop or cereals for themselves is the reason of it? Why they have not produced enough for their people?" (V (12), 12.3.1987; 159).

On the issue of subsidy and loans with compound interest, he said, "Now take the case of cultivators and the amount given to them what you call subsidy. You raise the price of a commodity and then you give subsidy. This deviously was a funny system of tax collection. In colonial administration, the administration was different type. When we are giving more and more power to them, the people are neglected more and more by them. There is interference by political people and ready oiling by officials. The sufferers are the farmers or the poor men. What is the subsidy? Does it ultimately go to the farmers? The loan they are taking, you have compounded the interest on them, but you call that is a help. You have moved them from money-lenders to *kabuliwalas*. This compound interest on loans should be stopped. If Andhra can do, Haryana can do, and Karnataka can do, why not Odisha? The Government in Karnataka waived ₹108 crores of interest" (V (12), 12.3.1987; 161-2).

On Odisha's need and strengths, he said, "What you need is you have to create major point of growth, for which the State has facility, we have unlimited mineral resources, coastal resources, water resources. We have everything, but no funds. We need funding. The State does not have strength for funding, hence the Central Government has to do the funding" (V (2), 24.2.1987; 80).

Expressing concern for the poverty in Odisha, he said, "I would like to quote some authorities, like that of the *International Agricultural Commission* which is a part of the World Bank Advisory Board. It has examined the question of poverty all over the world, in the poor countries and in the under-developed countries. I comment that India has now at the moment more than 30 crores of people below the poverty line, poverty line is drawn by the Government of India's *Planning Commission* at ₹6,400 per year income basis. They go on to say that the agricultural labourers forming a part of it, almost the entire 30 crores, are below poverty line. In proportion Odisha is below the poverty line and the income is less than ₹300 a month.......Why is it that our labourers mostly go as cheap labourers, 8-10 lakhs a year, it is not a small number, and do not find work in their own homes? This is a great slur on the administration and on the policies of both the State and the Centre. They have forced the people to leave their homes and hearths to go and seek work there......The *International Agricultural Commission* said that these are the lowest income groups in the country which amount to nearly 30 crores of people engaged as agricultural labourers in the country of which Odisha's share should be 1.5 crores. Which tells very poorly of all our efforts in this direction.... All I am saying is that Odisha must agitate to get out of this business. We have got 19% irrigation potentiality, where as Andhra has got 64% and Punjab has got 80%. How long things will continue like this? All the money is going there, nothing is coming to Odisha. We are the poorest of the poor. We have to get up and fight" (VII (2), 25.2.1988; 118-22).

On a Resolution of the House regarding *Special Category State status* to Odisha, he said, "This House made a Resolution. That was thrown away by the Union Government. Is this all you can do? By this can you raise the standard of living of the people? You neither get steel plant nor the ample opportunity for the irrigation. Nothing. We gave in writing. This is from two or three years ago. You sent a note and Chief Minister also mentioned it in the NDC. Now what steps you have taken? How you contradict this thing? Now for the whole State what steps you have taken? You only say that you are writing, but what action thereafter? What are the impediments in the way, what are the constraints which prevented Government of India or NDC to accept the proposal". He also said, "I want to remind the Chief Minister, that in 1961, when I happened to be the Chief Minister, that was the mid-term of Third Five-Year Plan. Two years had already passed and yet, I got special disciplination from the Government of India to the order of ₹250 crores extra what was allotted in the Plan. You must be straight to fight for your proposal; otherwise you will not get anything. Except the routine, which cannot raise the people of Odisha?" (VII (12), 14.3.1988; 4-5).

On the social and economic problems, he said, "This Government is unable to do even simple things. It is dipped in corruption. Young man and woman who are jobless are in a state of revolt, farmers are in a state of revolt, landless people are in the state of revolt. They want somebody to ignite it. I shall not ignite it, but would request it. I shall certainly revolt against the Government till it goes out of office. I shall give a call to the youth, women, farmers, landless workers and others, to rise against this Government till they are thrown out of the Office" (*OLA Debates*, Vol. IX (27), 31.3.1989; 82). He also stated that how the Government Departments are spending beyond the budget sanctioned amount and said, "The House has not sanctioned a

Budget provision, and this Government goes on spending money outside the scope of the sanctioned Budget. I will give you just instance of one single Department. Let us take the PWD or the Works Department. In the year 1980-81, the budget provision was ₹42 crores and the excess was ₹34 crores. In 1982-83, the budget provision was ₹47 crores and the excess was ₹61 crores. In 1983-84, it was ₹49 crores and the excess was ₹30 crores. Sir, if the Ministers would like to go through the books, which actually are the business of the Finance Department, they will find such excess expenditure outside the sanction by this House to the tune of ₹1000 crores, which has been pointed out by the AG in their reports submitted to this House. When such a situation is there, one Cabinet Minister, made a statement that the Opposition should be wiped out by using Bofors gun. He has not apologized for making that statement. How a Government can wipe out the Opposition at the point of a gun? This Government is now sitting in a boat, which is leaking pretty heavily and very soon it will drown. Therefore, this Cabinet Minister wants to shoot down all the Opposition by use of Bofors gun. I am quoting it from *The Samaja*, dated 1 September 1989. Probably, this gentleman has never used a pipe gun but wants to use a Bofors gun" (*OLA Debates*, Vol. X (5), 13.9.1989; 84).

Critically examining the financial position and the depth of excess expenditure of Odisha, he said, "In 1980-81, it was 118 crores, which was pointed out by the Comptroller and Auditor General of India. 1981-82, it was 101 crores, 1982-82, it was 164 crores, 1983-84, it was 245 crores, 1984-85, it was 179 crores, and so on. The financial position of this Government is such that it is virtually bankrupt. Net year if you see the budget any provisions, you will find that the Government has to pay 1,200 crores towards repayment of loans. This works out to about 60% of the State revenue. When the financial condition of the State is so bad, how you can think of developmental expenses. From where it will come" (*OLA Debates*, Vol. IX (27), 31.3.1989; 75)?

Commenting sarcastically on the claim of Odisha being a progressive State of the country, he said, "Are you proud of the fact that while we are sitting in this luxurious air-conditioned hall, young little girls are sold by their mother's for ₹40 or for 20 Kgs of rice? Do you feel proud of that Mr. Chief Minister which is the performance of your stability? Are you proud of the fact that thousands of our men and women are leaving the State to look for jobs elsewhere? The other States can provide life and vital to our people, what we cannot provide ourselves in our State. Are you proud of it? Is that the blessings of your stability? Are you proud of the fact of a total power crisis in your State not because there is too much demand, but because there is less production with existing apparatus? Are you proud that Talcher Thermal Station is a total bluff? Are you proud of the fact that you have not taken any step whatsoever to ensure that power plant is in full operation?

Are you proud of that stable Government for nine years, Mr. Chief Minister? Examine it yourself Mr. Chief Minister. Do not try to wash away the whole system that is developed in your continuous ruling. But you have certainly progressed in laying enormous foundation stones" (*OLA Debates*, Vol. IX (2), 22.2.1989; 95).

On the issue of economy and making Indian rupee free currency, he said, ''We are talking of Indian rupee. I said make the rupee free currency. Only then we would know our strength. In Indonesia, they made free currency and today they have eight-lane traffic going from one end to another. Their money is free and it move freely. Anybody can invest anywhere in that country. We protect us against what? We are a big country. Nobody can take away our country anywhere. We have never tried to use free money for the nation's benefit. I said investment prospects should be encouraged. For example, the Chinese Minister of Steel came to India and said that they produce 62 million tons of Steel. Whereas we produce only 13 million tons. They produce five times more of our production. They went round the world for shopping of various second-hand plants. When we call second-hand, we think old. But they are not old. Suppose a furnace is dead and 60 years old, it is not old'' (*OLA Debates*, Vol. II (22), 6.7.1990; 64-5).

He further elaborated on the above and said, "There is no poor-man in Thailand. Their *per capita* income is ₹25,000 per month. This is the position today. You know what Gorbachev is doing and *perestroika* is something. So fresh idea must come, fresh technology must come. Without making the currency free we do not have to wait for sanction from the bureaucrats sitting in Delhi. It needs free movement, idea, concept and everything. That is what makes your nation grow. Now foreign technology is our policy. Self-reliance is good. Self-reliance in foreign technology is better. Now Japanese money is stronger than Dollar. Today seven rupees is called one German Mark. But, at one time one rupee was one German Mark. Now these are the history of movement of strange.... Finance Minister of Hitler, who is equally Chairman, Finance, was called upon by most of the countries of the world to give lecture and was asked how Mr. Chairman, you recovered so rapidly? He said that it is a simple thing. I have three *mantras*, that is the work, hard work and hardest work. That is the secret. Can you imagine this in India? The freedom of currency will facilitate because we shall see and we shall work like that, we shall learn like that, Koreans are working like that, Japanese are working like that, so, we shall work like that. Unless we work like that, nothing will be done. In NDC meeting every Chief Minister agreed to develop our work equally not gossiping and trying to juggle here and there. That is all it meant in my address to the NDC meeting" (*OLA Debates*, Vol. II (22), 6.7.1990; 67).

He said, "In 1944, when the British conquered and took away their machines, the Germans told that it was better and with their brain they would produce better machines whereby nobody could compete with them.

This is the way the world moves and that is why the Russians went on to *perestroika*. I told the Prime Minister (in National Development Counil meeting) that you have no money and I have no money, but the world is full of money. Leave it to the House to discuss and adopt it. No Chief Minister objected to this and the Prime Minister three times told the Finance Minister, to examine it carefully what Biju Patnaik told" (*OLA Debates*, Vol. II (22), 6.7.1990; 64-5).

Presenting a case history of Odisha, which is under poverty-line always, he said, "Not one mile of railway line has been built in Odisha. So, I made an appeal to the Council (National Development Council) there that when the British came, they first landed in Madras and my dear Karunanidhi's ancestors surrendered to them and they settled there. Then the British took their little ships sailing on those days and went upto North along the coast line. When they came to Odisha coast, our jawans with bows and arrows threatened to kill them and they fled away. While moving forward, the British landed at Hoogly and settled at Sutanati and Kalikata, two fishing villages. That is why, Calcutta is built where Jyoti Basu is the Chief Minister and their forefathers surrendered to British. Because, Odisha did not surrender before the British, the British did not build railway line in Odisha. So, I told the Prime Minister that the British were blood-suckers and for the last 44 years of independence this State was sucked. I do hope our present Prime Minister will not continue to do that. It is a part of satire and joke and that is the case history of Odisha which is under poverty-line always. I said that when the British made Calcutta their imperial capital, they built railways line from Calcutta to Madras and Calcutta to Bombay. Calcutta to Bombay was built because the little hamlet was sold to British for sixteen pounds only. So, these are the histories and the history of the last three hundred years. With the imperial capital moved to Delhi, then the railway line went from Calcutta to Delhi, Delhi to Bombay and Peshawar and all over Delhi became the hub-centre of imperial India and Odisha still went far behind inspite of its mineral resources, water resources and forest resources. I also said that Odisha has 11% of water resources of India and the total development towards irrigation in comparison to other States of India in the last 44 years has been only two per cent in Odisha. These are all my recorded speech in the National Development Council. How long we will survive with this step-motherly attitude and how do we linger to sustain in this fashion" (*OLA Debates*, Vol. II (22), 6.7.1990; 64-5).

Criticizing the dependence on foreign financial institutions for money, he said, "We are born of modern times. We decided to go for scientific development at the cost of the nation. Result, we have to bow, borrow, take loan from IMF, World Bank, from all these little so called World organizations, which are largely worth nothing. You call it neither WHO, you call it this or that, these are all International Humbugs operating not only in Delhi or in India, but everywhere, where there is possible scope. So we have become slaves of another colonial party. That is the saddest part of it. So, how I would be proud of being an Indian if I don't sacrifice. Be strong and avoid use of foreign products. Say, I will not buy it, take it away..... I remember when I was a Member of Lok Sabha and Venkatraman, later on he became our President of India, then he was in Indira Gandhi's Ministry, he came to the House and said why are you cheering me. I have got five billion dollars of loan. Why are you cheering me? So, I got up to say, Mr. Venkatraman, you are really a good South Indian Brahmin. But, whoever is going to pay that loan and with what interest. If you get five billion dollars, would India die? He by-passed the question. So, it is all done step by step. Now, we have to borrow for interest charges. To borrow capital, to pay back interest. This is a national economy and this Dunkel is nothing, it is as such to squeeze the downtrodden people of India and you are bound to be squeezed" (*OLA Debates*, Vol. XIII (3), 24.12.93; 103).

On the issue of liberalization, he said, "This is not a question whether a multi-national comes here to do his trading, whether it is Pepsicola or Cocacola, whatever it is, is a question that it is a conscious decision taken by a Government for its open-sky policy, what you call liberalisation. He took a decision, why did they take a decision like this?..... Sir, there is something inherently wrong in ourselves. We fought for the Nation's independence, independence from British rule. But we have today by means we can say, we have reached a situation which is worse that when we were under British rule. Let us say, the British rule gave us various systems, gave us judiciary, gave us railways, gave us communication, gave us telephone, roads, education, we also got the thought of liberalism, also communism. Different thoughts were generated by the British education by our class of people. What did Gandhiji do? He said, give up what is foreign. By and large, the Indian mind was for foreign goods. Anything that was foreign was good. Foreign meant English product, British product at that time. But today we lost sight of that thought. How to become self-reliant?" (*OLA Debates*, Vol. XIV (6), 2.3.1994; 97-8).

On the Stock Scam, Biju Patnaik said, "On the 15th of that month, Harshad Mehta was going for a Press Conference. In that morning, I was dining with Shri Sharad Pawar. At that time, I came to know that Harshad Mehta with Jeth Hajari is going for a Press Conference in Taj Hotel and 500 correspondents are coming there. He said there that he had given one crore of rupees to the Prime Minister. My answer to them was very clear that time. Biju Patnaik said, 'you cannot rely on the statement of a crook'. This came out in great broad headline in papers. In the next morning, I talked to the Prime Minister and said, why did you not put this fellow in prison? If I would have been in your place, I would have held the horse whip. He told me, '*Hum aisa kar nehin sakte, aap kar sakte hain*' (I cannot do like that, you can do it). I said you are the President of the Party, if somebody has donated something to the Party, you say, YES, I have taken that one crore. You could tell it, so nothing is wrong in it. Net morning, I was flying back to Bhubaneswar. After serving, an Air Hostess asked, Sir, I want to put one question. How Harshad Mehta, the villain of the scandalous of 4000/5000 crores of rupees of public money, still is not yet put behind the bar? When Harshad Mehta said that Prime Minister has taken money, how the Prime Minister is continuing as Prime Minister without clarifying his stand? The net day, I faxed the exact word to the Prime Minister that this the observation of one person, an Air Hostess, who is a First class in Political Science from Delhi University" (*OLA Debates*, Vol. XIV (29), 7.4.1994; 10).

On the Dunkel proposals, he said, "Sir, this is a very strange thing. Strange thing, because it is called a treaty. Why it is a treaty? Only it is an agreement. It is not a treaty. Treaty is during war and peace. This is not a treaty, this is an agreement. Why you call it a treaty? The Government of India said, it is agreed, the whole nation, 90 crores people have been consulted. But is has not been discussed and debated in the Parliament, no legislation is sought to be brought before the Parliament. It has not been discussed in the Legislatures of the country. Such a thing is this. With all such ramification this has been brought by the Multinationals. It is a matter of serious concern to this country. This country has been a colony of white men for a long time. I have suffered a lot during those days. I was in British prison for thousand days. One of our brothers got killed by Englishmen. When I was Chief Minister here, Mr. Narasimha Rao was a Minister of State in Andhra Pradesh at that time. I know Shri Narasimha Rao very well. I respect him. But this is a matter where I must discuss with him, debate with him and try to persuade him. This cannot be in the best interest of the Nation" (*OLA Debates*, Vol. XIV (29), 7.4.1994; 11-2).

On the issue of the increase in the entertainment tax and its use for development purposes, Biju Patnaik said, "In fact in civilized countries it is the essential duty of every citizen to pay for all the amenities. Here we do not pay for any amenity. We are used to living near dirty and filthy *nordhamas* (drains). By introducing this Bill we are going to have a small increase of about twenty to fifty thousand rupees and this small income will always remain small if we stop at that. In other civilized countries people pay heavily for living a planned life in the City. Take for instance the City of London where they pay very heavily to get better amenities. Sir, for a first class cinema seat they pay something in the neighbourhood of ₹10, whereas, here in this country we pay only ₹2.80 for the same. This taxation is not considered as a normal one. So, Sir, we should not discuss a great deal about a very small measure that the Government are trying to introduce. We shall not only support it, but shall ask the Government to bring in other similar measures" (*OLA Debates*, Vol. X (2), 11.10.1949; 51).

On the poor economic performance, during the General Budget discussion, Biju Patnaik said that there was nationalization of coal industry but corresponding infrastructure support was not provided to consume it. The Food Corporation operation was chosen to be financed from banks and not from the Consolidated Fund. The previous Government, under Mr. Subramaniam, started two sectors-industrial and commercial and it was known to provide millions of jobs. The Government got ₹2100 crores from banks and paid ₹200 crores as interest annually, and this was never told to the House. The cost was borne by the consumer. "These are the contradictions of a shattered economy left behind by the Government which was manned by Mr. Subramaniam as Finance Minister of India although he had only a part of it. The other part, the revenue and taxation-he was not concerned with. The Finance Minister of India would not be knowing anything as to what were going to be the revenues! This is how the Indira Government was functioning" (OLA; 47). He also expressed concern about "how much small tools has science and technology really given-in the hands of the small farmers? The answer is nil.... So, Mr. Subramaniam, it may have been your desire; it may have been your wish. But the entire machinery of science and technology has not been developed to the extent to serve the national purpose of 400 crores of poor people. We have developed scientists; we have built up engineers at great cost to the nation but, most of them are unemployed or underemployed. You have not provided the infrastructure to see that the national resources and manual labour are combined to create wealth" (OLA; 50).

On inflationary pressure, he said, "If you cannot improve the efficiency, then you raise the fares to match the cost. By doing so, you have only raised the cost of all commodities-you have raised the cost of industrial goods, coal, steel and cement as well. Industrial activities will cost more and more. By so doing you have only brought about more and more inflation in this country. We have been hearing the old story that there is only a marginal increase in the cost of living of 0.04 per cent or 0.05 per cent. This is the old story by Planning Commission and Finance. Actually, it comes to 10 times more, only the decimal has to be shifted behind-not forward". When the Railway fare cost goes up, the prices of all commodities will increase correspondingly. "So every time when you raise the tax a little, there is a general upward movement in the index price. As a result, you have to pay dearness allowance to your employees" (*Lok Sabha Debates*, 17 June 1980; 258).

On national interest and to get benefits from the depression, he said, "My personal thinking would be that as long as we can protect the interests of our country, as long as we can find international market-till such time my own consuming market goes-up-I have to find ways and means of utilizing my enormous dormant natural resources and enormous dormant number of trained personnel and put them together. This is my problem. I do not wish to be reduced to the position of an exporter of the raw material. I do not want our people to be their *hewers of wood and drawers of water.* I reject the idea. I must have an added value whether you call it billets, pig iron or sections or whatever you may call, semi-finished or something else. I must have added value at different stages.... But the world market of steel is a most depressing market for the last 40 years. Today Japan has 35 million tons of idle capacity. But the very fact that there is a depression in steel market shows that it is time for this nation to plan. Now, I can get credit. I can get the machinery cheaper. Now I can get services cheaper because there is unemployment in those countries as against boom. If we have courage and if we plan now, probably we will lay the foundation for all the things that many of the Members have wanted the Government to do" (*Lok Sabha Debates*, 28 June 1977; 294-5).

On the non-tax source of revenue as an alternate for development activities, Biju Patnaik said, "We must augment our non-tax sources of revenue because our people are poor-not only poor, we say poor but have been kept poor during the past two centuries. We have to have non-tax sources of revenue. Therefore, when I said *Gandhamardan* (hill) can be bartered, the Chief Minister said Biju Patnaik says he wants to sell away *Gandhamardan*. The meaning was far deeper than what the Chief Minister could understand. First thing I had taken an estimate of *Gandhamardan* as to how many million tonnes of iron-ore it contains. Its present value ex-port Paradeep is about Rupees Five thousand crores. If I have an asset of Five thousand crores, people of the world are prepared to give us credit.... If I have Five thousand crores asset, why can't I utilize it for my development which is a part of India's development? How politics comes in here, who will deal with it? Is the little Odisha nothing but a municipality in terms of New Delhi? Certainly not. When I say my people cannot grow by your gifts, I say because I have natural gifts and allow me to transform it to wealth within the national framework. Do you think what I have said just now is against the interest of the country-leads to disintegration? Or do you think it will strengthen the backbone of the country? All I am asking the present Government is to get away from the slogans; start looking deep into what you are, what is your asset, what is the measure of your poverty, measure of unemployment. Where is your prospective thinking, where is the direction of thinking at the end of say, 10 to 20 years?.... If I may say so, the hill of *Gandhamardan* of ₹5,000 crores value today can be negotiated with Japan or Holland or any other buying country or with ten different countries for getting steel plants, for making Paradeep a free port where you can invest foreign money for steel plants, jute mills, and hundreds of other things and get the credit from them to get all your factories all down the line as against export quantity of iron-ore, pig-iron, etc. Therefore, a whole chain of development can start on the basis of one asset called *Gandhamardan*" (*OLA Debates*, Vol. II (24), 10.7.1974; 110-1).

On land reforms and consolidation, Biju Patnaik said, "This measure is a scientific measure for greater productivity. Land reform is not a ceiling; it is for all practical purpose, *Chaka Bandi* (consolidation). If we want more production, we must speed up *Chaka Bandi*.... Let the Opposition and the Government sit together and chalk out a programme as to how quickly it will be done, at least within 10 years. It is not a question of employing two thousand people, it is a question of twenty thousand. Let us jointly ask the Government of India to give us extra money by way of grant or loan. Since the productivity of the State is suffering, this must be done. If land consolidation is considered as a progressive policy of your Government, you must find out money..... Now you have provided one and half crores for land consolidation, saying that no further money is available. It is the business of the Government to find finance for the policy they have announced. Instead of doing that you are saying that with this one and half crores we will do this and that. Only by slogans you cannot make any real progress on land. In this connection, I will draw your attention what the undivided Punjab Chief Minister, Mr. Kairon did. He provided funds for this land consolidation and finished the job within 8 to 12 years time. Now there is record growth of agricultural produce in the Punjab and Haryana" (*OLA Debates*, Vol. III (9), 19.12.74; 127).

He expressed concern for the poor and landless people in the villages and how they will rise above poverty-line. For the development and employment of these landless people, there was a National Planning where in every village a handicraft and small-scale industry would be set-up. In this address, it is stated that there will be industrial estate in the towns of Bhubaneswar, Rourkela, Dhenkanal, etc. "Revolution will not come in this! Planning of small-scale industry for every village of every Panchayat should be made. There should be central planning of purchase and sell and central management to be continued till these people know how to manage their own affair. It cannot happen in propaganda, but thinking is needed. Industrial planning cannot come by cursing Industry Minister, Biju Patnaik, or Mahatab babu.... I find there is no total planning of industries for the villages, one requires time and concentration, sensitization for the landless people. It cannot be attained by clever and high-sounding speeches, but by thinking and planning only" (Vol. IV (2), 1975; 96). Commenting on the Governor's address, he said, "it would have been little more enlightening, it does not have any productive balance-sheet, profitability balance-sheet. No mention of any equitable society, progressive society. It only states democratic value" (*OLA Debates*, Vol. IV (2), 19.2.75; 97).

On the food policy, he said that we have 14 lakh tons less production, and "Odisha will not survive unless you get Central assistance" (*OLA Debates*, Vol. IV (2), 19.2.75; 97). He also said, "If the House Committee should have discussed this food policy, it could have found ways and means. Food must be outside politics. The Chief Minister is saying that

Lok Dal is inciting people. When land records are not examined, the levy is wrong. Those having not even 2 acres of lands, levy is charged on him. This is the mistake.... You will have the courage to face it, to correct it. I am ashamed of it. We are slaves in an independent country. Government servants have become more than slaves. They have no concern for the citizens of India. They think they are paid by the state. At the same, I do not want to blame the government servants. The fault lies with political party in power. They want to be autocratic. They do not want to consult. They want to be partisan. I want to ask the Chief Minister that how many rich farmers have been charged levy by the Congress party. There is a wide gap. What is there in this Governor's address? Nothing, it is a cry in wilderness" (*OLA Debates*, Vol. IV (2), 19.2.75; 98).

On the issue of subsidizing things like food, Biju Patnaik said, "But food is not a public enterprise; food is very much in the private sector; no public company produces food in this country; it is the individual producer who produces. You talk of subsidy. But the actual price is far beyond the subsidy-plus everything-when it comes to the consumer because you have no distribution system. So, the less you talk about prices of food, sugar, textiles, etc., the better" (*Lok Sabha Debates*, 11.12.1981, OLA; 163).

Biju Patnaik, addressing the Motion, said that in the last session we had cautioned the government that "Levy on the basis of land records will be valid, because land records themselves are valid" (*OLA Debates*, Vol. IV (2), 19.2.75; 117-18). At that time, the government replied that they are arranging Camp Courts so that people are not troubled. But this will not solve the problem and registration of land records is required. He said, "I say, as the Leader of Opposition, this method of levy on the basis of land records will not succeed. This is faulty because your land records themselves are faulty. You had made procurement last year on the basis of production. Why do you not do it again this year...This system of levy based on land records is quite defective and faulty and it continues litigation, the people will resist. This is what happening. I told the Minister last time of this bitterness which will come out if you pursue this.... You are pursuing a policy which is totally an inconceivable project. The project is levy on the basis of land records. The scientific method would be on the basis of production which you had attempted previous years. In previous years the surplus was purchased from the people by the purchasing agents. We have collected as much as 3, 4 or 5 lakh tons in good years. Nobody had sent a policeman. Sir, it stands to commonsense that when procurement has to be done then incentive has to be given. It is human character that when production decreases, everyone will save for personal consumption for a month or two. This is human nature, human psychology" (*OLA Debates*, Vol. IV (2), 19.2.75; 118-19). Illustrating the use of brutal force and violence by the police on the villagers of Kankhinda in Sambalpur, he said, "This attitude is totally opposite to the democratic norms stated in the Governor's address" (*OLA Debates*, Vol. IV (2), 19.2.75; 120). In conclusion, he said, "I have categorically opposed this method of levy. I support procurement. Levy and procurement are two different things. I support procurement to the extent of 5 lakh tons, but not this method of levy on the basis of land records which is simply not there" (*OLA Debates*, Vol. IV (2), 19.2.75; 126).

Planning

On the issue of proper planning of industry, he said, "We must examine and plan the development of industries in this State accordingly. With all that we are doing here in the State as well as we are getting from the Centre, we are creating bottlenecks. We must have real planning committees so that within a period of five, ten or fifteen years. We should aim at revenue which may come up to ₹30 to 40 crores. We know we have tremendous natural resources. Although, time and again, I have raised the issue that if we set up a planned body for developing these minerals with a view to increasing the revenue of this State, nothing has been done, except the issue of a few licenses for mining or industries or some private enterprise. The real wealth lies underground unlike some Members of the Opposition who went underground. This wealth must be brought over the earth and analysed into rupees, annas and pies. Therein lies the real wealth of the State. I may suggest Sir, without any delay, we should form an Oriya Mining Syndicate and take up the survey of mines most thoroughly. Then we should work out these mines and thereby have as much revenue for the State as possible. This is my conviction. If we do so in five years, we will add five to six crores of rupees to our revenue. To corroborate this statement, I am ready with facts and figures and I am prepared to show them if any Hon'ble Member so desires. Then again there are several other industries in the deltaic areas. If Government take up the chemical and salt industries in a big scale, it will add one to two crores of rupees to our revenue within a space of two or three years. The question of finance will not stand on the way because Government has ownership of these areas. All that they have to do is to invite capital either from inside or from outside the country to work these mines on royalty basis. All these are State mines and State money.... If we set up Planning Committee and that Committee functions properly, within a period of five or ten years, we could have double or treble our present revenue. To that effect, I urge upon the Government to form a Planning Committee which could really function for the benefit of the State" (OLA Debates, Vol. XII (24), 30.3.50; 1282-3).

On the issue of share-cropper cultivator's interest and bringing legislation to this effect, he said, "Government would be tempted to bring about land legislation almost immediately where there would be no intermediary between the tiller of the soil and the State. In fact, Sir, the more we analyse the problem of the cultivator, the more we are convinced that unless and until we remove the intermediaries between the tillers and the State, the question of large increase in our agricultural production in terms of incentive of private ownership of the cultivator himself, will never be fulfilled. Sir, we are thinking in terms of providing small machines for the agriculturists. We must make up our minds as to whom we are going to define agriculturists.... The man who produced has to own the land. We have come to this conclusion after a great deal of analysis. In USSR after forty years experimentation of collective land farming, they have now come back to the individual land ownership of 4,5 or 10 acres for kitchen garden and so on for greater production because private initiative at the lowest unit would produce maximum result provided the man is also trained and he also gets the necessary equipments and other chemicals, seeds, and various other marketing facilities and so on. Now, before we start planning agriculture, it has almost become imperative that land legislation on the basis of the removal of all barriers between the actual cultivator and the support of the State's apparatus must be removed. Therefore, Sir, in the 68th Session of the Congress here at Bhubaneswar, we have decided that within two years, land legislation on the basis of maximum production for maximum incentive at the hands of actual producer has to be brought about and therefore, if the Hon'ble Member from Kamakhyanagar, while making his unusual good speech, projected the same thought or has been influenced by the 68th Congress, then I would welcome his speech. I will welcome it more if his speech in the House represents the established policy of Swatantra Party. Then I would enjoin on the Government to bring about legislation of that nature which he has advocated within the shortest possible time and establish the basic requirements of increasing output of agriculture on the basis of removing of barriers between the State and the cultivator" (*OLA Debates*, Vol. VI (8), 26.2.1964; 15).

On the important issue of rapid industrialization in Odisha and how to manage and sustain the industries, he said, "We talk of 3,000 small-scale industries. We talk of development of industries in every Panchayat. It looks alright on paper or it can be arithmetically established. But the human factor of management of such industries has to be streamlined if you want to make it a success and the streamlining of this human factor in an under-developed State like Odisha becomes the direct responsibility of the State. The simple reason is that we do not have entrepreneurs in the State. That is not the fault of the people of the State. It is a historical truth. During the 150 or 200 years of British rule, they created some points of growth by creating Calcutta or Bombay or Delhi or Madras or Poona or Ahmadabad. None of these were existing before the British came. The entire area of Odisha, parts of Madhya Pradesh and other areas were totally left out. Hundreds and hundreds of crores of investment has already taken place over the last two centuries in these points of growth. It is simply impossible to turn the tide by trying to attract the capital into Odisha, to attract the entrepreneurs into Odisha, unless the points of growth are created within the State. This is a fact this House will do well to realize. We are at the wrong end of the line. We have to create the points of growth. How? Paradip port is a point of growth, Rourkela Steel Plant is a point of growth, Sambalpur-Hirakud complex is a point of growth. Talcher complex is a point of growth. Sunabeda-Balimela complex is a point of growth. Obviously, it does not meet the bill. You may build a town. You may build an industry. But you do not create the industrial atmosphere of enterprise unless it goes through a certain phase, a generation phase. Industrial development in and around the points of growth planned by the British took two centuries, about 20 generations before the mind has been built for organizing industries, organizing commerce, trade and so on. We have not even that mind here. Therefore, the Industries Department, the Industries Minister and the entire House have to apply their mind as to how soon we can create this mind. Would it take us 150 or 200 years or can we shorten this period? Then only the fear of commerce will go. The fear of building industries will go. As announced by the Industries Minister, we would have 3,000 small-scale industries spread over the entire State. I would say, how do you propose to go about it. Until and unless you have in this State at the State level built up managerial personnel and put them at different points in the State, these proposed industries are bound to fail" (*OLA Debates*, Vol. III (23), 21.3.1972; 48). He also suggested certain mechanisms for strengthening and sustaining the industrialization, and said, "A central managerial pool has to be developed by the State. A Central Purchasing Organisationhas to be developed. A Central Finance Institute has to be created. Not this Odisha Financial Corporation as it is constituted, which does not meet the requirement. Until all these are done, you would not know what industries you have to set-up, what is its marketability, where to locate it because of the need of the area and the development of that area or we can shift it to somewhere else till that area becomes a point of growth. All these factors have to be taken into consideration. Today, as we are situated inside the State with our limited capacity, machinery that we have in the Industries Department and our Odisha Finance Corporation or the Small-Scale Industries Corporation are so terribly limited in their capacity that it is not possible to generate that quantum of enterprise as the whole House seems to desire. Much more original thinking has to be done in this State if we are to make even the smallest dent. Far more risks have to be taken by the State. These are the imponderables which this House has to question, settle and determine before we can go further. It is easy to quarrel with our tools. We have a set of IAS chaps and a set of other officers. If they are incompetent in certain fields, I will say that this is all the goods we have.

If collectively the House and the administration are both incompetent and we expect to achieve miracles, obviously we are barking on the wrong tree. We have got to use the tools that we have. Reorganise or sharpen them may be, but we have to take chances and risks. We have to make up this gap of couple of hundred years of backwardness to compete with other areas or points of growth. Without taking into account this vast gulf of difference which we have to make up and without putting all our energies and heads together, if we go on breaking each other's heads and trying to pass the buck to the next chap, whether he is a Minister, or a MLA, or a trader or a customer or an entrepreneur or the Bank of the Industries Department, then we are getting nowhere and we will get nowhere. This is a gigantic problem" (*OLA Debates*, Vol. III (23), 21.3.1972; 50).

On the subject of mixed economy and planning, he said, "Our country is a developing country, like many other developing countries and we have a system what we call mixed economy. When I was the Chief Minister, in my Budget speech, I said mixed economy was an unusual thing. In this mixed economy, it is not possible to provide equal benefit to all sections of the community and we see the result. Mr. Rajiv Gandhi came before he was Prime Minister and he came after he became Prime Minister. He went to the areas where there is abject poverty. It is a mixed economy and we ought to be part of this social order. The thinking is that we concentrate on development, or we have got concentration on development and hope that in this period, the miserable period of time, the spread effect of this development will reach the lowest strata, the people, the people living under abject poverty. But Sir, this is not possible in this country, for the simple reason that for example, take the development of industrial locations around this little town, Bhubaneswar, like Mancheswar, Chandaka, etc., will we expect this kind of development will reach to the poorest people, i.e., 80% to 85% of the total population? There is rapid expansion of population. So, the investment on industrial concentration can never have the spread effect to reach the poorest part. Even after 37 years of independence, what is the fate of antidote of poverty? There is only one dote that is to fine productive employment and to have a minimum income, which will raise the percentage of family above the poverty line. Income is the key factor to destroy poverty and income to be permanent is to be productive, so that the labour of the labourer can be sold and he can get the regulated income by his normal man-days. Therefore, should it not be the State policy to form this priority of planning. Is there any priority that the State policy can be implemented in this planning.... The good planning must have two imperatives. One is *hard monitoring* and the second is *accountability* as to the performances and targets fixed in planning. Priority is to be fixed and State policy should be given such priority, that can only provide productive employment to raise the people above the poverty line and such priority must be monitored" (*OLA Debates*, Vol. I, 30.7.1985; 57-8).

On the critical issue of planning and its consequent result of development, he said, "When the nation became independent, there was protracted discussion whether this country would come under the 5-year plan or 7-year plan or whatever. At that time the leftist elements in our party i.e., the Congress party, not Congress (I) party, were insisting on planning because in the Preamble of our Constitution, the people of India adhered to make India a welfare State. At that time, the difference between the rich and the poor was very high as Nizam of Hyderabad and a poor man earning at that time four *annas* and so as daily wages. Such was the condition then. The progressives, what you call them today, I had the privilege to belong; we demanded that the nation must be declared as a welfare State and socialism must be its objective. Now, nearly 40 years have passed and following that under the Constitution, we decided to have plans. Instead of 7-year plan, we have decided for 5-year plan. There has been an occasion when the 5-year plan could not operate, between the annual plan. When it was thought of, then there was a non-continuous plan, rolling plan and so on. So, Sir, a nation which was in abject poverty in rural India and which was wallowing in filth, dust, and sore of illiteracy, because in Punjab and West Bengal, where crores of people are refugees, they converge at different parts of India and create inseparable problems, administratively and economically. It made the nation running more difficult and led to more abject poverty in certain areas. When the first 5-year plan was born, you will notice that it was a very small plan, a very poor plan. Sir, from then onwards, we have proceeded. Now we are in no way out of the woods and the population growth and the investment do not even run parallel, it runs tangentially against each other, never likely to converge at a point of affluence and under such conditions, we have to plan very carefully. We have to plan with priority, clearly set in our minds and we have to plan in such a manner that every rupee becomes a sacred piece of equipment to help the poor to get out of their poverty and this House where we all of us are representatives of the people and we know the condition of the people where we have come from. We must insist on no wastage of any type either administratively or economically at national level. Planning assumes the greatest importance for the multitude of the poorest of the poor. So, I propound certain situation, it must be taken in the spirit of planning for the greatest good of the greatest number. In this context, I would like your attention to some interesting things happening around the world, even in some countries where planning is part of their religion. In Russia, from which we borrowed the idea of five-year plan, *Pravada*, their official paper, has published and I want to quote, 'Moscow, July 15 that several senior officials have been dismissed and punished for squandering millions of public funds'. What squandering? Because they failed there on account of industry, agriculture, constructions, etc. Their type of officials including

Chief Minister and the executives in the rank of Chief Secretary, Director, Chief Engineer, etc., have been dismissed by the Soviet Government under the new Secretary-Generalship of Mr. Gorbachev. It is an interesting thing. What you call misuse of public funds...... When you enter a plan, there is no scope for frivolities. The first need is how to make these millions of poor people live, live with dignity, to be able to feed themselves and clothe themselves. Gorbachev has come out with this kind of things for planning and it goes on to say how many Ministers have been dismissed. Ministers for twenty years have been dismissed for not achieving the targets at the national level. The planning must presume priorities of the type which the Russian Government is giving focus, and must achieve the targets" (*OLA Debates*, 25.7.1985; 86-7).

On the subject of the philosophy and the basis of plan preparation, he said, "In our State, we are rich in natural resources but why are we poor? As things go on and for historical compulsions, Odisha remained and continues to remain, one of the poorest States in India. There are certain things in planning, two major things-what is our per-capita investment? And how do we stand there in comparison to other States in India? What is our per-capita income? According to the Reserve Bank bulletin in 1978, we have only growth in per-capita income. As regards domestic product, from 1961 to 1965, it was 7 per cent. In the subsequent planning, it went down to 0.4 per cent and for the whole of 10 years, it was 2.4 per cent. Now coming to the per-capita expenditure, in 3rd plan, I draw the attention of the Planning Minister, the per-capita expenditure was ₹39.11. At that time, Odisha stood No. 1 in the country so far per-capita expenditure is concerned. In the sixth plan, our per-capita expenditure was ₹41.55 i.e. about ₹2 more per head and now Odisha stands way down at No. 13, in the list of 15 States, major States. I do not wish to draw the attention of the Planning Minister to these figures on any manner in deprecating the situation but mainly to bring home to our honoured colleagues here, the situation where we are really in. How can we collectively come out of this situation? And this is planning" (*OLA Debates*, 25.7.1985; 88).

On the question of planning and providing employment accordingly, he said, "Planning should entail employment of engineering personnel. Whether it is in irrigation Department, whether it is in Electricity Department or whether it is in the Transport Department or whatever, provided you have an expanding economy. We do not have an expanding economy that is the whole crux of the problem. We are unable to epand for various restrictions that we have imposed on ourselves. World is a big place. We are restricting ourselves only here, not getting into the world market which we can as a State or as a Government. Not World Bank or IMF, but now the Indian business houses are going and seeking loans in the world market not guaranteed by the Government. Today more than ₹15 crores dollars have been ear-marked for Indian industrialists who are borrowing from the world markets to develop their own industries. But we have neither knowledge, nor the interest. We are dead-locked. The whole Secretariat is moribund. They are busy in their own affairs. These kinds of meetings are held by the Chief Minister all the times. Wishful and woeful thinking are produced all the time. What is the result? Result is you have taken up this only on the last day of the last month because there is howling outside that we are unemployed, otherwise you would not have bothered about this. This is not planning. Planning should be suh that you can develop your man-power and investment should be such that man does not look for the job. Job should be there for him. All over the world this is the situation" (*OLA Debates*, Vol. IX (29), 4.4.1989; 58).

On nationalization of Kendu leaf trade and development, Biju Patnaik said, "The idea of nationalization of this trade (Kendu leaf) started ahead of socializing the country. Only for this reason in 1961, I started Public Corporation; only to develop an undeveloped State like Odisha. Development means development of managerial capacity, engineering capacity, business capacity, which we do not have, not because of our fault. Calcutta was built 150 years ago; so also Bombay or Delhi. Many were built like this. But we have been neglected. There was no energy for enterprise in our State. There were no men or women worth the name who could build the State. Therefore, in a place like Odisha, even Singhdeo agrees with me that in a place like Odisha, Government is the moving force who can create the energy. Government should do it till such enterprises develop. Government should take the initiative till such enterprises develop. Therefore, Kendu leaf, fishery, or construction, or Industrial Corporation, small scale industries corporation and other corporation should grow in the State. Government has to take a vital and major interest of managerial control and create the manpower before thousands of young men take up further enterprise" (*OLA* Debates, Vol. III (2), 4.1.1972; 44).

On the issue of distributing 1 acre of land to each of the landless SC and ST by the Government, Biju Patnaik raised the question that where the Government will get the revenue to develop around 2 lakh acre land and make it cultivable as free barren lands are available in the districts of Mayurbhanj, Kalahandi, Keojhar, etc., and not in the fertile coastal districts. Further, to convert barren land into cultivable land ₹1,000 per acre is required. For distributing 2 lakh acre land, approximately twenty crores rupees would be required. The Revenue Minister can judge it. I would request the Ministers to experiment in field what they are saying. This is called "planning and that is realistic planning" (Vol. I, No. 2; 44). He said, "this is nothing but distribution of poverty. If the Government wants our support, we will give support, but you must tell in what constructive works you need support" (*OLA Debates*, Vol. I (2), 25.5.1974; 42). He said,

"People have decided differently, vote boxes have been used differently. Day will come when truth will come out. People of this country will know everything. Now there is no time to discuss those things. They have reached bankruptcy of ideas stage" (*OLA Debates*, Vol. I (2), 25.3.1974; 43).

The Governor address stated that the 5th Plan outlay tentatively fixed is ₹567.01 crores, and for establishment of industrial projects in the Central sector during the 5th Plan a total outlay of ₹489.34 crores have been decided (Vol. IV (2), 1975; 92). On the industrial front, while expressing concern for the Fertiliser Plant at Paradeep, expansion of Rourkela steel plant, Sukinda nickel project, Ferro-Vanadium project, heavy-water plant, argon recovery plant at Talcher, and Indian Rare Earths complex at Gopalpur, he said, "the so-called 489 crores investment by the central sector in the plan may not truly exceed even a couple of hundred crores during the 5th Plan so that even this 567 crores of the 5th Plan devolution for the State along with the 200 and odd crores of central sector investment bring the total to about 800 crores in the 5th Plan which is the total investment from all possible sector as enumerated by the government in the Governor's address.... What kind of devolution that this government fought for that we did not get any priority even though we are the poorest. In the allocation of funds, we did not get any special consideration because we are poor. We did not even get the very normal consideration on ratio of devolution of national plan by population alone" (Vol. IV (2), 1975; 93). He said that Odisha has 4.3 per cent of the total national population, and the Deputy Chairman of Planning Commission, Haksar has said that the Plan expenditure will be rupees fifty-one thousand crores. Taking the 4.3% population rate, we should get rupees 2150 crores, but we are not even getting a thousand crores. What plan and development they will do for the progress of the country? Only by saying or writing about *progressive government, progressive planning* will not do. The Communists beat the drums about progressive policy of government. "Every progress is investment" and these Communists should visit Moscow for 2-4 months to know it. He said that in 1964 he led a delegation on behalf of the Prime Minister of India, to Moscow to study their Planning Commission. In their Planning Commission discussion "a whole chart of their national development right from the Arctic up to the deserts was prepared, and in every sector the rate of investment and return is seen". He sarcastically said, "You Russians are no better than Americans, because you can only think in terms of profit" (Vol. IV (2), 1975; 94). Their Chairman of the National Planning Commission is also a Minister, and what did he said to me, "Mr. Patnaik, money has no colours. Before we invest one ruble, we want to ensure how it is coming back as two rubles. Otherwise, how can we pay for social over-heads? Where is the question of planning and investment, if you do not make one ruble to two rubles, where is the balance-sheet of progressive development" (*OLA Debates*,

Vol. IV (2), 19.2.75; 94). They say this is progressive view, this is Moscow-oriented improvement. He said, "Russian society is very progressive apart from the policy and methods of administration, no democratic thinking there, single party rule, etc." (*OLA Debates*, Vol. IV (2), 19.2.75; 94).

Industry and Industrial Policy

On the industrial policy of the State Government that according to him was grossly neglected, he said, "This province can easily grow into a major industrial State in the country because it has got all the necessary mineral resources and the river and power resources. It simply has got to be harnessed but for the inadequate supply in the way of finance, men and training some of my friends there have drawn attention of the Government about the efficiency that is required in an Engineering school and the engineering workshop. This should be multiplied in hundred fold, if this State is to live. For example, this valuable thing which has been found in our Paris and German laboratories out of our Talcher coal. Talcher coal is the second-grade coal. It is not metallurgical coal but now this coke which will come out of this can easily be put in furnaces for putting up steel plant. This is a vital problem for us (*OLA Debates*, Vol XII (22), 28.3.50; 1151).

In the discussion during the Second Five Year Plan, speaking on the significance of heavy industries and technical education, he said, "When we think of producing steel, it is unwise on our part to believe that the steel in this country could not be utilized in consumers industries and the people cannot get the requisite materials. Sir, on the body of the Plan I would make a few observations as this is going to give priority to heavy industries in the next five years. It is very likely that every plan should give importance to agriculture or other cottage industries and for education and health. They have not only given emphasis on heavy industries for the next five-year plan period, but along with other things, more emphasis has been given to heavy industries and it is in the right way. I can give you one instance. We are importing thousand crores worth of machineries from foreign countries. If we can stop this, our per capita income will immediately go up. This is one major point. Apart from stepping up import of manufactured goods, we can give employment to our people. Looking at the plan, about building up of heavy industry, I find one lacuna, i.e., lack of technical personnel. I do not understand, Sir, why our planners have not taken into consideration this thing. They planned for the steel industry, paper industry, cement industry, etc., and the total increased output of each specific industries. Why was it not possible for the Government to specify also that so many technicians would be taken in by these very industries and therefore so many boys should be trained in different branches of production, so that as and when new plants are installed, these boys can take charge of these industries? Our universities are not producing such students who can be useful to industries. We do not want graduates for our industries. We want skilled workers, we want foreman, who can work in production industries. If a production factory is not attached to a university, it is not possible for it to produce such students...... The fundamental and basic success of the State's economy lies in the establishment of heavy industries. But still we have not laid stress on the training of our people as teachers and designers" (*OLA Debates*, Vol. VIII (31), 7.4.56; 56). This is what he spoke about the necessities of heavy industry and spread technical education.

On the criticism of the inefficiency of the working of the Industries and Mining Department, he said, "Although it may be said that they are not fast enough, still the main deficiency remains and in fact there are not sufficient man-power to man this vital department of Government particularly in a backward State like Odisha. If we in this State have to come at par with the western countries and more modern States around us like Bengal, Madras, and Bombay, we have not only to think in terms of collective work, but we shall have to positively think in a completely changed and ruthless manner before we can set our house in order. It is true as many Members from the Opposition pointed out that it is always talked that Odisha has the best and vast mineral resources and they have rightly asked what is being done about it.... It is not enough for us in this House to tell a Department inefficient. It is not enough to tell in this House a Department ineffective. The real question is that with the collective wisdom of this House, we must formulate a policy by which this Department should function as we all of us want it to function (*OLA Debates*, Vol. IV (15), Part II, 10.3.59; 28-9). He further urged the Industries Minister to consider, if possible, to set up departmentally various process industries like ferro-manganese, graphite, etc., and concentrate on them. He said, "If a Department of this State can start these industries slowly even one such plant can give a couple of crores of rupees of revenue. We must think of new sources of revenue and not go back to the small people for taxation, just now for fifty years. That means, we must have to apply our minds and with courage and determination think of new sources of revenue. We must be afraid of the *Public Accounts Committee* and others who may ask this question or that.... It only needs human energy, human intelligence and human courage to bring this situation into being in the State" (*OLA Debates*, Vol. IV (15), Part II, 10.3.59; 29-30).

On *Kalinga Tubes* factory that was once owned by him, he said, "The *Kalinga Tubes* is a big company, with nearly three crores of rupees of investment in which I do not now have even one per cent of share. My wife has only about seven per cent. There are Directors who are big industrialists from different parts of the country. They frame their own rules and policies. The purchaser of *Kalinga Tubes* products by Government during the last four years accounted for less than three per cent of its total sales. It is a fact that the *Kalinga Tubes* make lot of money, its profits may be beyond the comprehension of the Hon'ble Member form Rajnagar. Would you consider that a company which has crores of rupees worth of production every year and whose total sale in Odisha does not exceed three per cent, would at all bother about these transactions? In fact, had it not made these sales in Odisha, it would have made much more profit. If the House decides that the tubes from the *Kalinga Tubes* should not be sold to the Odisha Government and they should buy from the Tata's and Birla's or outside agents at higher prices, I can assure them that the Government would have no objection if the House would vote me that much of extra money. We welcome the suggestion. The Hon'ble Member from the Swatantra party is suggesting nationalization of industries. If that is approved by the Swatantra party, I shall have this done tomorrow. As far the Low Shaft Furnace, it was given to the Government as a gift. The Hon'ble Deputy Chief Minister made a statement like that in the House the other day. They have said that the Deputy Chief Minister had said in the House that the Opposition would be consulted before the purchase of the Plant. That has not been done because it has hardly been purchased and a gift has been made. Payments will be made out of the profits" (*OLA Debates*, Vol. V (13), 18.9.63; 49-50).

On the usefulness of Panchayat industries to provide alternative employment, "In America, the nation which produces the maximum food content of the world, the number of men employed directly in agriculture is 6 to 7 per cent. In our country, it is over 80 per cent. We have a long gap to make up. Therefore, they say that it should shift a sizeable part of the rural employment from agriculture to the secondary and tertiary sectors. In this context, further development on an extensive basis of agro-based industries is of great importance. Mr. Chief Whip, you were joking about Panchayat industries. This is what needs to be done, and I hope, it is not done as it has been forgotten. And if it is forgotten, never mind. You do it. This is the plan - my plan is what Planning Commission says. We have it at that time; subsequent governments neglected it. You have continued to neglect it, and therefore, I said, Panchayat industries. If a Panchayat has got two thousand working population, thousands of them could be shifted to localized consumer industries. Hence, I say, every Panchayat must have industries of one lakh rupees, every block must have industries of one crore rupees and that was the thinking in 1971. The values have gone down; the rupee has gone up. If you plan it like that, if you get the rural population in the rural area and give them productive employment then only, we can think of removing some amount of poverty line, irrespective of population explosion.... Two things are required to remove the poverty, taking the people from agriculture to rural industries, by raw materials being supplied by the Government and buying the finished goods by the Government. This is where the Government should come in a big way" (OLA Debates, Vol. I, 30.7.1985; 63).

On the question of effective monitoring of industries, he said, "Mr. Finance Minister, you have invested so much money in this SSI units and medium industries. Have you ever monitored or your Finance Department has monitored that on your investment, what is the return from these? Have you ever bothered? You are the giver of money. Just give money and forget it. Is it not your business to check it. You have invested 100 crores, but what is the return? According to reports from Minister, Industries, small industries at Jagatpur and Mancheswar, out of 270 industries, 200 are sick and the rest are going to be sick. Why? No power, finance is not coming in time. They are not able to pay for the machineries in time. But the interest goes on accumulating" (*OLA Debates*, Vol. IX (27), 31.3.1989; 78).

On the second Steel Plant, and its justification at Paradip, he said, "Mr. Pranab Mukherjee, the Minister of Steel, categorically stated in the Parliament that the second Steel Plant will be port based and both the Chairman and the Britishers have approved the Paradip as the best site in the country. He went a step further to say that all the financial decisions have been completed and the Steel Plant will be under production in 1985. I am sure the Chief Minister is aware of this.... In the Parliament, when I was there, and the Congress was in the Government, when Mr. Venkatraman took over the Ministry of Finance, on a pointed question raised by me on this issue, whether the loan of ₹5,000 crores that the Government of India is seeking from the IMF will restrict the borrowing capacity of the Government of India in the world market and care has to be taken to see that the Steel Plant will come up with the borrowing finance either from German or UK, etc. His answer was categorically, *YES, a steel plant and a major Power Plant of 1,000 MW in UP, and on those two accounts the expenditure will be met out of the international borrowing and this will not come under the purview of India's proposal for borrowing ₹5,000 crores from the IMF....* I would like to know from the Chief Minister, shall we try collectively with the Government of India to bring this major integrated steel plant to Odisha? In my opinion, we should try collectively to get it. Government is saying that power supply will be a problem.... Mr. Chief Minister, we both should take up this matter with the Government of India..... Paradip is a beginning of major city. It is a major port, a deep port.... If the major steel plant will be put here, then the ship coming here with other goods can carry steel. It will not return vacant. That is why Paradip will be the best site" (*OLA Debates*, 17.7.1985; 57-8).

On the topic of Second Steel Plant in Odisha, for which Biju Patnaik had a cherished desire for the development of Odisha, said, "Mr. Pranab Mukherjee, the then Steel Minister emphatically said in the House that best effort has been made to put up 3 to 4 million tons steel plant with an expenditure of ₹4 thousand crores, all the funds arranged by England and Germany. It is our misfortune and also misfortune of the State of Odisha that you have not mentioned about setting up of the second Steel Plant in the Address. It is a matter of misfortune for the State on account of which I do hope that you would revise the same. So, the fact remains that Paradip is the best site for Steel Plant. It is in the records of *Lok Sabha*. For the non-implementation of the steel plant at Paradip, so also in any part of Odisha, the present Chief Minister of the State is solely responsible. With the consent of the then Prime Minister Smt. Indira Gandhi, the then Steel Minister who later became the Finance Minister remarked that this Plant is at Paradip and all the benefits will go to the people of Odisha. Do you realize that this Plant which will be three times as big as Rourkela Steel Plant will bring about a city of more than ten to fifteen lakhs. You see this will give employment to at least two lakhs of young people who are trying for employment, which is one of the major factors of poverty, because they have no income.... Should you or this Government not fight for this massive mandate? Should you not use your mandate? You have 20 Members in the Parliament. Should you not use in the Parliament. Should you not use your muscle power there in the Central sector?" (*OLA Debates* Vol. I (2), 15.3.1985; 13).

On the item of projected impressive industrial growth by the Chief Minister, he castigates it by saying to focus on power generation and said, "Mr. Chief Minister you have proposed to have industrial growth without the use of electric power. If this is so, then the House should be enlightened on how you have achieved an impressive progress in industries without power. What I think you have showed a total negligence towards the development of power potential. If the priority is given to anything, then it is to the power, which must be the base for either the agricultural or industrial development. I regret to say that this Government has neglected the power base.... So the Chief Minister knows it very well that we are in a very bad situation for any development of industries. Unless we back it up by power, we cannot make true industrial development. Long ago, 23 to 24 years ago, i.e., in 1962, when the Khosla's Decade of Destiny was prevalent, if the Chief Minister is keen to know what really would develop the State, I recommend him to go through it in great detail. Power is the base for agricultural and industrial development. The total power need of the State is to be generated from both the hydel and raw materials like coal. Until that is done, Sir, all kinds of industrial growth will remain just a talk. The slogan, *thousand industries in thousand days* (given by the then Chief Minister J. B. Patnaik) is very nice to hear, but in real sense has no meaning. You talk of Industrial growth when the numbers of hotels are increased. In your sense, the industrial growth is related with more hotels which are termed as industries. You are giving loans and subsidies to the entrepreneurs for new hotels and cinema halls. Cinema halls and hotels are all for pleasure sake of the people" (*OLA Debates* Vol. I(2), 15.3.1985; 11-2).

He was more interested for industrialization arising out of the mineral resources, rather than only selling the mineral resources. He said, "The Hyundai Corporation, South Korea, have given a proposal to shift six million tons of iron-ore to South Korea for their Steel Mill. I dislike shifting of our ore to other countries for making steel and selling it back to us. If it is on limited purpose, Jakhapura Bansapani Railway line, I think Government of India is justified in not giving money because there is no project behind it" (V (27), 4.4.1987; 32).

On the issue of foreign financiers financing for Steel Plant, he said, "The Foreign financiers are saying 'wait' we will watch. No one is coming with big investment. Big corporations came and they have all gone. They have seen, they have accepted and they have admitted the potential of the area but when they go back home, talk to financiers. They say your policy sounds good but the implementation does not look good at all. This is the crux of the problem. Prime Minister announces liberalization policy, liberalizing, it gets stuck in every department how not to implement that liberalization. One Minister told me, 'We told your Minister also that we agree with the terms and conditions what do you say-but we cannot fill up 40 forms, and we have no time. This is worst'. So who will like to do business with us? You have civil servants those who have no interest on creation of wealth right from the top, Chief Secretary down to your clerk, peon, nobody has any desire to ensure that the nation throbs with vitality. What to do? This is how we are measured" (*OLA Debates*, Vol. X (7), 26.2.1993; 116).

He disclosed one secret with regard to Steel Plant and said, "I am telling you one secret. When Panditji was alive and Sri T. T. Krishmachary was the Finance Minister, we had planned in that area from Dubri to Keonjhar, to build up a comple of 10 million tons of steel. Panditji dies, Mr. Krishmachary left, I left the whole thing just collapsed. After all ideas come from the minds of men. Man changes, ideas die" (*OLA Debates*, Vol. X (7), 26.2.1993; 116).

He gave an instance of two top Australian executives of a company named Broken Hills who visited him. The company breaks hills and mountains for iron-ore. This company supplies 42 million tons of iron-ore to Japan. He said, "We were discussing about the prices. Japanese are squeezing us, they said. I said, you cannot squeeze them? They said no, Japanese are clever. They have got resource supply from every country in the world, including India. Japanese produce maximum steel in the world and they have maximum engineering industries in the World. But there is not a single ton of iron-ore in that country nor coking coal and these wonderful people without any raw material are controlling the sources of raw materials and its prices. I said why cannot you go on strike? They said, who will go on strike? What about Brazil, what about Africa, what about India-what they will do with their labour? The labour will say you cannot go on strike. How will they live? We are all tied in this great vicious circle. Sir, all I wanted to say, within this circle we have to live, we have to struggle and we have to prosper. Within this wickedness of the structure, we have to make it alive. How can we collectively deal with such problems? Ofcourse, in a democratic society, we can snag at each other. It is specially for the Opposition to snoop at the Treasury Bench. It is normal. But when it comes to the issue of removing poverty in the face of multiple number of problems, which becomes so fast that no Government even if God is in the Government, he cannot solve the problems" (*OLA Debates*, Vol. X(7), 26.2.1993; 117).

On the resolution of having the second Steel Plant in Odisha, he said, "We should know that we are sitting on the mountains of iron-ore. Take our neighbor country China. Twenty-five years ago, China was producing steel the same quantity as India is producing today. Today China is producing six times more steel than India. When the Chinese along with one Indian promoter came to set up a plant at Daitari, half a million ton steel plant, a small one, the Chinese Ambassador very proudly said that twenty-five years ago, they had the same tonnage of production what we have now. Eighty million tons they are producing and they are importing more steel. We keep on poor, we remain like poor. Because our consumption of steel per capita is the lowest in the world. Steel is the emblem and yard stick of modern civilized order, more the steel consumption, the more civilized the people are supposed to be. I asked the Chinese Minister for Metallurgy, who came eight months back, how do you find a market for your steel production? He said that their central committee which is the real planning committee, decided to give every firm a wheel barrel made of steel and that increased the demand of steel by 5 million tons over-night. This is the difference. By this way, the demand increased more and more in steel production resulting 80 million tons and they are planning for 100 million tons by the turn of the century. What is our position? We produce only 16 million tons inclusive of everything, Tata and HSL. You see the forecast of the Steel Ministry, they have said, by the time 2010, India would produce 45 million tons of steel, roughly 30 MT more than what we produce now, in the next 17 or 18 years. But effort is nil. Everything is discussed in the Parliament and reports are placed in the House, but nothing is being done. That is the end of the story. A Nation does not grow like this, it needs determination" (*OLA Debates*, Vol. X (7), 26.2.1993; 115).

On the problems of having the second Steel Plant, he said, "The problem of getting land is the biggest problem and on top of that getting clearance of Forest and Environment from the Government of India is one of the biggest problems. Secondly, this Plant steers midway between Keonjahr and Paradip. Since all these plans depend in deepening of Paradip Port and connection of railway line from Paradip to Banshapani that was held up for the last 10 years" (*OLA Debates*, Vol. VI (3), 18.12.1991; 5).

On the development of making affordable steel, he said, "So, experiments have been going on round the world by various firms like Lurgi of Germany, Allis Chalmers of USA and some others to find a method by which the non-coking coal can be used in making what is called sponge iron and then go over to steel. But it has not yet been a success story and there are many deficiencies in the working of the process. We are trying to put up one in Andhra Pradesh as an experimental measure with the help of UNDP and one little plant is going on in Jamshedpur with many varieties of coal. But the whole process is not yet fully satisfactory, but we are trying to find out the best way of doing it, because, that is ultimate answer for India if we want to use our own resources. If you look at it, not politically, but only by economic considerations, which this House must, to produce the cheapest steel, as everybody wants or both sides of the House want that the nation must have the cheap steel, the steel companies in both the private and public sectors must have adequate profits for their own expansion, for their own replacements, and so on. And then, we must also locate any future expansion at localities or at areas where the steel production would be the cheapest. The second consideration is that the gestation period should not, like the Bokaro, take us to ten years. It must be concluded within three years or at the maximum within three and half years from the time the first rupee is invested till it starts its production. Unless you are able to do that this long interest charge goes on being capitalized and capitalized in the case of Bokaro from ₹600 crores to ₹700 crores and it goes upto ₹1500 crores and then the cost of production will go up from ₹2000 to 20000 and so on. Then that cannot meet the demand of the nation. Therefore, if expansion has to take place the minimum capital cost expansion has got to be at the existing plant level. Obviously, it is so. The land is there, the infrastructure is there, some housing is there, power set-up is there, water is there, Mines are there, and they are working already. So, Bhillai can go up from 4 to 6 or 7 million tons, Bokaro can do the same, Durgapur can do that, Rourkela can do that. Tata can do that although they cannot do it alone, the Private sector cannot do that. Obviously, that involves big money investment. Neither Tata nor anybody can do that. This should take us to 20 million tons from the present figure of 10 million tones, by using our own coke" (*Lok Sabha Debates*, 28 June 1977; 290-92). He also continued to say that for the the pressure of this expansion what we need is low ash-content coal from Australia, US. Australia coal has 11 per cent ash-content and our coal has got an ash-content of 24 to 27 per cent. "We have to put up coal-washeries, another expensive industry to reduce the ash-content by 20 per cent" (*Lok Sabha Debates*, 28 June 1977; 292). He again said that his predecessors like Shri Chavan, Shri Pai, and Shri Subramaniam and others worked under difficult situation and could not streamline the steel industry. "This is one of the major sectors of public investment".

On his assurance to revive the dying mini steel plants, Biju Patnaik said, "I can assure the House that shall ensure that they are not quite dead, we shall take necessary fiscal measures, in consultation with my colleague, the Finance Minister, and other measures which we can think of through the Steel Authority of India for obtaining the raw materials like scrap and so on. The industry which was born out of an euphoria of delusion of grandeur, of a great deal of surplus money has suddenly found itself like a plucked hen. Even so it happens to be on the soil of India we will ensure that it does survive....because the House desires so" (*Lok Sabha Debates*, 28 June 1977; 282).

Expressing his support for the small-scale steel industries, Biju Patnaik said, "I have great deal of sympathy for that little man who is making little plates, *katories* and things like that from stainless steel, he buys stainless steel rods from the government factory at Durgapur, he has introduced his own engineering, he employs his whole family for making steel, for polishing it and for making little pot and pans. I have and my Ministry has, after considerable deliberation with all these little indigenous manufacturers, come to the conclusion the policy of substantial reduction of import duty on stainless steel has, perhaps, been a little hasty. Therefore, I and my colleagues, the Finance Minister and the Commerce Minister, are trying to put our heads together to ensure that this small indigenous industry not only survives but also flourishes. That will also incidentally save Durgapur Alloy Steel Plant because, I have learnt that, the moment the policy of reduction of duty was announced all the sales orders on government stainless steel plants have been cancelled. Therefore, a certain amount of rethinking is required, and we shall ensure that the correctives are applied very soon" (*Lok Sabha Debates*, 28 June 1977; 282-3).

On development of rural electrification, Biju Patnaik said, "I say rural electrification is a waste of expenditure unless at the end it produces some wealth. Rural electrification does not mean an electric-pole with a bulb on top of it. With it, industry, irrigation will go to villages. Otherwise, the whole line is a waste of public expenditure. What are you going to do about it? I am merely pointing out the points of areas of development. Your engineers cannot even run a plant. Steel prices are rising; cement prices are raising, no electricity, no coal, whatever is coming to hand is going. No wagon. Strike, indisciplinein steel plant, power plant, fertilizer plants won't produce. Transport system dead and still. How do you propose to run the Government? What do you expect from us? How do you expect to remedy the essence of discipline in production and distribution.... Political cross-siding apart, as long as you are in the Chair, we will like to know from you precisely and exactly how do you propose to govern the State?" (*OLA Debates*, Vol. I (2), 25.3.1974; 47-8).

On the issue of fall in aluminum production due to power shortage, Biju Patnaik said, "It is a very distressing situation that the production of aluminum has fallen because of shortage of power. I wonder what made the previous Government not to allow large aluminum projects to have their own captive power plants. Power must be in public sector, and like that iron must be in public sector was their view. I do not understand what prevented them to allow these power intensive factories to have their own plants. I have allowed them. I have asked them to work it out quickly. They will give output in full. His situation has been corrected as Mr. Pai mentioned. There was a weakness in the previous Government. But Janata Government is quite strong and pragmatic (*Lok Sabha Debates*, 28 June 1977; 287-8).

In another instance, expressing concern for the poor people, he said, "There is no doubt that while we have been developing the engineering industries, the technology and everything, we have neglected the growing number of people below the poverty line. The numbers of such persons stand at 40 crores today, whereas it was 25 crores in 1967. Therefore, Sir, there is no alternative but to pump more and more money in that sector to give them necessary minimum facilities like drinking water, cottage industries, etc. They have to be nursed. They have been neglected. You may call it lop-sided planning or whatever else you may like to call it. The Janata Party has decided that maximum amount of funds must be made available to the agriculture sector, small-scale sectorand the cottage sector" (*Lok Sabha Debates*, 28 June 1977; 293-4).

On the issue of governance and policy, Biju Patnaik said, "The foreign policy of this Government has been very ably represented by our External Affairs Minister and the Prime Minister. It is based on self-reliance, a simple thing, not much to talk about, dignity and national self-respect. Before we came to the Government, you signed away ₹300 crores of Bokaro Steel Plant to the Russians. I retrieved it and gave it to our own engineers, Indian business; too plain and small a matter, ₹300 crores. Would you call it a self-reliant economy? Would you call that a dignity of our own? In every sphere the Janata Government have decided not to depend for any critical item on any particular power; even in the case of heavy water, we are going to make our own, whether the Americans give it or not. The Prime Minister has made it clear that whether they give it or not, we are not going to bow before anyone. This kind of authoritative assertion of a nation's interests was given over to the House or to the country and you should be proud of that if you are patriotic" (*Lok Sabha Debates*, 10 May 1978; 392-3).

On industrial potential, Biju Patnaik said, "It has boiled our hopes that if a Congress Government came to power in Odisha, the rate of growth of Odisha in the field of industries as well as in other fields would be far greater than if a Government is installed here which is opposed to the power at the Centre. The party in power, which is in the Centre, and now in the State, although a minority Government is the Government themselves. They must fulfill the promises they made to the electorate, otherwise democracy has no meaning at all. We are creatures of democratic institutions and if we give an undertaking we must either fulfill it or walk out and give place to another set up who can do it. But here we see that somehow to win the elections by any means seems to be all the morale in Indian politics today; by any means we must win the elections by lying, by cheating, by buying, by making fraud, by making false promises, by laying down false foundation-stones and any such thing. And that is why we are unable to make any headway, any planned headway of this nation, because we are not as serious as in other countries. Look at Europe, America, Russia, China. We are not a serious people like them. That is why the world over we are not taken seriously. We are talking a lot; we are having a lot of conferences, a lot of conventions. The result is, we are great talkers with little performance. You ask a German, you ask a Russian, you ask an American, he will speak the same thing that India is a land of talkers with very little performance.... The Industries Department is a critical Department of the State. Why do we build industries? The philosophy of industries is to produce goods and to provide employment. If these two things, which are vital for any backlogging of the plan, are not provided then what is this paper-work? It is merely narration.... The minimum objective is quantum of production, value of production, employment potential created and actually employed" (*OLA Debates*, Vol. IV (23), 24.3.1975; 61-2).

On small-scale industries and growth areas, BIju Patnaik said, "Rourkela is a growth area and therefore must have small-scale industries around it. But we seem to forget that small-scale industries are not only for production and employment but also for dispersal of production and employment potential around our villages. When this idea was originally mooted out by Manubhai Saha, when he was the Minister, Industries at the centre, I personally told him that it may be good in some areas but if this be the pattern of the entire industrial development of the country it will be faulty and it will not serve the purpose. I want to draw your attention to this simple situation. Odisha has 50,000 villages. We have three thousand Panchayats. Now in a Panchayat, on an average, the population is five thousand. Leaving aside the children, the old, infirm, women, the working population is roughly one thousand. Therefore, the Planning Department of the State should take into account how to absorb atleast 500 out of this one thousand into industrial activities oriented to production based on consumption industries to fulfill the social needs on one hand and providing social justice of minimum employment on the other. There is no point of talking socialism unless you provide social justice to people who are in starvation and whose number is more than seventy per cent. Nearly one crore seventy lakhs of people in our State, who are living in villages, mostly have not got an average income of even one rupee a day.... Therefore for any type of socialist planning in the State of Odisha, total intervention of Government at all stages is required.....Where my despair is infrastructure is lying dormant and there is no force" (*OLA Debates*, Vol. IV (23), 24.3.1975; 63).

Regionalism

On the significant debate of regionalism, he said, "Unless that mind is not changed from an age-old of defeatist to that of conquest, of fearlessness, Sir, this State nor India will ever grow. This is a task which we will not achieve by bickering. This is a collective task of every thinking person in Odisha, in India. In this context, I disagree with limited view that we should not regenerate regionalism. I do not agree with Indira Gandhi's description of policy while she says regionalism will disrupt India. I say, on the contrary, this is the only positive force raising of which will make the people of India through the people of the States where they live for positive action, definite sacrifice. The question is how do we reconstruct our Constitution so that we can have stronger States and a stronger Centre, not weak States and an economically destroying Centre. Not that Centre which can rule. That is not a stronger Centre of a strong nation. Twenty-five years have proved that we still remain as a nation of poor men. Every other country in the world we approach for aids. This is our position. What is required? The genius of India, I am sure is not lacking this positive force of patriotism through the linguistic States which was designed by Nehru to shuffle into a national thought by which India should live in the States and can grow and the people of India, and not the Secretariat of New Delhi, can participate, can become partners in the whole thing. Actually, India is constituted of different races, different States. But United States of India would have been its proper definition. Now we should have the engineers here to reconstruct our Constitution only because twenty-five years of experiment has shown us that this has not given us the satisfactory result and driving this Constitution in such a way that this positive force of result, patriotism that exist in different parts of the country can act as a force of construction, not as a force of destruction, as we see between Bengalees and Odias, between Assamese and Bengalees, between Andhra and Telengana. Today there is disruption. If we can bring it out and baffle it, I submit, we generate a fantastic force for total reconstruction of India (*OLA Debates*, Vol. V (10), 23.2.1973; 29-0).

On the regional balance, development, and ratification of the decision of merger of Telugu speaking areas of Telangana with Andhra Pradesh by the State Re-organisation Commission, Biju Patnaik said, "I want this Resolution to be passed because this Resolution aims at social and economic welfare of the State and the country as a whole. But in the peripheral discussions some references have been made which need a little clarification. The Hon'ble Member from Ersama belonging to the Communist group of this House, mentioned about vested interests. He said that Andhra as a State had been onesaliz after the sacrifice of one of her able public men. But he has forgotten perhaps he chose to forget that it is his party who created the base in Telengana for revolution in India to throw out the properly elected

Government of the State" (Vol. II (8), 1974; 102). To this Shri Loknath Choudhury retorted that the Leader of Opposition is supposed to know a little bit of history. The Nizam was there. Biju Patnaik in reply, said, "No, Nizam was not there. It was not the Mulki movement, it was the movement of the Communist Party of India at that time to create the so-called revolution to throw out the properly and duly elected Government of this country. The reason for the attempted division of Telangana and Andhra was not started so much by the existing Mulki rules. It was started by the internal dissipation of the Congress Party itself, the question of local leadership fanned it into the same manner of thinking as has been from time-to-time recorder here – South Odisha, North Odisha, West Odisha and things like that. That is how the whole Andhra movement started. Now firm step was taken by the Central Government and this is going to be one Andhra Pradesh and this Resolution is good for Andhra Pradesh because it seems to have removed certain anomalies in area of development or lack of development. Therefore, we in this House, welcome it but as some Hon'ble Members have pointed out that it is necessary from the point of view that it is now well known that there is a feeling here that certain areas of our State also get preference at the cost of other areas. Such a feeling must be studied in full details and the causes of such feelings must be removed and it is the duty of the Government in power to see to the development of the whole State equitably and leave no one with any feelings that this area is being neglected" (*ibid*; 103).

While commenting on regional imbalance that Odisha is suffering, he said that "Kolkata planned for 250 crores for the underground railway, and Bombay planned for 500 crores investment for water works alone, but our plan is confined to 560 crores only. On what basis this is being done? We are not thinking of America or London or Japan or Russia, but in which century shall we be comparable with other states of India? Therefore, for the development of the state, the per capita income of Odisha should improve, and this is now one-fourth of the per capita income of India. In order to bring it at par with national average, we should adopt *parallel development* with all our available resources, like minerals, forestry, water, and this will not only bring welfare of Odisha, but also of India. For this we require minimum investment. If you want to make a common cause for the development of Odisha we are there. If you want merely to survive to the national devolution of the finance, then you will go down in the history as having stopped the growth of Odisha. We can together sweat where the development of Odisha is concerned, there is no politics there. It is only the question of accelerating the growth of the state. For that and in a federal type of administration as is obtained in India today, it is a question of capacity and efficiency of lobbying and enforce and on top of that the capacity and efficiency of the administration of the state" (*OLA Debates*, Vol. IV (2), 19.2.75; 101).

Development of Odisha

Biju Patnaik, said, "What is Odisha? Odisha is a land of rivers, a land of hills and forests, a land of long sea-coast. These are Odisha" (*OLA Debates*, Vol. II (24), 10.7.1974; 108).

On holistic development, Biju Patnaik said, "I can only request that if we all 140 Members from either side, if we jointly work out plan for the development of the State and accordingly direct the official machinery then there can be holistic development for our State. The Opposition Members must consider this very seriously. Odisha is a great sufferer due to the type of politics in India. There is imbalance for the last 150 years. Our State is a predominantly tribal state. Our State has forest resources, mines, but we are neglected for the last 150 years. We have everything, but we are poor. We only think that if we belong to the party of Indira Gandhi then we can get more from the Government of India. Whatever finance Government for India gives is based on the economic angle. We are not getting the quantum of share from the Government of India as the other States are getting. Even if we are vocal for this, we are unable to raise our State to that level. To bring Odisha at par with other Sates, I would sincerely tell to my friends please find out any mechanism by which we can ruthlessly plan and implement the programmes, otherwise it is not humanely possible" (*OLA* Debates, Vol. III (2), 4.1.1972; 46).

On the development of Odisha, he said, "We are projecting for the all-round development of Odisha. Odisha should not remain as a hinterland of Calcutta which is the creation of the British. We are the citizens of India and we want to be equal citizens with others in India. Historically, Odisha has been the vassal of Bengal or Calcutta for over 150 years. It is well known that it is a historical fact. We wish to get reversed from that situation. For a very little thing we have to go to Calcutta. Everything is made in Calcutta. Now we are not only doing this. Bihar and Assam are smarting for the same thing. It is a historical fact which has widened the gulf. We must have to fight for our cause.... It is a question of people's demand. As Shri Banka Behari Das and the Leader of Opposition has said it is the people's demand and wish to be equal among the equals. We wish to be citizens of India. This must be understood. We should not remain indifferent here. The people of Odisha should not lag behind. They want to be at par with others. People want that their case should be sympathetically considered. We say this is our birth right and we shall have it. That is what the Father of the Nation, Mahatma Gandhi told the British Government. But we are now developing all the imperial British policy. By the same policy the points of growth or the centres of growth have concentrated in certain palces. Shri Siddharta Shanker Ray's attitude is to develop by imperial policy. But we want to change that attitude. As Shri Banka Behari Das has advocated because there are rail heads at Madras, Vizag and Calcutta, what is produced there, are being sent outside through Bay of Bengal. Those are historical growths. Therefore, we have been left abandoned by the British imperial policy. But after independence there must have been natural urge to create growth in Odisha like Calcutta. But we are far away from Calcutta" (*OLA Debates*, Vol. III (33), 6.4.1972; 36-7).

On the situation in Odisha, he said, "In a State like Odisha, we are collectively in access pool of India, the filthy part of India as far as poverty is concerned. One of our Advisers to the Finance Commission, former Chief Secretary of Haryana, Mr. Gupta, he went round the districts of Koraput and Kalahandi. Mr. Gupta came and told me that, 'I have not seen so much of poverty anywhere in India. Whichever house I went, I saw they have no grains to eat'. I told him, this is one part of life and we belong to another part of life" (*OLA Debates*, Vol. X (7), 26.2.1993; 115).

On the developmental transition of Odisha, he said, "Now we are changing over our administrative system from a feudal system to a modern industrial system which necessarily brings new pressures on the State exchequer as our police force must be modernized with modern equipments not only to maintain law and order but they must be in a position to provide direct security so that every man live without fear. Similarly our road system develops and more vehicular traffic comes along, you will find that until and unless civic sense properly develops in the pedestrian as well as slow moving vehicles, the accident, the rate of accident, are bound to mount. There is a changeover from one system to another system" (*OLA Debates*, Vol. VI (17), 10.3.1964; 22).

Speaking on a united approach for the development of people, he said, "Why not we in this House sit to decide the destiny of the people. Let us at least join our intelligence resources, our capacity to fight the battle for the people. If you do not combinedly fight the battle for Odisha, you as Government have not done justice, we as Opposition are not doing justice and ultimately people will suffer. Therefore, let us frame issues, but not present this accountant's dilemma to us which you call Budget Speech" (Vol. II (2), 1974; 27).

Biju Patnaik said that every member of the Treasury Bench promised to do lot of things during election and said that they will do all things as they have the keys with Indira Gandhi in Delhi. Biju Patnaik cannot do anything. They themselves are saying that 1 crore 20 lakhs people are affected due to drought, but for that the demand for grants is an amount of Rupees Three crores 58 lakhs. If they would have said this during election time that an amount of ₹2.50 per head will be spent, then people would have beaten with shoes. For this I always say from experience that whether we are in government or not, we should not say to people what we cannot do. If you have will to do *democratic development* and initiate bi-party system in the country, then form 'shadow cabinet' for either party not in power. It may take 20 years or 30 years, or 50 years, does not bother. If we have such democratic pattern of "development of major two-party system or two and half party system, then every party should responsibly chalk pout the chart for developmental work. They should have performance and accountability that will be judged by the people. Else we will continue with this system of telling pack of lies just to win votes. It is not happening here. It is happening all over the country. Even though this is a party discussion, I am generalizing this for those who are telling all these stories. He questioned what rectification has the government done on the present drought? You have not even started scratching part of this national calamity. Basically and fundamentally, if we cannot counter the drought, then it will occur every year for the next 500 years. "For this when I was the Chief Minister and Dr. Khosla was the Governor, we prepared a chart of development works which was called *Decade of Destiny* plan for Odisha..... I am sorry to say after 1964, all successive governments are not able to catch even first part of those ideas" (*OLA Debates*, Vol. III (6), 16.12.74; 93).

On the point of integrated development, he said, "You are talking of food, electricity, irrigation, you talk of revenue, supplies, agriculture, everything. Therefore, unless there is coordinated effort, unless all these Secretaries concerned with food and food production comes under one single authority in some form or the other, you cannot do anything. I would request the Hon'ble Minister to consider this problem and make all the Directorates come under one authority so that you can have a targeted achievement, you can reach the target" (*OLA Debates*, Vol. III (6), 16.12.74; 94). For giving maximum price to the cultivators and subsidized price to the poor consumers, the profit-margin has to be wiped out. He said about nationalization of all rice-mills that he also pointed out in the Congress Session of 1964.

Biju Patnaik's ever zeal for the prosperity of Odisha was reflected when he responded to the Finance Minister's query of 'given a cooperative and constructive hand', that he will always be there on the question of prosperous and radiant Odisha..... I am prepared to give my cooperation to bring the economy of the State to a higher standard. Where the economy of the State is concerned there is no question of politics. When it is question of bread and butter, when it is a question of malnutrition, it is the duty of the politicians to find out the cause and the remedy. It is their duty to eliminate all these from the State" (*OLA Debates*, Vol. II (2), 25.3.74; 24). Biju Patnaik said that financial resources "can come from infrastructure, because infrastructure can raise revenue" (*OLA Debates*, Vol. II (2), 25.3.74; 25). He referred to what the then Prime Minister of India exhorted the people of Odisha, "if you vote for the Congress, then your condition will improve, economic condition of Odisha will improve otherwise not" (*ibid*). While criticizing the taxation policy of Odisha as "increasing regressive taxation in the name of progressive economy" ..... He said, "Finance is an art and not a science. It is a question of how much our people can sacrifice and pay"(*OLA Debates*, Vol. II (2), 25.3.1974; 25).On the natural resources of Odisha, he said, "Odisha has abundance of natural resources, why do not you exploit it. Madam Chief Minister, you promised to exploit the natural resources of this State. The great GandhaMardan hill is there, why do not you take steps to sell these iron-ores to some foreign countries through the Government of India and the Reserve Bank of India, it does not disintegrate India. It will increase our non-tax revenue. It will help us in reconstructing Odisha. In the name of radicalism, you have brought untold miseries to the poverty-stricken people of Odisha. You say you are radical;I am reactionary" (*OLA Debates*, Vol. II (2), 25.3.74; 25-6).

On the issue of development and investment in Odisha, he said, "A very simple fact that if Odisha is to come up economically it would mean a great deal of maneouvre and investment for many years to come........ As I said before that is during the course of last 100 or 150 years a great deal of investment has been made in those areas (Delhi, Punjab, Madras, Bombay, Calcutta) whereas nothing has been done within the boundaries of what we know today, as State of Odisha. When hundreds and hundreds of crores of rupees were invested in certain areas in all fields of human activities, i.e., education, health, roads, buildings, factories, electricity, agriculture or irrigation, an easy base is created from where it is easy to jump. Madras or Bombay or Punjab can develop much more rapidly than we can today because they had all this investment for themselves during the last 150 years. Therefore, our first interest in this State will be how to attract or force investment within our boundary, taking care of sizeable investment on man for science and technology as well as concurrently marshalling of our raw materials and power and to see to its successful implementation. The Governor in his address has given a clarion call to us to apply our minds and take resolute steps so that we can marshal all these factors and go about our own development with single-minded dedication. It is not very important to my mind what a Minister does or a Member of the Opposition says or one group says or does. To my mind, of greater importance is to understand or assimilate the grave danger of non-progress of our State, if we do not clearly perceive the risks and dangers involved in our lack of understanding of the programme. If this House, Sor, which is destined to provide the motive power for the State's development, fails in its duty to understand and see that all that is standing in the way of our quick development are removed and harness its thoughts and action towards removing the disabilities in a clear manner, I would submit, Sir, that this State stands very little chance of paralleling itself to the more advanced States of our country" (*OLA Debates*, Vol. VI (2), 18.2.1964; 42-3).

On the Tikerpara Power project feasibility and utility, he said, "Certain views have been expressed.... Certain eminent journals or newspapers of India, Calcutta paper editorials reads, 'It is a maneouvre in the battle of funds', and the editorial again reads, 'Mr. Patnaik succeeded in maneouvring the Prime Minister to lay the foundation stone'. I think the House ought to know that nearly two years ago when I was the working as Chief Minister there was a meeting at the Prime Minister's house with the Planning Commission, the then Finance Minister and myself were present. The Tikerpapa Dam investigation was going on which was one of the priority investigations approved by the Government of India. The Prime Minister asked me how long it may take for this investigation to be completed. My answer was that it is a big affair; it might take two years. The Prime Minister was irritated and said why does it take such a long time to investigate? Can you not make it one year? After that order of the Prime Minister, the State Government put its best people on the investigation. The details were prepared in consultation with the engineers of the CWPC in Delhi and top American consultants were brought in to vet this investigation, and these top consultants were also consulted at Government of India level for various other dams and power projects. Only after these were done and the preliminary report was prepared and it was discussed with the Prime Minister, the Prime Minister agreed to give it his blessing. It was not a maneouvre. It was a race for getting priority of allocation.... Wherever there is a massive national project, there is bound to be certain dislocation because we have decided our Government has decided that the people who would be dislocated would be treated as privileged people and all their conveniences should be looked after first before submergence. This is a very big promise by the State Government. It means a tremendous amount of work to be concluded by the State Government and therefore the Government and the Chief Minister have requested for active support from all Members of this House" (*OLA Debates*, Vol. VI (8), 26.2.1964; 17-8). He also said, "While dealing with such a massive project, I submit that there is no place for sentiment. It must be cold calculation of our capacity, of our finance, of the returns, of our preparations and the reconstruction of the area for the people who would be submerged. We must find better place, better employment, better opportunities for them. This can only be done by calculation of our capacity and our implementation methods" (*OLA Debates*, Vol. VI (2), 18.2.1964; 46).

On the issue of resettlement on account of the Tikarpara power project, he said, "When the State Government is convinced of the feasibility of this power-project and has decided to embark upon it and has enlisted the blessing of the Prime Minister of India. I have no doubt that this massive project will find a place in the thinking of the Central Government, whatever may be the resistance to this project here and there. As far as our people are concerned, who would be directly affected by this project, Government have said here in this House, on the platforms and in the press that this area has been earmarked for reconstruction. It is not a question of limited rehabilitation as has been understood in the Hirakud rehabilitation. It shall not be so. Government has made it expressly clear that all the defects experienced at Hirakud would be rectified and improved upon. That was the first work of submergence. I do not say that the Government was incompetent then. It was a question of knowledge. Everything you do not know at the first working. Everything is learnt in gradual process of working. We now know the defects of the administrative machinery, and the time that takes to implement. Therefore, Government have already ordered adequate administrative action which will plan adequate advance actions to construct new villages, new towns, new roads, factories, electricity, agricultural land reclamation, so that they may not really feel that they have been shifted from hovels to far better homes and hearths. All this would be implemented by Government" (*OLA Debates*, Vol. VI (2), 18.2.1964; 44-5).

Discussing the precarious situation in the expansion areas of Bhubaneswar and to provide amenities and development during the 1980s, he said, "Bhubaneswar, you call it Municipality and now you want to convert it to a Corporation. Whether you have the adequate number of citizens here to confirm to the needs of a Corporation? Perhaps it will take a long time before you reach that number within the precinct of a Corporation. Bhubaneswar Municipality is now extended to Patia, people call it Patia with five Panchayats where the conditions are truly horrible. There is no road inside the village, which is full of mud, filth, and stone. Nothing has been done to provide electric lights. There are no canal systems, no ordinary proper bridges are there, where children can walk. Only little bamboos are used. Government has not done anything there; your Municipality has not done anything there. This is the picture in the rural areas. Now in the town itself you can get areas where the people live in filth. People who have helped to build the town, which is now called city, are the most neglected. This is a travesty. Can I call it welfare State when this is the situations.... I would like to know is there any justice in this so-called welfare State thought by the founding fathers of the nation? For 25 years these people have served for us. Whether they are rickshaw pullers, labourers, nothing you have got to settle them. You have got HUDCO, you have got BRIT (Bhubaneswar Regional Improvement Trust).... I would like to know, is it not the responsibility of the Government to take special care to give people their rights and build 2-3 storey buildings even on a small piece of land to accommodate them.... The problem is, we rulers are so greedy for our own benefit, for our own extension of wealth, for our family's wealth that we want to grab every available thing that comes our way and throw away the poor people who cannot go to court of law, who cannot prevent from being thrown out" (*OLA Debates*, Vol. I (6), 21.3.1985; 47).

On the development of the State, he said, "I must admit that for an impatient person like me, who wishes to see the development of the people in the State and resources rapidly, to my utter dismay, I find that we are crawling at snail's pace speed. This was my regret in 1961. This has been my regret in the last 30 years. It is my regret even now. I do not know what has happened to my administration. I think, the exercise of corrupt practices of last decade has made the people somewhat spineless" (IV (3); 21.2.1991; 170). He suggested to give highest priority to the power sector for bringing in industrial development, and said, "We can raise our power potential during this Plan period by more than 2000 megawatts which is double the present production of the State. Then only we can look forward to develop all industries based on our mineral resources. We have unlimited coal. We can develop unlimited power. The only shortage being financial resources. Without bilateral arrangement we are lagging behind the competition" (*OLA Debates*, Vol. IV (3); 21.2.1991; 170).

He said, "When we say that we have got independence for the last 40 to 45 years, at that time my poor people did not have anything to eat. What does independence mean to a poor woman who wears torn clothes and carries a load of wood and walks ten kilometers to sell it in the market for a livelihood! We fly the national flag and do march past, what relation does it have to her? There are 90 per cent of such people living in the country. What relation does such a person have to what we are talking here? Then consider this. If a citizen of this country does not take part in the Constitutional functioning of the country, then the Constitution fails, then and there. But we are not concerned. We have great lawyers of Constitution. We have Constitutional experts. What is happening at Delhi? All the culprits who belong to the damn State that is Uttar Pradesh have brought this country to the brink of ruin. That is Rajiv Gandhi number one culprit, V. P. Singh number two, Chandrasekhar number three culprit-all from UP. Number four Indira Gandhi, mother of all culprits. Now, if these are the people who think the Uttar Pradesh is India, why the devil all of us follow it? I would like to know. All these three Johnnies do not run the Government of India. Why are you going for election again? What for? People voted for five years. Are the electorates cattle or sheep or slaves-what? When we some leaders want, we will say go for election, or stop elections, who are these leaders? UP the damn State produces this kind of people. There is chaos in UP against these people. It is my personal opinion ad it is also the public opinion. It has become a joke-for stupid cause, two constables were moving near your house. Therefore, break the Government. This is too much. There are fifty *chowkidaars* in your house, so what if two more *chowkidaars* are there? (*Interruptions*) Hence, for the two, do you think to reduce the whole Government of India to a farce? Now the whole fortune of the nation is at a disastrous stage and you bring this nation to the brink of ruin for two damn constables, supposedly to be constables or whatever it is. This is not tolerable. These are the people of UP. UP is producing leadership and the whole country is trying to follow them. This is the misfortune of this country. Why they do not want to break up the UP into small States? They wanted to keep it as a big State when Mr. Charan Singh was Prime Minister. Yesterday proposal came to Government of India to break-up the UP into three States. When poor people who have majority, get disappointed, then revolt starts. At that time, they do not obey rules, regulations, Constitution, law, Judge, etc., and clear all these! This is what happened in France. The King, Queen, and other descendants were all beheaded. In Russia the same thing happened, in China, the same thing happened, and in Vietnam, the same thing also happened. Everywhere the same thing. What is the guarantee that it will not happen in India? Every year, India is adding 1.5 crore population that is equivalent to Australia's total population. For this unemployment will increase, crime will increase, what will the students reading in colleges and schools do? They will loot, commit crimes, frustration will increase. We will ask them to give vote! Foe what will we ask? We will say we have broken the Government. Give us vote again? There was the V. P. Singh Government which was broken by the BJP. Their Advani told that I am going on Rath Yatra. If I am arrested, I will break the Government immediately. Is it a daring talk?" (*OLA Debates*, Vol. IV (16), 14.3.1991; 91).

Emphasizing upon the natural resources of Odisha and development, he said, "But I have not lost faith in the vast natural resources of our State. Let us struggle together democratically, constitutionally, within the system and within the Central limitations to be the masters of our own resources. You will see the picture vastly changed and you would be almost able to do what you want to do for the masses. You have to have three harbours, Paradeep, Chandbali, and Goplapur. These are the infrastructures you must have before Odisha can be elevated to the position of Calcutta, Bombay and Madras. We were under the British regime for 300 years. This is the reason for our backwardness. You must get the money for it and you must give it to us. You must raise your voice and you must demand it" (iOLA*Debates*, Vol. II (2), 4.6.1974; 30).

On the various aspects for which our Corporations are failing, he said, "There is to be coordinated management in financial structure of these Corporations. If this is done, there would never be any shortage of working capital. This is one weakness in the financial structure that we find. Atleast, to me mind, this is a weakness.... We are to depend much on men of ours. If the men are inefficient or uncontrolled, then you cannot get success in any field. Those who are in control of management of the Corporations, if they are inefficient or open to temptation because there is a lot of money rolling in those Corporations, then nothing can succeed.... Now, after formation of

Odisha Construction Corporation, every year we are sustaining loss, only because we encourage parallel construction companies, whether it is local company or outside company. We do not even help the local companies. I would have been happy, if our own men or local people or Odia people would have been given preference in doing the work. That is not being done. Most of the work is done by the outsiders. Where is the scope for Odia's development or Odisha's development? All the business in the Odisha State is controlled by non-Odias. All the business is controlled by outsiders, we are fighting among ourselves. But all the creams of the State are being taken away by non-Odias or outsiders.....In our little Corporations the scale of officials, such as IAS officers, Finance officers and Audit officials are too much " (*OLA Debates*, 7.2.1986; 136-8). He also suggested to the then Chief Minister, J. B. Patnaik, and said, "Mr. Chief Minister, if you have a sincere desire for the development of Odisha, then the industrial development must be backed by and large by the promoters of the State. I regret to say that the promoters with the bulk of investment from any guarantor or any financial institution like IPICOL, etc., are from outside the State which I am not talking in totality" (*OLA Debates*, I(2), 15.3.1985; 12).

On building entrepreneurship skill for Odia persons, he said, "Just to give a fillip to the mind of a latent Odia who is always afraid of doing something or initiating something, I will give an example which is very interesting. You talk of Odisha Construction Corporation. The contract for siphon under the river Birupa was to be taken up by a company called Hind Construction Limited, which is a Birla owned company. Our engineers had drawn some kind of design for the work of siphon. Later, it was found in consultation with Government of India that the design has to be changed slightly. With slight change, the moment that was put to Birla, they raised the quotation by ₹2 crores. At that time the then Chief Secretary was Mr. Sivaraman. I called him and asked him, you form a corporation here, now that is called Odisha Construction Corporation, and that corporation would take up their job. The moment Birla came to know about this, he came to me and requested to give the work and indicated that he will do the work at previous rate. But, I did not give him the job. I said, you have lost the job. This Corporation built 67 bridges in Paradip and Express Highway. Our able engineer was Mr. Khosla, whom I hoped, the Prime Minister would be kind enough to send as a Governor of the State to assist or help us in all these engineering developments. Similarly for Corporation, so many things were started at that time. Purpose was, one would help the other and resources of the State will remain mobilized within the State" (*OLA Debates*, 7.2.1986; 135). He also said, "Growth of Corporations was the need at that time for Odias development or to involve Odia entrepreneurs and Odia enterprises directly, whether small, big or medium, so that Odias can grow out of moribund mind, helplessness, inferior complexity. Why we cannot compete with Tata and Birla. We can, we could. I proved that we can do textile as efficiently as Birla can. We can do tubes as efficiently.as Tata can. Just to prove ourselves that we can do it, it was necessary (*OLA Debates*, 7.2.1986; 135).

On the implementation of the twenty-point developmental programme of the Government, he said, "You have said in Governor's address that Odisha is in second place in implementation of twenty-point programme. May I ask Mr. Chief Minister can any other Minister read all the twenty-point programmes? I do not think anybody bother to study it. I do not think can any of you assimilate it? They think just as failure of the programme. This is a misuse of the programme. As I found this is completely a failure programme, during me exhaustive tour of the State....As I found, more than half of the money is going to the pockets of Congress (I) *dalals*" (*OLA Debates*, Vol. IX (2), 22.2.1989; 95). He questioned whether this can be stopped and said, "There was one V. P. Singh, who resigned from the Chief Ministership because of this fact. There was one Union Minister like Lal Bahadur Shastri, who resigned from the Ministership because there was a train collision. But would you resign? No. You have said on record Mr. Chief Minister, that even if 115 MLAs will oppose, you will continue as long as Rajiv Gandhi wants you to. How can then you claim to be the Chief Minister of the State? I think people of Odisha have abandoned your Chief Ministership. It is my belief" (*OLA Debates*, Vol. IX (2), 22.2.1989; 96).

He also said, "This motivation will give thought to build factories of small, medium, and big. Motivation will give thoughts to build roads and tanks in periphery areas. Is it possible to motivate them by giving labour? They work for 6 hours for themselves and 4 hours for the State. These are certain items on which we should give our thought and put them in the body of our legislation. Government of India will give us a framework, we will introduce that framework for us. Where there is insufficient leadership in village area, where there is insufficient motivation amongst the people, we will have to think new ideas which will motivate them. Perhaps the prize can be a motivation. Perhaps they can be motivated by other things also. We should change the hearts of the people to do things more than what they can do, so that the nation can be built. Two crores hands of poor Odisha will but itself work outside the wage labour without that Odisha cannot come to the level of Bombay, Calcutta or any other State. These are the thing, these are the matters, the House must think of and come to a conclusion" (*OLA Debates*, Vol. II (21), 5.7.1990; 65-6).

Speaking on the Railway development in Odisha during the British period, he said, "Those were imperial necessities by British Raj for movement of their troops, goods, their men, their officers, army and so on. In those days the engines were locomotives and run by coal. So wherever they located coal fields, they also built few miles of railway line to get into the coal fields like Talcher. They could get coal because the locomotives were then run by coal. At the beginning of locomotion engineering available to the world in those times there was burning of timbers in the locomotive engines to raise steam which in turn moved the wheels of the engines" (*OLA Debates*, Vol. VII (28), 2.4.1992; 68).To push forward the demand for development of railways in Odisha, he suggested to the Hon'ble Speaker that the House should lead a team of Legislators belonging to all Parties including some Ministers to Delhi and sit with the Minister of Railways, Finance, and the Prime Minister and say that unless you commit yourself to build the Koraput-Jeypore-Malkangiri lines, Lanjigarh-Ambagoda line, Gopalpur-Talcher and Bolangir railway line through Boudh, we are not going to leave thus place (*OLA Debates*, Vol. VII (28), 2.4.1992; 70).

On the neglect of development in Odisha, he said, "Here (Odisha), Congress had a Government which ran for last 10 years. Why didn't you give us more power plants? The coal was there. We are suffering today for lack of power. You know a power plant takes 4 to 5 years before it can go. But they don't bother to do it. They don't bother to give us Railway line, power, money for irrigation canals. It was all happened when you were in the Government. Why don't you suggest for the development of Odisha because Odisha is never counted? You must remember this. This is the fact. You must recollect; you must remember whether it is J. B. Patnaik, Chief Minister, Nandini Devi, Chief Minister, or Biju Patnaik, Chief Minister, it does not count. For that purpose, we the Members of this House must collectively suggest for the development of Odisha and we can only fight collectively for the good of Odisha. I don't care any ends of the party because people have voted us for the development of Odisha. Let us see if we can do so" (*OLA Debates*, Vol. VII (28), 2.4.1992; 69).

Lamenting on the neglect of Centre for development of Odisha, he said, "Planning Commission has not given adequate priority to Odisha's mineral resources. This is largely true. The development of Paradip port and the railway line from Daitary to Banspal, and another 6 million tons for the proposed Steel Plant at Daitary has been hanging, hanging, and hanging with the Government of India for the last 7 years.....NRIs are coming for mineral industries, but there is lak of adequate power. In the previous ten years, we had not taken steps to add even one MW of power. The main thing is power and I am trying to increase it. Odisha is rich in minerals. So, its development can only take place if we have adequate power (*OLA Debates*, Vol. VII (26), 30.3.1992; 85).

On the infrastructure development, he said, "Today we do not have sufficient power to develop Industry and agriculture....Unless we have enormous quantity of power all our minerals will be wasted. Any mineral needs power, to smelt, whether it is iron, whether it is chromite. Any minerals for smelting require enormous power. Therefore, we have to produce enormous power so that our prosperity can really make headway......We should have thermal power and hydro power mix it together, so that we can have cheap power and encourage industries to come for steel, aluminum, chromite, nickel, etc., and thus Odisha can advance. So, industries and power are synonymous today. If we can develop power, then only we can go for industries in Odisha to develop" (*OLA Debates*, Vol. XVI (8), 26.9.1994; 79-80).

On the question of making Steel Plant, he said, "I have started my life as a steel maker at Barbil, which most of you do not know. The Steel Plant which I have given to this State earns a profit of more than ten crores. Therefore, on modern technology we have to be very careful and think as to how we can have that technology through which we can use our own materials. So, what our imports are minimized because we do not have sufficient foreign exchange to buy foreign materials. So, all these have to be considered before I say – Yes. In the meantime, lands have to be acquired. Land takes a long to acquire, to pay compensation and all these things take long long time. Swaraj Paul is coming in the first week of next month (March) to finalise it at Bombay or elsewhere and will discuss with me to finalise the technology and financial package and then get on to the work" (*OLA Debates*, Vol. X(3), 22.2. 1993; 130-1).

On the point of development, Biju Patnaik said, "The point is can you collectively look after the people, the weaker section of the people and give them time. What changes are required in our cropping pattern? It has not yet been decided to set-up a jute mill. We talk that we do not have capital; whether it will be in joint sector, or private sector, or public sector, but still we will have industrial development! You have got a harbor. I would request all Members to see the port and also tell the Chief Minister to send all Members to Haldia, Vishakhapatnam, and Paradeep. By this they can know that even if we have a deep harbor, how much attention is given for its development, and how the others are advancing. I am not against anybody. I am for myself and for my people. I am not against Bengal, Delhi, and Madras, but in comparison to them, if we are not allowed to rise, then I will revolt. I have no other option than to revolt. I prefer to die thousand times. It is nothing parochial. Similarly, this is an area which is undeveloped. Your own address says this, what does the Governor says, so rich in natural and human resources and yet continues to be one of the poorest states. Are we poor because we want to remain poor? What are the forces? I would like the Chief Minister to examine herself what are the internal weakness and eternal forces that continue to keep us poor? What prevents our growth in comparison with the other areas? If we don't know what the forces are, how can we meet those forces and how can we make the people like those in other developed States? These are not mere words. Unless you go to the essence of things, by merely saying parochial, reactionary, progressive,

SarvaBharatiya, we will go nowhere. The poor man will remain poor" (*OLA Debates*, Vol. I (2), 25.3.1974; 45-6).

On the Odisha's needs, he said, "The House should know the proper assessment of things. What does Odisha need really? We could not expand our power projects in the last 10 years, when my colleagues were in the Government they did not apply their mind to power generation. They must have their own calculation. What they thought it was enough. But now it is not enough. What we see our production is going down. So, we are going to renovate it which costs ₹700 crores to ₹800 crores" (*OLA Debates*, Vol. XV (5), 26.7.1994; 86). On the power reformation, he said, "We want money for the system development, for improvement of the system to make it a growing concern till such time we have divided the Corporation. Ultimately the Electricity Board will be a regulatory one. Power generation would be in another Corporation and transmission and distribution will be in another Corporation. So what Hon. Member from Balasore said it is confusing, it is not confusing. It is the process of change. The World Bank says we are good boys and we are doing good thing. The process of change requires more and more capital" (*ibid*; 87).

In the same discussion, he said, "Odisha needs power, much more power than it has got. It has got raw materials, it needs power. The mineral industries need power. Not the pretty power of 500 MW, 600 MW, fir its survival. Odisha is destined to grow. In net 60 years, it must have 50,000 MW of power and we have to produce that power. We have coal, we have the resources, and we have some hydro possibility. Therefore, if we take something to get something more, I think, there should not be any objection. If the American company, with whom I am discussing to build a 500 MW plant at Kalarahanga, another two 500 MW plants in the Ib valley area, apart from the 210 MW plant that is being discussed with AES Corporation in the next 50 years we must have 50,000 MW of power generation, whoever it is, the Government that does not matter. Therefore, anything we do is in interest of generation of more power. If we have got distribution system defective, for which we need this money (₹500 crores to ₹600 crores) whatever we need, it is just chicken-feed, for your distribution system, it is nothing, you need much more than this.... I think the House has the capacity to give much more than what we are asking for. We should dream these big things, because we have resources, we have water power, we have mineral resources, we have the sea power, and we should develop, we have to develop and I have no doubt about it. I know what it matters. One company produces more than half the power of the whole nation's consumption. One company which had come here for discussion produces 37,000 MW of power, that is an American company and the whole country's need is 80,000 MW. I amtalking about my State. I have the resources, raw materials, but I do not have the money. I want power to develop. If I get foreign support, foreign investors to introduce, I must see that they come and the whole House must welcome it and see that they come without swindling us, and with reasonable profit, they should come and generate powerin the State. I am sure the House should agree and accept that position. You see, we have a possibility" (*OLA Debates*, Vol. XV (5), 26.7.1994; 97-8).

In the context of development and surplus power in Odisha and its sale to Andhra Pradesh, Biju Patnaik sarcastically said, "Although we are selling a certain percentage of our power, I consider it a matter of deep shame for a State that it is surplus of power. It only depicts a crippled state of our economic growth. In all the developed area all over the country where they have got 5 times or 6 times more installed power than Odisha, they are clamoring for power, but here is a State which is under-developed in so many ways and which need a lot of power for its industrial and rural development and for the development of its resources, boast that we are surplus in power. Neither the Industries Minister, nor the Mines Minister nor any other Minister concerned with development cannot say that even for some years to come there will be surplus in power and there will be no demand for more power for our industrial progress because there is no prospective planning with this Government and because they have not thought in terms of prospective planning; they have not worked out in terms of industrial investment; they have not worked out in terms of industrial employment and have not gone deeper into the question of power of total production-the total value of production. None of these have been taken into account by the Government" (*OLA Debates*, Vol. II (24), 10.7.1974; 108-9).

On the development of power infrastructure in Odisha, he said, "Talcher Thermal Power Station was built some 30 years ago and it has become old and derelict. It has to be renovated. I said to renovate, it will cost ten or fifteen times more than the original cost. This is all approved by Government of India agencies, Central Electricity Agency and so on. But the question is, how to create a condition by which the air pollution and water pollution will be totally removed, which will cost atleast ₹200 crores. Neither the State Government has got the source nor does the Central Government have the ability. So, when this question was raised by the Central Government through the Ministry of Environmental Pollution, a letter was written by me to the Minister of Energy, Government of India, pointing out two things. I said, you have two options, either to close down this plant and throw away the employment of 2,500 people working there or fine money to do it or try to do it.... I want power. If I do not get power, whatever little industry I have got, that will be closed. Till such time we have to wait for alternative power. We have to put that power into the system. Then only think of closing or repairing or renovating it. So, all these will take time" (*OLA Debates*, Vol. XIV (18), 22.3.1994; 9-10).

On the mineral resources of Odisha, Biju Patnaik said, "You had gone on records Mr. Finance Minister that Odisha is rich in mineral resources. We must develop the mineral resources. You know that without power, it cannot be developed. So first thing my Government did was putting up two power plants each of 210 MW. Now 420 MW power is under production. I said that in my last speech that I have put up this plant and you can inaugurate. Nothing wrong in it. Governments go and come. It is nothing new. Some Government does something else and some Government inaugurates that. That is not the credit. He brought the Prime Minister of India to inaugurate it, anyhow. He again said, "Your Finance Minister has stated on record that this State is abundant in mineral wealth. It is the richest State in the world. But he also said therefore we need more energy. I agree with him also" (*OLA Debates*, Vol. II (12), 14.7.1995; 99).

On the Irrigation projects in Odisha, Biju Ptanaik said, "Irrigation project is a time taking job. It takes generations to build Irrigation projets. Unless you do that there is little scope for development of Irrigation projects. You can develop L.I points, for that you must have power" (II (3), 1995; 132). Emphasizing upon the completion of power projects in Odisha, he said, "If all the power projects are not put up, Mr. Finance Minister, all your dreams, all your talks of development of Odisha by whether it is aluminum, whether it is steel, whether it is Chrome or whatever it will be, just empty talk. As it has been for 10 years, it will continue for another 5 years" (*OLA Debates*, Vol. II (3), 3.7.1995; 133).

Biju Patnaik was more interested for the development of Odisha, even by the private sector investment. He said, "My only point is that when my Government has tried its best to bring in as far as possible private sector investments but now unfortunately either that is lacking or it is being delayed or deferred. Even your own thing like TTPS (Talcher Thermal Power Supply) may be handed over to National Power Corporation, even that is being delayed" (*OLA Debates*, Vol. II (12), 14.7.95; 99).

On the development of Odisha, he said, "Because this is Congress plan. Planning is not by the Congress Party. National Government is running it. Planning Commission is running by National Government. If that Government changes what will happen to the National Plan? 38,000 MW in 8th Plan has come down to 22,000 MW. If this be the position, Mr. Chief Minister, please consider, ponder about it and find out Odisha is not your Government or anybody's Government. Odisha is Odisha. Odisha has 3 crores and odd people, can you do anything? Can you take care of them and can you take care of the Rural Odisha? Can you take up industry which must be developed for having a focal point of development? There are serious problems which no doubt is working in your mind and I have no doubt that right answers will be given. It is not that we can do anything? Can we take care of Rural Odisha? The Hon. Member from Kodala says it is not a Party problem. It is a national problem. Can we put our heads down?

Let's sit down together and chalk out a plan together and work together? That is all I want to say" (*OLA Debates*, Vol. II (12), 14.7.1995; 101-1).

On development of railways in Odisha during the Railways budget discussion, Biju Patnaik said, "Neglected area continues to be neglected. The same thing happened when the previous Government was in power. With the limited funds, the Minister-in-charge wanted to develop the metropolitan areas. If Odisha was not on the coastline when the British took over this country, there would have been no railway line at all connecting Calcutta with Madras for imperial preference. Since then, Mr. Railway Minister, all the urges of the people of Odisha had fallen on deaf ears only. For example, there was a demand from the coalfield area of Talcher. The railways of course connected that from Cuttack to Talcher just to get their coal for running their locomotives. We have been pleading for a line from Talcher to Sambalpur. If this had been done the whole of Western Odisha would have been served and Chhatisgarh region would also have been served. We had asked for a connecting line from Jagpura to Banspani so that the whole of Bihar could be served; we wanted Talcher and Rourkela to be connected through to the Paradip port so that the whole hinterland could be served. But nothing has been done. Every time the demand is raised the Railway Minister had been saying that they were surveying it. My Hon. Friend said previously that one survey had seen a silver jubilee. It may probably see a golden jubilee. Take the case of Ganga Bridge. 15 Railway Ministers over the last thirty years had laid new foundation stones at the same place. But the bridge has not been constructed. I know Panditji (Kamalapati Tripathi, the then Railways Minister) is a devout man. At one time he was thinking of going and settling down at Jaganath Dham and I had promised to give him a *math* there. In the name of Jaganath, may I appeal to Panditji to ensure that some new railway lines which I have enumerated earlier come up in Odisha not only for the sake of Odisha but also to service the entire hinterland of South Madhya Pradesh and South Bihar, which are rich in minerals..... Sir, the major portion of South Eastern Railway passes through Odisha that is Calcutta-Madras and Calcutta-Bombay route. I know that if the British could takethe railway line over the sea they need not have crossed Odisha but since major portion of South Eastern Railway passes through Odisha, the South Eastern Railway Head-Quarters should move into that area. That is also not there. If Odisha people want the Head-Quarters to be in their State, the Calcutta people will not agree to it. This is not the dispersal of wealth or dispersal of jobs or dispersal of opportunities. I hope the Hon'ble Minister will consider these points and especially when their colleague, the new Chief Minister of Odisha who has just taken over has said probably on the floor of the House or somewhere that the new railways lines will be built, at least to keep up his face-if not my pleadings-you will construct these lines" (*Lok Sabha Debates*, 17.6.80; 258-60).

But in the case of Steel Plant, I do not understand Mr. Finance Minister, why that Chief Minister is making wild promises? Steel Plant is not built up in a day! I caution the Chief Minister through you Sir.... Steel Plant takes 10 years to build up. So, I would request the Government not to make such wild promises" (*OLA Debates*, Vol. II (3), 3.7.1995; 131-2).

Giving a united approach for development in the House, Biju Patnaik said, "If we look at one or two essential things, the failure of this Government in that direction will be quite apparent. We have failed to obtain a Ship-building Yard for Odisha. Government of India decided not to give Ship-building Yard to Odisha although they decided to have one in eastern belt, one in western belt and one at Haladia port and I would like to know from the Chief Minister what steps the Government have so far taken and what further steps they want to take in this matter and what support the Government want from this House and I have said earlier during discussion in the House that where the points of growth are concerned and so far as the interest of the State is concerned, the House is to function as one unit irrespective of our Political affiliation and ideologies. Similarly, Government should also note the facts that during the last ten years, Government of India neglected Paradeep to the extent that even one cargo berth is not yet completed. Whereas Haladia, which started much later, ship carriage berths are completed there. I have cautioned the people of this State and its Government that in this race that Paradeep, which was started long before Haladia and long before the expansion of Vishakhapatnam, has been left behind because other Governments have been able to influence the Government of India, of which my friends are well aware, resulting now that they whittle down the importance of Paradeep, although it is one of the biggest ports. Unless this particular point of growth is accelerated there would be no hope for Odisha to develop its economics because a major harbor is created at Bombay in Maharashtra, at Calcutta in Bengal, and also in Madras or Cochin or whatever it is. We have a harbor but without any facility, there will be no point of growth because to this harbor will go all the railway lines, all the national land, express-ways and special ways through which will pass a lot of traffic carrying cargoes which is essential for commerce. It is only the commerce that is essential for or growth, '*banijya basanti laxmi*', (Laxmi sits in commerce) as the saying goes. Therefore, this is the point of growth on which the State, the Government, the Opposition can have no difference as this is so to say the life-line of Odisha" (*OLA Debates*, Vol. II (24), 10.7.1974; 107-8).

4

Social Issues

The society constitutes the bulk of the political and economic issues. The society has to be build is such a manner that it contributes a healthy economic system with a robust political structure. If the society, as a whole is neglected, then its ripple effect will be observed over all other systems. Hence, social aspects constitute the core to all the ills, and it also has to be addressed in such a manner that it leads to positive impact over all. The social issues have a tremendous impact on the political structure functioning and continuance, in a democratic system. Biju Patnaik, being himself a mass leader, knew the pulse of the grass-root democracy and the mood of the people. He addressed all the social issues with great care and dedication. This is evident form the debates he delivered in the House.

Welfare State

On the issue of successful implementation of third Plan period and its requirements, he said. "We have simply got into a habit of attacking each other on party platforms whenever we get certain opportunity. That, Sir, somehow or other diminishes the seriousness of the problems that we are facing today and more serious problems that we will have to face tomorrow.... At the end of the Third Plan, we will have 20 million unemployed and we think in terms of Panchayats and development schemes to employ these people for acquiring community assets, such as improvements of tanks, bunds, making village roads or various other things like that and pay them only a meager wage of 12 a day, which means that Government shall have to spend every year 450 crores of rupees. We do not have this money nor can we make this capital investment and give work to the growing population of the country. At the rate it is growing now every year, a new European nation is born in India and no Government in the world can plan successfully for a new nation every year. Therefore Sir, while I am forced to the conclusion I cannot without my tongue in my cheek, agree with the view of my young Communist Member that planning of this magnitude and democracy of our brand is not hostile to each other. We have got am ultra-democratic Constitution. Every man has the inalienable right to do what he likes and pursue any trade or profession he chooses. But here we are caught in a vicious circle. We are called a welfare State. We do not have the funds, we do not have the resources, we do not have the capacity to find the resources either by taxation or by any other means to break through this vicious low level. We have to reduce the population by means of drastic enforcement. I do not think for a moment that through the process of democracy we can achieve the result within a measurable period of time at least well before the danger level of population is reached in this country. My Communist friend says that if people are taken into confidence and if this idea can be sold to the people through democratic process, they could voluntarily get in to face these problems and try to solve them on individual and national basis and not through bureaucratic method. I would like to confess that such a possibility does exist. It is true that such a large plan cannot be implemented through the meager bureaucratic administration that exists in the country today. The administrative set-up that we have got in this country, whether in the Centre or in the States, are unfortunately ill-equipped to counter and solve such tremendous problems" (*OLA Debates*, Vol. IV (6), 25.6.59; 26-8). As a solution to all the problems stated above, he suggested, "We are the representatives of the people, we have come to the Legislature, and we have to do something. The Leader of the Opposition, the Leader of the PSP (Praja Socialist Party) and the Members of the Communist Party here in the House as well as in the Centre should be prepared to work together for the implementation of the Plan. They should say that we are prepared to pool all our resources for the national cause, because here a single party is not in danger, but the whole of the nation is in danger. The country is going to face a rebellion if something is not done in time. It is not the problem of a party. Let the Opposition say that they are willing to do their might for achieving this task. Let us leave of these bickering on small things and sink our difference for the time being, and work unitedly for the plan. This is the problem I would ask my friends to consider seriously. There may be political differences; even if we want to break one another's head at the slightest pretext, can we not keep it off for ten to fifteen years and get down to work. If there is wastage of Government money or public funds let us form vigilance squads and see that such things do not happen. That is the duty of every Member of this House. There is no need to dilate in this matter. Let us form vigilance squads and sit in every department and scrutinize the expenditure" (*OLA Debates*, Vol. IV (6), 25.2.59; 28-9).

On the functioning of welfare State, he said, "The question, therefore, comes in Welfare State-what should be our attitude, how should we frame our laws, so that the man to whom we have given the funds from time to time, knowing him to be poor, knowing him that he is unable to pay it in due course, what should be attitude of the Government, whether of this side today or of that side tomorrow, what should be the democratic thinking in a Welfare State" (*OLA Debates*, Vol. III (3), 23.8.62; 16).

On the question of Muslim personal law, Biju Patnaik was highly critical of the *Nikaah* system and the Muslim divorce system. He said, "Muslims are not angels. It is not a caste. What is a Muslim law? Muslim law *nikaah, nikaah, nikaah*! You take thousand wives. It is a degrading law. It has become personal law of few Mullahs. The Koran didn't do it. Mullahs have done it" (*OLA Debates*, Vol. XVI (4), 21.9.1994; 72).

On the issue of tribal women, he said, "to prevent atrocities, we thought a new idea of giving *Adivasi* women police powers, and I must tell you that this has started acting in salutary way, particularly in *adivasi* areas. The other day, I went to Nawarangpur. Five thousand women, I counted them, came and sat there in the meeting. That meeting was having 25,000 people. I asked, why have you all come? They told, we are going from here to break all the liquor manufacturing centers. Amazing awakening of women" (*OLA Debates*, Vol. XVI (4), 21.9.1994; 72).

On welfare, he said, "It was written in the posters with photos of Chief Ministér and Prime Minister that give vote to Indira Gandhi for the welfare of the Tribes and Scheduled Castes. There is no Congress except Indira Gandhi. Have you got the courage to deny this? I am asking what is the meaning of the tribal and scheduled castes welfare. Does giving wages of ₹2 to 5 during vote time means welfare? Giving 2 acres of land does not mean welfare. I can show you with proof that without infrastructure there is no welfare" (*OLA Debates*, Vol. I (2), 25.3.1974; 46).

Labour Welfare

Speaking on the welfare of labour and Trade Union, he said, "I have been connected with the labour more intimately than all the Members that have spoken today. Sir, I have a general grouse on all sides towards the labour. First because that is more prime necessity for the industry. I must refer to it and elaborate it later on that the Trade Union movement in this State and in fact many other States have not yet reached that state of responsibilities for which this movement has not got the status it has got all over the world. Our Trade Union movements in this State, like our industries in this State are very young and inexperienced. Although some of the speakers wanted to remove the political colours from the Trade Union movement we must admit that so far, they have used these Union more or less to advance their own political ends and not so much for the cause of the labour. Today in this democratic age in our country, the labour does play an important role and would continue to play even more important role. Therefore, there is scramble by various political parties in this State and in other States to get hold of these Unions and in that process, I think, the first mistakes are made when the political parties get hold of these Unions. At the same moment, the whole attitude of trade unionism is vitiated, because at that moment, the only important factor that remains in the minds of the leaders is primarily that this Trade Union or that Trade Union should not get out of their hands. Therefore, Sir, I must submit that is the cardinal error in proper health growth of trade unionism and admittedly political leaders who wish to control are aware of the strength of the Trade Union movement. No doubt, this is the history of the growth of Trade Union movement all over the world. But, when it comes to the question whether they can maintain the growth of trade unionism and maintain their political requirements, the trouble begins. I would humbly submit that let Trade Union in this State, like other States, grow, be allowed to grow with responsibilities. Trade Unions have distinct functions of productivity, of improved efficiency, improved methods of production, as well as, protecting the rights of the workers, who are the important part of the industries. When my previous speaker, here accused the Government of suppression, may I also put at this doors, that it leads to conditions which calls for suppression. May I also lead to his doors the accusations that because he wishes to manage his political requirements to the requirements of the Trade Union, he does create conditions which demand suppression? It must be very clear from that a healthy Trade Union growing on proper Trade Union lines cannot be suppressed. No Government in the world has the right to suppress the legitimate demand and growth of a proper Trade Unions unstinted by political requirements. But Sir, the very moment such colour is given to it at the same moment comes the necessity of suppression and comes the necessity of all the bitterness that goes with it. By saying this Sir, I do not absolve the Government machinery from the great responsibility which they must shoulder in advocating and nourishing proper growth of Trade Unions in this State. In this connection, Sir, I strongly object that the Minister of Labour is absent from the House and he is not here. He may be called" (*OLA Debates*, Vol. IV (31), Part II, 29.4.59; 28-9). To this Hon'ble Member Dinabandhu Sahu replied. "The Minister for Labour has entrusted me to note down the points". Biju Patnaik said, "It is not a question of noting down the points. He must be present in the House to know the sense of the House. I submit that the Labour Minister should come to the House. In this connection, we are also prone to dub this movement, politically we are prone to suppress, we are prone to take the labour task. I must also submit that equal to the labour movement in the industries, our labour department is similarly young and inexperienced" (*ibid)*. Hon'ble Member Dinabandhu Sahu said, "The Labour Minister is young and inexperienced". Biju Patnaik then said, "That is true for all of us in this House. Sir, I will give one isolated case. A labouer working in an industry gets certain amount of provident fund. Certain contribution by the employer and certain contribution by the worker are deposited. In my knowledge, over the last four years, the provident fund has been formed and not a single employee in any employer which has over ten thousand

and has yet got any benefit from the Provident Fund Commissioner. They have not got any answer from the Provident Fund Commissioner. I think Sir, this really very depressing that such a Department of Government which is supposed to function for the benefit of the workers does not be so in the interest of the workers. The workers are entitled to take advance from this fund, but not a single worker has got it. When a worker died, his dependents went on breaking their heads in the Department of Provident Fund Commissioner, but no satisfactory answer has been received. I hope the Labour Minister should look into these matters. At present hundreds of workers are coming to me for an advance from the provident fund deposits. This is only an instance from which the inexperienced and the inaptitude of this Department can be illustrated. Behind this odd, Sir, is the basic fundamental fact that in this country, in the socialistic set-up that we have today in this country, we do look upon our labour as something inferior. When we analyse our own minds, thus one fact comes clearly before us that any workers whether he is in the field or in the factory, whether he is a domestic servant or a public servant, no worker comes under the category of somebody inferior. This is in our mental set-up and from this mental set-up, begins all the evils. While we from our Congress platform have declared that ours shall be a socialist State. It begins with the premises that worker is the most important citizen of the State. The worker either in the field or in the factory produces wealth and is by far the most important citizen of the State. That is what we have declared from the highest party platform in this country and yet the inertia of our social system, like caste system, like the religious system, and so many other systems. Inspite of all the provisions, a worker remains something like a *coolie*. From this set-up of mind, come all our troubles. We have a Labour Department which is manned by people like us, our colleagues, by people from our State, in whose mind the idea is fixed that it must be the labour which is wrong. Unless we change this attitude of mind, we cannot help the worker or improve the factory or the administration of the State because in the ultimate analysis the prosperity of the administration depends on the productivity and efficiency of our workers. Unless we change our whole attitude towards the well-being of the workers, training of the workers, education of the workers, building the health of the workers, by which we can improve the productivity of the country and no State administration, can prosper with improvement in the production. Therefore, Sir, would humbly request to the political parties and leaders to cease the use of the Trade Union as political machine to justify their own existence. I would also request the Government Department which deals with labour to be much more vigorous than they are today. The employer has nothing to do with the relationship between the labour and the State. Employer is only an instrument a means of production. Very soon, I hope, long before our friends in the socialist party think possible, the instrument of production will be taken from the individual hands. I do sincerely hope that when it is done and in no distant future it shall be done then relationship will remain directly between the State and the worker. Therefore, the administrative machinery should be prepared from today to plan and lay down the foundation to enable a nealthy growth of this relationship so that people will understand what is production and the labour should also understand what is their relationship. They do understand what is quality, they do understand their own responsibilities and they do take pride in their work. Sir, coming back to our administrative affairs, I am surprised to note that the Minister in-charge while intervening to my previous speaker said that it is not his business to look after the workers of Hirakud or in the mines. It is the business of the Central Government. I thoroughly and whole-heartedly disagree with him. Any labour question within the boundary of the State is the responsibility of the State concerned. Whether the instrument of production belongs to A, B, C category or individual private firm or the Central Government is not their concern. The State is concerned with the workers working within the boundary of the State, they are taken care of, are given their dues, are looked after as the Act provides and there are no two opinions on this. If he thinks just because mines, Hirakud, Rourkela, etc., are the property rights vested to the Central Government and he is not responsible towards the workers. I would humbly submit that he should very quickly his reviews on this. The instrument of production may remain in any hand, but as long as the production remains within the boundary of the State, the workers become his direct responsibility. Therefore, any dispute that leads to break down of production machinery, he must take cognizance of. The first necessity in any dispute is to see that production does not suffer. The labour machine should be so geared that before they could force down the growing of the dispute, they should be able to judge well ahead that disputes are likely to arise and they should solve the dispute before it explores and even if it explores they should see that it is set right within 24 hours of its explosion. After that if the production continues to hamper in any field of industries, then only comes the question of conciliation, tribunal or various other things and if I may add so various inadequate and ill-typed machineries which are badly in need of replacement by setting up new apparatus. But the moment these disputes take place and production suffers; it becomes the immediate responsibility of the Labour Department to see that production is resumed by any method. If the law is unreasonable and if the leaders of the Trade Union are reasonable, they should explain it to the people. If the employers are unreasonable, I humbly submit. Then again, Sir, on the question of labour benefits, we have in this country in the Central Government made tremendous legislations. These legislations are run into thousands of items. I wonder whether these legislations are made the spirit under which legislations are made, whether they ever thought of giving it any practical shape. Under these legislations, the workers are supposed to live in paradise. But while these legislations are made the necessary resources required to make such legislations effective are not simultaneously looked into. The result is that most of these legislations remain paper legislations. A worker should have a house, should have a minimum standard if requirements, should have schools, hospitals, time for cultural growth, etc., are provided in the legislations. But if I ask the Labour Department, can you build house for a thousand workers, the answer is we have no funds. I do not understand why these legislations are formed without providing resources for it. It is true. I do feel and cent per cent agree with my previous speaker that most of our labours in our mines are living in inhuman conditions. In fact, it is a constant surprise to me that these poor people do not revolt and cut throat of every official. Every time I am seeing that. The Government must work hand in hand for these things. I always wonder why there has been not sufficient agitation to draw Government minds towards this fact. Whenever Government has planned to carry out these projects of housing schemes, the labour leaders have not participated in these nor have they focused the attention of the Government on the urgent requirement of the houses. They have created difficulties, they have created conditions, as I have said before, which lead to put obstacles in settlement. But I have not yet seen the labour leaders sit with the Heads of the Government and ensure that the minimum conditions of the labour are fulfilled. I would humbly request again to the political leaders who have so far made use of the Union to sit with the Government agencies and the Government parties and evolve a formula by which the workers in the mines can be provided with houses, school for children, hospitals, drinking water, electricity, etc. I have not yet seen any demand and I do challenge my previous speaker to produce before me any demand he has pursued and substantiated for the basic needs of the workers. Therefore, summing up the whole thing, I would suggest again that let us get away from the attitude of the mind that the workers who shall ultimately be the producers of wealth of the country be treated as something fairly. Let us begin to treat them and begin to build them as equal partners for the development of the country. When that old caste system from our minds vanishes and all of us, including Government parties, public men, employers, leaders, et, change the way of thinking then only something can be done for the well-being of the workers and producers, which alone would lead the country into prosperity and lessen the bitterness and attacks and counter-attacks" (*OLA Debates*, Vol. IV (31), Part II, 29.4.59; 29-32).

Discussing on the problem of labour and the facilities provided to them, he said, "I would like to emphasize on this because I have got special knowledge about this and apart from that I have seen in other countries of the world what they are doing. They have laid emphasis firstly on educational training, secondly on teachers and designers and thirdly on workers. In this country where it is a state enterprise or a private enterprise, our workers are still thought of managers and the topmost men as nothing but *coolies*. Really, I am very much ashamed to say so. But now things are being changed partly by workers themselves and partly by planning. Sir, here I would give one wonderful example what is done by Germany by Messers Krupps and Demag, the expert producer of steel. They have found out the secret of production of steel. The first factory they established with some workers and the workers also knew that secret. They planned a basis by which these workers became the producers of steel. Today the Krupps have made a pension scheme in which they are giving pensions to their workers much more than what our Union Government are giving to their highest paid officials. Immediately after the war, the first thing they did was that they gave six crores of rupees as arrears of pension to their workers who had not worked for five years during the war. The facilities with regard to Provident Fund and housing which the workers of the Krupps organization are enjoying can in no way be compared with the facilities that are afforded to the workers of any of the best factories of Bombay and Calcutta. The disparity is abominable" (*OLA Debates*, Vol. VIII (31), 7.4.56; 57-8). Speaking further on the labour issue, he said, "Whatever plans are being made for labour development, we must give fundamental rights, like right to work, right of training, right to strive peacefully, right to manage, right to organize, etc. Then only the plans will be successful for them. If the labourers are not given fundamental rights, then the plans meant for them will not be successful. For this, the plans need to be changed thoroughly. Otherwise, equality and development cannot be established in the country. The way plans are prepared if any fact is placed before Magistrate of Government official, then they suspect the worker. In this relation, I am reminded of a constituency where the labourers were not paid for their labour done in a road in 1953/54 (*ibid*; 65).

He was of the opinion that we must have compulsory labour programmes for all citizens, and said, "One very important thing that was discussed in the Planning Sub-Committee of the All-India Congress Committee (AICC) that every able-bodied man and woman in this country, whether hi is rich or poor, whether he is a Maharaja or beggar, it does not matter, must give so many days labour for increasing the assets of this country. If this is called regimentation or subjugation of our type of democracy, it does not matter it is being discussed at higher level. We do not have the resources, we do not have the money to pay, but we have the man-power. How to use this man-power for improving the condition prevailing in the country. This can become the law of the land by general agreement in the Parliament and in the State Legislatures that every able-bodied man or woman shall give one month's work in a year for acquiring new assets for the country, for development, for giving employments to others. We shall have to do it. If we do not work at top most speed then within five to ten years time that we will be faced with the worst type of revolution, which nobody can prevent. The Congress Government, both at the Centre and in the States, will have to face this problem and we attack them at their roots. That means we must have to work very hard to avoid this catastrophe and properly manage our affairs. Therefore, I would once again request that let us not fight over minor issues.... We have to make a great sacrifice and then we can benefit the people and can build up ma nation of which we may be proud" (*OLA Debates*, Vol. IV (6), 25.2.59; 30).

On the issue of engagement of contract labours and for their welfare with a wage policy, Biju Patnaik said, "I have been trying to operate on the whole canvass of the mines all over the country, which are under the purview of this Ministry. How to get these men a living wage, a home to live, education for their children and all the rest of the things? The organized sector is fleecing at the cost of the disorganized sector. Is it the sort of society which we want? I hope this House will utilize its mind to find way so that this scourge is eliminated for all times from the entire nation, from everywhere. I do not know what previous Government did. They claimed they removed bonded labour from the Adivasi area. But what we see now in the entire country is nothing but bonded labour. Contract labour is taken to tea gardens. From my State of Odisha they are taken to tea gardens of Assam as contract labour over a period of the last fifty years. In fact, it is through their blood and sweat that the tea gardens of Assam have been developed. Contract labour are taken even outside the country, all over the place. A reference was made to Section 10. A Committee has been set up on this question and it is going to submit its report next month, in September. But what is the use of that report? How do you implement it? How will you pay the wages? Where is the money to come from? All these things must be seriously debated in this House and a firm policy established if you want to give the smallest comfort to the poorest sections of the workers". He also expressed his anguish while saying this as there was very little number of Members present. "Nobody sits when such questions are raised. You can see the interest of the House; never mind the newsmen; this shows where we are. I am interested to know how many Members of Parliament are truly interested in this. All the empty shouting you will find in the headlines, because empty shouting interests the people. We are interested in heap popularity, not in any serious effort. That is why I am worried. I am grateful to Shri Vasant Sathe for having given me this opportunity to unload myself. You have to find out a machinery, a way, and we will implement it" (OLA; 41-3). This shows the commitment and sincerity of this dedicated leader towards the welfare of the labour class.

Educational Development

On the issue of technical education, he said, "We have just started few schools and colleges. Today, I would urge upon the Minister-in-Charge to think in terms of getting top class personnel from anywhere in the world for at least five to ten years to train up our boys. We can only prosper if we produce really good civil engineers, mechanical engineers, production engineers and so on. They must be, really best engineers in the country. Then only we will have better trained men to develop rapidly. We have to make a race with the States which are fifty to hundred years ahead. We are not getting good teachers from other States. They are only second or third-class Professors. We should get best people from Japan, or from America or any other place of the world to teach our boys for a period of ten years during which period our junior Professors can get training. Some days or other, States also paid heavy price for its development. We should not also mind for paying a little heavy price for our development" (*OLA Debates*, Vol. IV (15), Part II, 10.3.59; 30).

On the issue of maintaining autonomy of Universities and the process of democratic operation, he said, "Therefore, to make it operative and proper, it is my considered view that this Bill should go to a Select Committee for proper consideration clause by clause, keeping in view the practice of democratic operation of the Universities and the total autonomy of the Universities. Sir, the recognized Universities in the world have become great, because they are autonomous. Oxford University, Cambridge or Harvard University, whatever University you can mention, though they are autonomous they have produced great men and women. We should seek to produce excellence in the Universities but not to make them subordinates. But you have reduced the entire status of excellence to the level whatever level you want to have. Whatever is required for excellence and whatever is required to support the independence and the autonomy of the University, we should examine it carefully in this Legislature through a Select Committee and then try to find out a proper answer to this. Sending the Bill to a Select Committee is the only way to find out an answer" (*OLA Debates*, Vol. IX (23), 27.3.1989; 89). He also said on this autonomy and democratic tradition, "Government has authority to supersede him (Vice-Chancellor), supersede the University. It is the unanimous opinion of this House that you can recall the Vice-Chancellor because he happens to be an employee of the Government. Supersession I would like you to avoid, because when you set up an autonomous body, it is always painful to supersede it and does not help the situation. Because the way it is created, what that is required is to find an appropriate Vice-Chancellor and able Vice-Chancellor; even perhaps, senior most Officers of the Education Department wherever it is, can function as a Vice-Chancellor" (*OLA Debates*, Vol. V (18), 23.3.1987; 66).

On the issue of engineering study and providing employment, he said, "Out of this bunch of engineers, a man like Dr. Khosla was born. From this type of engineers, a great engineer, Dr. Bishesarayya was born...... Just now, I learnt that in Burla Engineering College, they have reduced the civil engineering seats. They have got sufficient engineers, but instead of producing employment for them, they have cut the seats. So they do not have the interest or they do not have the capacity to build the infrastructure for them" (*OLA Debates*, Vol. IX (29), 4.4.1989; 59).

On the development of the Education Department, and more relevantly in the context of what is happening in 5T intervention in the present times in the schools in Odisha, what Biju Patnaik said was was absolutely true. He said, "Take the case of Education Department. The problem of settling some teachers has been found to be very very difficult for them. What about the Education system? What about modernizing the education? What about technology from Class I onwards? How will you change the teachers and students and create a new environment? These are vast problems. Would this Government tackle them? Have they got the capacity to tackle them?" (*OLA Debates*, Vol. II (24), 10.7.1974; 109).

While discussing on the educational development in the state during his period of governance, increasing the number of colleges to 92, establishing 2 new Universities apart from Utkal University, he said, "since then, education in this state has not only been stagnant qualitatively and quantitatively, it is also deteriorating proportionately to the population increase in the state" (*OLA Debates*, Vol. III (11), 20.12.74; 76). He cited the instance of teachers' agitation over certain demands that were fulfilled today by amendments. With this, he opined, "that people have got an impression in the state that this government is not only lethargic, it is not even sensitive to the people's requirements and tries to impose its will at all time on the people in a most undemocratic fashion, resulting in a resistance that is being built up against the government, especially against the party which is leading the government" (*ibid*).

Speaking on the tribe education, he said, "The only problem with the tribes is to de-tribe them" (*OLA Debates*, Vol. III (11), 20.12.74; 79). This by taking the tribal children from the age-group of 5, and putting them in separate school till the post-graduation level, in universities – one each in Mayurbhanj, western Odisha, and in Koraput. "In two decades, you will see there will be no *Adivasis*. That is the manner by which you modernize education" (*ibid*).

Prohibition

On prohibition and revenue source, he said, "Sir, I also fully agree with the Raja Bahadur of Khallikote, friend of mine that prohibition should be scrapped. I and Raja Bahadur of Khallikote are a company of persons who proclaim that prohibition should be scrapped. I have the courage and conviction to feel that the provision made in the Constitution in this regard is wrong and outmoded. If any of my friends is of the opinion that it was in the Congress manifesto, I admit that it is a mistake which is not beyond correction. This has been tried in various other countries and has failed. It may be a social stigma. Let us not make a law to regulate it. Let the people drink. But unless they themselves realize that it is social stigma, whatever legislation is there, it would not have any effect on the people. Let the social reformers work in this direction. I would request the Chief Minister to consider this matter. By adopting this prohibition we are simply losing nearly two crores of rupees as revenue, but the people are doing as they were before" (*OLA Debates*, 1957; 26).

On the control of production of liquor, he said, "One Hon'ble Member mentioned that the Excise Minister had made some discrepancies in his statement, when he said that the control over production will be control over consumption of liquor. I as Chairman of the Board of Directors in the Aska Distillery know from my experience that control of production means control of the quality of production. If you go through some of the town of Madras and Bombay, where they have prohibited production of liquor and consumption of it, there some people are reported to have gone mad by drinking home-made stuff which is not scientifically or chemically made. Therefore, it almost amounts to poison. It is one thing to exercise complete prohibition and it is another, to stop the human instinct from going through all the disadvantages of producing bad type of liquor. Therefore, when the Hon'ble Minister for Excise mentioned control of production, he meant control of quality of production, with which I agree. If we produce liquor in the country, we must produce the best quality that we can, so that the people who insist on drinking should at least get proper liquor and not poison" (*OLA Debates*, Vol. XII (24), 30.3.50; 1282).

Reservation

On the issue of reservation and the Scheduled Castes (SC) and Scheduled Tribes (ST), he said, "I had tried to bring to this House the importance of undoing the mischief that has been perpetrated against those people whom we call Scheduled Castes and Scheduled Tribes for over five thousand years. This social stigma is not easy to remove; it has gone down into the blood of the system-he is tribal, he is *harijan*, he is *sabarna*, he is brahmin, he is *karan*, etc. All are individual sects, just like Hindu society has been divided into 2700 sects, just like the *harijans* and tribes have various sect among them. For this all the tribes and *harijans* are now being club-up. There are many divisions among the *harijans*. Just like the Hindus have divisions, tribes and *harijans* also have the same. By and large, when we are making legislation with objectives, those steps are faulty steps. Some of us who have been educated since the British period and belong to brahmin, *karan* castes, got good positions in the society. But the real fact is, these people, are unwilling to leave their place. The Government will say a person does not have merit for any job; he is not fit for any promotion; we had advertised, but suitable candidates were not available, etc. Earlier this was not the situation in India. When there was the Constituent Assembly, we had thought that even though not in ten years, by twenty years, all these people will come up; and this reservation will not be required. This was the thought then. Now we are in fifth decade of reservation, but there is no sign of development of these people, how many have become MLA, Minister, and officer. Once a person becomes MLA, he stays here and gives speeches, but does not go to his area and mixes with his community people. They have already become declassed, what is called in tribal language as *diku*. That means they do not belong to the society anymore. For that reason, last session, I had said, if we can make two Universities with fifty thousand students-like Moscow University-when it started first, it enrolled students from different States to create a different system of people, altogether for three to five years, boys and girls were admitted and educated upto Post-Graduate, to be away from their social environment. Like that, if this Government is prepared to consider this matter to open two Universities, one in Mayurbhanj and another in Koraput to create fifty thousand children from one University, then in three generations, you will have no *Adivasi-Harijan* problems and with whatever civilized human beings of the top most level people, he can complete with any *Sabarna*, let it be brahmin, *karan*, etc. Without this, whatever we are doing, it is a begging question. But the House should consider seriously how to de-tribe them; how to de-scheduled caste them; for which education is the only way, but nothing else, to bring them together to the mainstream of the social structure. It is the only answer and I hope the House will consider that and I am sure, Government of India will play the game with us. And because we are heavily populated with *Advasisi and harijans*-nearly 40 per cent of the population-and I am sure the machinery of the Government of India will go the whole hog with us to create two more Universities, one for boys and one for girls, or one for *Adivasis* and one for *harijans* and I think the House will consider this" (*OLA Debates*, 2.4.1986; 110-11).

Favouring women reservation, and during the discussion on the Eighty-first Constitution Amendment Bill (Insertion of Art. 330A & 332A) on 12th September 1996, Biju Patnaik said, "We started the reservation of women. When I was in the Government of Odisha in 1991, at the Panchayati Raj level, long before this Parliament passed this Bill, we have had it established. There, we had given one-third proportion to the women. What I want to tell you is that.... Wherefrom you will get woman candidate, they will not come forward. You will not get women leaders. The moment reservation was made, there was a parade of women claiming to be there, right from the bottom level. There were 100 women contesting for one seat. That was my experience. When I called a Panchayati Raj Conference in Bhubaneswar there came 27,000 women who were all elected representatives. There were representatives from Panchayats, Nagarpallikas, Members and Vice-Chairman, etc. All of them, some 27.000 women, came. So, there will not be any dearth of women representatives once we have the system as we are proposing to do in this Bill. The other thing is that it is true that only a few ladies are getting elected here on their own strength. By and large, ladies are not being encouraged by men. They talk of male chauvinism or whatever you call it, it is there. Unless there is reservation for them, they will never come up. Since there is reservation for Scheduled Castes and Scheduled Tribes, they have come up. There are hundreds of Scheduled Castes and Schedules Tribes in Parliament, in the Legislatures, in the Cabinet and everywhere. Therefore, they must have an opportunity to come to Parliament, to the Rajya Sabha. There are difficulties as to how you will elect Members to Rajya Sabha.....So I would suggest, Mr. Chairman, if we have the requisite numbers, let us pass the Bill today. I think the Chair should give a call to everyone to be present here. Then only you can pass the Bill. Otherwise, you cannot pass this Bill" (*Lok Sabha Debates*, 12.9.96; 531-2). Biju Patnaik strongly favoured women representation in representative institutions. He started the policy of 33 per cent reservations for women in panchayati raj institutions in Odisha. He understood that the social fabric is such that women had to be given assertive legislative provisions in order to overcome the male dominance.

Social Justice

On the issue of social justice, Biju Patnaik said, "We are against slavery; we are against so many things like ill-treatment of *harijans*. We are against these have been borne out by facts. A few things have happened, unfortunately. Nobody supports it this Government least of all. The entire power and authority of this Government goes behind the down-trodden and the *Harijans*. We have said that. But in the implementation by the police administration that you ran, because of the police morality that you created during the Emergency, the hangover is still there. It will take time to control, direct and train them. If the people have suffered for 30 years, my friend, will they not suffer us? They will bear with us for atleast30 years more. So, you need not worry about that" (*Lok Sabha Debates*, 10 May 1978; 393).

On a very substantial debate of 'ism', Biju Patnaik said, "Therefore, this commitment to 'ism' is something which you must move out of and the only 'ism' should be what is good for the country and pragmation should be the only 'ism' that we should adopt. I do not subscribe to the view of some of my friends that 'ism' pervades everything. I have therefore decided, as a matter of policy and I have instructed my Ministry to clear this cobweb of little fellows with ten acres, twenty acres, and thirty acres. There is something called peoples sector or national sector, where they do not make a great deal of money. They are not capitalists, they are not monopolists, and what is more important is that these thousands of little fellows can provide employment to ten twenty or thirty thousand people which is very important for the country today. I am telling the House very clearly that as far as public sector is concerned, large areas like manganese, chrome or whatever it is, and iron-ore, shall be reserved for the public sector, but little things must be released fully. There is such a thing called peoples' effort which must not be smothered in a policy which is not workable" (*Lok Sabha Debates*, 28 June 1977; 284).

On the welfare and social justice issues and matter of Ministers putting pressure on the Collectors not to take action against hoarders, Biju Patnaik said, "This is the moral human weakness reflected in the political apparatus of a democratic set-up but whichever party be the Government, they must rise above these things, otherwise it causes failure. The question, therefore, is we have in our country advocated that the bare necessities of life must be supplied to the poorer section and the weaker section at concessional rate and rice must be supplied to them at ₹1 per kilogram. It was not a lose statement, it was the minimum philosophy of any social justice of any Government which want to put up a welfare state, not a question which is something to be thrown about. The philosophy is simple. We have said two things. The minimum wage in Odisha, whether one is working in land or in factory or anywhere else must be paid ₹3.25 a day and rice that will be given to the poorer section, the weaker section at ₹1 a kilogram so that a man getting ₹3.25 will get 3.25 kg of rice per day. That is the minimum need of the poorest section of the society. We, the legislators get certain allowance, we want to increase our allowance because the rise in prices pinch us, but we have not yet brought about this minimum social justice. From the point of view of social justice, I want to ask the Supply Minister and the Government as a whole, can you or can you not provide job to the backward people, the under privileged people and the workless multitude at 3.25 or not and one kilogram of rice per rupee to let them live atleast the life of a human being. Therefore, I submit that, all of us, whether on this side or that side. I submit to the House collectively that I am really ashamed on your behalf and on my behalf. If I were the Government, I could have taken the House into confidence and work out a system by which the minimum social justice to the poorer and weaker section of the society could be assured without whichyou see the specter of death, malnutrition or starvation or whatever you may call it, which bring about a general reduction in their vitality and which is going on all over the country at an accelerated pace. My friends in the CPI benches have gone round the whole State some time ago with the slogan, *chaula kilo tankaye ne hele Nandini Sarkar ku nikali debu* (If rice is not ₹1 per kilo, Nandini government will be ousted). We do not say to *oust*, we want to say that we are behind the theory of the same social justice, the same theory that the weaker section of people should get one kilo rice per rupee.... You call yourself Socialist and yet you are not prepared to build the instrument of social justice. Socialism is not a slogan; it has to be translated into action for the benefit of the backward people. That is not only the duty of the Government, more so your professed policy which needs to be implemented" (Vol. II(10), 1974; 127-8).

On the two-price system hindering social justice, Biju Patnaik said, "The Congress Government at Delhi introduced two-price system on wheat, sugar for various reasons. It is known to them and also to us. This two-price system of some commodities has been introduced not to give social justice to the people, but to raise political funds" (Vol. II(10), 1974; 130).

Corruption

On corruption, he said, "The Leader of the *Gantantra* party has said that at one time there was corruption at the top. Let us think less of corruption but think more of efficiency. Swami Vivekananda said that when we build the new India, he would rather have strong and wicked men than hundreds of good and weak men. I think that holds good even today. If a corrupt person would deliver goods for the benefit of the State, then I would say that he would be preferred to hundreds of good persons who do no good to the country. There is nothing wrong in it" (*OLA Debates*, 1957; 26).

On the issue of corruption and the colonial administration, he said, "There is tremendous amount of corruption in our State. Corruption is nothing new. Sir, corruption started in the Garden of Eden with Adam and Eve. But in public administration and public finances corruption is eliminated to some extent as the target has progressed. Corruption is nothing but leakage. If the money is not leaking out then you achieve your target alright. Sir, this system which we employ today in our administration developed as a colonial system of administration. This system is the legacy of a colonial system of administration. This system is the legacy of a colonial power, who administered a country from five thousand miles away; it was a system which was based on mistrust. Therefore, it is a system which has hundred checks and balances. The result is that we are intensely suffering in our achievements or targets. The operation of this system of checks and balances brings about the operation of *Perkinson's law*. Therefore, it would perhaps be wiser that we should trust our administrative machinery. It is likely that we may lose ₹500 in a scheme which is estimated to cost ₹1,000;

it is likely that we may lose the entire money in leakage. Because instead of doing a thing ourselves we are employing so many people on whom we may or may not have trust. Then shall we do away this system of administration here and now? This again is a matter to which the whole House must apply its mind in full detail" (*OLA Debates*, Vol. III (11), 5.9.62; 45-6).

On the allegations of corruption against him and CAG and its audit, he said, "The Comptroller and Auditor General of India is a statutory body on audit and no one can influence the Auditor-General of India. They are free agents and they have Constitutional responsibility and they are protected by the Constitution. One may differ from them, but one cannot influence them. The Leader of the Opposition who happens to be the Chairman of the Public Accounts Committee as well as many other Members of this House and of the Parliament belonging to the Opposition took up the matter outside the House and insisted on a separate agency to deal with it and managed to create a great deal of noise outside, in the Parliament.... We have a got a special body called the Public Accounts Committee who do their work traditionally year after year without any outside influence" (*OLA Debates*, Vol. III (6), 29.9.1965; 25). He said that the present Leader of the Opposition, Rajendra Narayan Singhdeo, who was the Finance Minister during 1959-60, and 1960-61, had 91,601 and 27,184 audit objections in the respective Audit Reports (*OLA Debates*, Vol. III (6), 28.9.1965; 20).

On the subject of political corruption, and allegations and counter-allegations of political orruption, he suggested, "These people are politically corrupt of the worst order that this country an ever think of. We have written to the Government of India, to the Home Minister of India; we have urged upon him that the People's Representation Act should be amended. One of the worst type of political corruption, as it is, which is visible in the country today is that spurious charges of all kinds are leveled against the men in authority, and against which even the Judges of the Supreme Court have expressed strictures saying that this is on the rise. Hon'ble Justice Mr. Gajendra Gadkar, the Chief Justice of India, in a judgment has said that it is on the rise now and most of them and sometimes all of them are found to be false. He has given this opinion in his judgment. Therefore, I say that this rotten type of political corruption must be stopped. How can it be stopped? We have suggested that the People's Representation Act should be amended. We have suggested that the Election Commissioner should be given the power of a Commission and if such charges are leveled against the men in authority and are not proved by the Members, may be of the Parliament or of the State Legislatures; they should suffer and come under the mischief of the law. If the charges are proved, the Ministers should be politically assassinated. Therefore, I would ask, Sir, why some of the Assembly and Parliament Members belonging to the Opposition have signed this petition in great gusto? I am sure, most of them do not know what is in it and the Leader of the Opposition on their behalf has given the assurance-no other person has given the assurance; he alone has done it on his behalf-that all of them would go to swear affidavits for disenfranchisement before the Commission. ...Just now a news comes which almost breaks my heart on their behalf, because Prime Minister has made a statement in the Rajya Sabha that the Odisha Chief Minister Shri Biren Mitra will continue in Office. How unfortunate it is for them? Because about charges against Mr. Mitra, Mr. Shashtri said, as yet he has not come to the conclusion that there is *prima facie* case against him. On behalf of my party and my leader and the Ministers whose permission I have sought, I request today the Prime Minister of India to forget about these enquires and appoint a Commission provided all the gentlemen sign an affidavit... that if the Ministers pass the test of these terms, those Members who have leveled charges should be disqualified for six years by the Assembly and the Parliament" (*OLA Debates*, Vol. VI (55), 22.9.1964; 42-3).

On the position of the politicians in society, Biju Patnaik said, "Somehow, we the politicians here inside the House and outside the House have been dubbed collectively by the people as a dishonest lot. Let us be clear about ourselves. We may wax eloquent; whatever we may say, but for the average man, we are a dishonest lot. Sir, when we fought for the nation's freedom. I remember, in 1940-42, we were young people, aged 22, 23 or 25 years. A lot of people were shot dead. My own brother was shot dead. We have gone through all that. But at that time, when we came out of the British prison after three years, people looked at us with respect. If I walk down the street in my town, the people just walk aside with respect and bow to me. Today it is different. We are responsible for anything that happens because we, the politicians, are decrying each other. We are trying to pull down each other" (OLA; 180). He continued to say about the international perspective of corrupt politicians being booked by Judiciary, "whether it is former Prime Minister who had landed himself in prison for five years for misdeeds or whether the former Korean President who landed himself in prison for seven years for misdeeds, impeached by the Supreme Court, all went to prison because of the Supreme Court. It happened in both countries. In Bangladesh also, General Ershad, the dictator had landed himself in prison again because of the Supreme Court. The question is-Does it adds to the stability or the honour or the dignity of the politician? How will we recover that dignity of the politician? How will you recover that dignity is a matter which we should discuss amongst ourselves quietly without making undue noises" (OLA; 181).

On election and funding, Biju Patnaik said, "election funds are the source of the greatest corruption in this country. Large sums collected by the Party in power or by other people, are spent in the elections. Those who say that this is a source of corruption in the country, I fully agree with them. I fully agree with Shri Jayaprakash Narayan on this point.... But it goes without saying that there is probably none who keeps within the limit of the expenses provided in the Act... Similarly, the Government in power would have the tendency to use its authority which indeed goes against the Representation of People's Act" (*OLA Debates*, Vol. II, (15), 27.6.74; 109). He said, "I am saying there is no bar to Ministers working as party-men but not as Ministers of the Government" (*OLA Debates*, Vol. II (15), 27.6.74; 110). He further elaborated, and said, "Minister must go on discharging Government work; but while going on tour in Government work, he should not engage himself in election propaganda, attending public meetings and delivering election speeches and doing other party work. I do not say Ministers are not entitled to do party work, election work. As party men, they are entitled to do that, but when they go in Government work, they should not do party work, attend public meetings and doing election propaganda for their party" (*OLA Debates*, Vol. II (15), 27.6.74; 119).

On the government implementation of development programmes, he said, "We have no doubt, the Chief Minister says the Government, must have the will, but have they got the apparatus to deal with it? You talk so much about rural development. I will just tell you one thing-a very small thing-where a very able economist said, 'if these development plans were stopped-the rural development plans-I think the poor people would be better off'. If this is stopped, they will be better off. There is so much corruption at all levels between the contractors, and the middle-men. Before the Government sanctions money by the Legislature or the Parliament, it should reach the poorest man. It is better to use money for structural development. In structural development, there will be a flow-back into the poor people. Supposing, we have massive education system; instead of spending 100 crores, here you put up schools for compulsory education, or a hospital building, etc., you will be more benefitted by this. This is total wishful expenditure; it is a very unfortunate thing. But it is a good thing that the Government of India in the Planning Commission-I understand-are seriously contemplating taking over this expenditure under their way, that it will be Central Government sponsored, and Central Government administered projects" (*OLA Debates*, Vol. I, 25.7.1985; 90).

On the Plan preparation by Officials, he said, "I find that the Community Development Department, Mr. Chief Minister, you have decided that the officials will do the planning, only officials. And they will put it up to the DRDA (District Rural Development Agency) or whatever you call it. Planning Commission makes the Plan or the officers prepare the Plan for the whole State? Even if it goes to the rural areas, it is the officers who plan-as you have said it, your Minister has said so-and it will be approved by the Committees, which is headed by the Collector. This is what he says. Rural community development should play a major role in framing their development projects, where he says that the village is a face-to-face area. So here we have abstracted, we prepare a Plan, it goes to Finance Department, so on and so on. But all is on paper. But the poor chap, he is nowhere in the picture we have just created an apparatus, Panchayat, etc., but we have not given the final key and that is what he says that there are flaws in the rural life. Yes, they have the flaws. Is the administrative system of India 'clean'? What the Prime Minister said that there is corruption at the upper level, but at the lower level, there is total corruption, and I understand that some honest people around the Prime Minister have very competently analysed this. But here they insist that there is no corruption.... Because, it is this corruption which grows social imbalance, and in that it makes the poor poorer. That is why, you say in the Janata Government, we did not do anything at all, so and so. The price was constant in the times of Janata Government.... Now for example, Mr. Chief Minister, you projected a plan of 5088 crores and you have cut down to 2700 crores in various vital areas your planning has been slashed. So, it is not that your planning is better. So, we have to make do with this little plan. We have to make do with resources; we have to make do even if the plan is reduced. So, this is a very difficult situation. Nothing, nothing, nothing. I do not blame anything of this sort. All I request is, it is not necessary to defend the indefensible situation (*interruptions*). Do not give wrong facts and figures. From 5000 and odd crores, we have come to 2700 crores. This is obvious that your total planning has been thrown overboard. It is a total picture; you have suddenly come down to half of your figure. There is therefore hardly any planning worth the name. So we have to make do with what we have. But in the process, let us tighten our administration; let us stop the corruption at all levels and let us see every rupee that we have goes truly for the benefit of the poorest" (*OLA Debates*, Vol. I, 25.7.1985; 90-1).

On the issue of corruption, he said, "The corruption of Rajiv Gandhi on whom the cloud of corruption is black. It is as black as it can be. I do not say. The whole country says. In Haryana, he lost; in Tamil Nadu, he lost; everywhere he lost......The same also is the case of Bofors and submarines. Mr. Arjun Singh one of your leaders, resigned for Churhat lottery scandal. We have not asked him to resign. Your Prime Minister has asked him to resign. You are a great supporter of Arjun Singh and he is also a great supporter of yours" (*OLA Debates*, Vol. IX (2), 22.2.1989; 99).

On the high handedness and corrupt practices of the vested interest in the society, he said, "Unfortunately, as in this country, perhaps in many other countries, the same thing happens that the vested interests the powerful and influential people always give help to the process and police officers in these areas and get the better out of it. Result is that poor always suffers, whether it is poor by caste or by profession or generally poor. Poor always suffers in the hands of the rich, land-lord or moneyed persons in one side and on the other side because they have a habit of corrupting all the officers. Perhaps this practice has been running from the British days. Unfortunately, that is the position today" (*OLA Debates*, Vol. II (6), 7.6.1990; 193).

On the controversial statement of Biju Patnaik to the public to beat the corrupt officials, Biju Patnaik clarified, "I was only voicing the will of the people. Sir, I will request the opposition to go anywhere they like and ask the people, 'what Biju Patnaik says, will you agree with him'? I think all will raise his hands. Sir, I only say the voice and will of the people. I have ensured that before taking the law into their own hands, people have to send telegrams to me. I must admit that people are maintaining that discipline. I have so far received 300 telegrams and letters from different parts of the State. All of them have been accepted. I am sure that the people would not take direct action without any prior concurrence. I would like to inform the House that I have not given prior concurrence to anyone. A High-powered Officer is going to investigate immediately with the case after case and report to me directly for necessary action. I think, some kind of control, however minimal, is visible in the State administration" (*OLA Debates*, Vol. IV (3), 21.2.1991; 169). He also said, "I have told only to put fearlessness in the minds of ordinary oppressed and poor people and told you have a right, you are a citizen of this country, you have a right to revolt against corruption, against injustice, you have a right. Therefore, they revolt against corruptions, but bring it to my notice. Don't take law into your own hands. I have a squad of officers. They will investigate and punish. Don't generalize my dear friend. Keep quiet Mr. Biswal" (*OLA Debates*, Vol. IV (16), 14.3.1991; 93).

On the development of Odisha State and curbing corruption, he said, "What is required for a backward State like Odisha is that the State must grow, nothing should be done to whittle or belittle the interest of the State. Now here a piece of legislation which has been brought by the Chief Minister, Member-in-Charge, why he is not in the House I do not know. He should have been here, unfortunately he is not there. What weighed to bring it to the House? At that time, the present Deputy Chief Minister was the Member of the Opposition. It was unanimously passed at that time which has been converted to Special Court Act. Why was it necessary to repeal? This has been brought only to prevent men in high places who have been indicated on corruption, to prevent them suffering the punishments that the court would give as it has been done in case of one official, large fine, three years in prison. Is it only to prevent something happening to high offices? There seems to be no other reason whatsoever. You have made it a weaker thing. From the High Court Judge you made it District Judge. From confiscation you have converted it to attachment. Why are you doing it? Are you upholding the dignity of corruption or abolition of corruption? Do not forget that what you do here today will be spread to the nook and corner of the State.... I have sold my house in Delhi to finance for the election in my State. The Hon. Members know that.... Now the other wrong thing is you are trying to abolish the Panchayatiraj System. I am not sorry because you are only assisting me and my group, my Party. My whole lot here today is to throw you out of power as soon as election takes place. I have no doubt about it. I say let this bill be withdrawn and discuss it once again. You discuss with the Opposition... send it to Select Committee or for the public opinion. You may commit mistakes if you do this thing in a hurry, better withdraw it, otherwise it will mean that you want only to support it for the interest of high officials who are known to be corrupt. You are doing so as you are scared of confiscation of your property or similar other punishments. So, you want to avoid it. But I want you; I appeal to you, please ask to your Chief Minister to withdraw this bill and allow the Special Court to function properly, so that people holding high offices irrespective of their position or party affiliation are brought to book it and when involved in corruption (*OLA Debates*, Vol. II (22), 27.7.1995; 175-76).

On the issue of corruption and use of money in election, Biju Patnaik said, "Here again comes the question of honesty and sincerity. The cost is honesty. The cost is misuse of Government authority. The cost is misuse of Government vehicles, misuse of Governmental powers. Again, increasing the ost of election at all stages means you have to accumulate money from some source or other which means the sense of honesty has vanished. Then if the Government, the party, whoever the party, has to collect this vast sum from people, how can you collect this unaccounted money without indulging in total corrupt practices? We need not deny this position. We, the political machine of this country is guilty of this crime and unless we collectively, instead of trying to blame each other, create the situation, we will not stop corruption. It is not possible, because it is we who generate corruption and all that. Therefore, we must do it so that we can hold our heads high as men of character and enforce our thinking on others. Right from the top to the bottom, corruption is being generated like this by Government patronage, by license and quota system, and generated deliberately because we need this fund for election. Until that is done, it is no use sending Vigilance Department, the CBI, or any other Department, because the men who govern, the men who rule are the culprits and we, the political machine of this country, are culprits. Therefore, you have to change the character of the Government, the character of the administration, if you want to give a new direction to the country.... If I am guilty, you are guilty with a greater measure because you are in power. We are collectively guilty. Therefore, collectively can we do this? Have you the capacity to do it, the mentality to do it, the determination to do it? Sir, at political level, we have dismissed with dislike, which I say strict discipline, and it has percolated to the administrative level. So what else is left for the country? Country after country has shown that when political machine has become corrupt, it has led to dictatorship. When the political parties become corrupt or when people feel that they have become corrupt, they invite dictatorship. I sincerely hope that this great democracy will not be reduced to that position. These days' democracies have become sick of corruption. The democratic Government also should function democratically. Democracy means Government by selection, not by dictatorship (*OLA Debates*, Vol. II (24), 10.7.1974; 112-3).

He spoke about the allegations of corruption against him, and said, "They charge Biju Patnaik as corrupt. I had CBI, I had Parliamentary sub-committee, I had Commission. None of them had said Biju Patnaik is corrupt, made money by being misusing government power. None of them had said so. These newspapers say Biju Patnaik corrupt. But they have not said that Biju Patnaik has misused government money for his personal gains or party gains.... I have gone through all the Committees to determine corruption by all my political opponents starting from whole Central Cabinet, whole CBI, whole State, whole vigilance, nowhere, it was found that Biju Patnaik has made money for his personal gains by misusing the official position. I always think for the people of Odisha and I can put them into action and I have come to the House for all these things. I want the progress of the people. Z. A. Ahmed has said that Biju Patnaik has committed economic offence, that Biju Patnaik has crores of rupees in foreign exchange. I say this is disgusting, disrupting.... You may talk of Indira Gandhi, Subramaniam, CBI, whole team. Let them come together; I can prove in the court of law. I am not one of those people, who can have a change in thinking" (*OLA Debates*, Vol. III (11), 20.12.74; 85-6).

Culture and Language

On the Odia language being used for Bills and for advancement to the cause of Odia, he said, "Language is a vehicle for expression. It is for the linguists, it is for the literary experts, it is for the experts of Odia grammar and all those that go to make a language and it is for them collectively or individually to improve the language. If the Hon'ble Members are keen and some of them appear to be keen, I do not for a moment believe that they can devote their life and sponsor the cause of Odia language. They should sit themselves in the society for the development of Odia language and I am sure any Government of Odisha would come to their help. They have neither done this nor have they been doing it except that occasionally they make it an excellent political football to indulge in this game. What is there in this Bill? The only thing is to permit a language to be used for legislative activities. That is all. It does not mean that Odia language is in any way being slighted.

Speeches are made in Odia; interpretations are made in Odia; questions are put in Odia and answers are given in Odia. If by merely printing the Bills in Odia, the great desire, the great ambition of the Odia language will be fulfilled, I shall order it now. If that is the aim of the development of the Odia language, it is something absurd. The language of Odia will not develop by merely printing the Bills in Odia. It may be convenient for a few Members to get on the business of the House. To that extent, I think it would be more convenient for those who do not understand English, if the Bills are printed in Odia. But that has nothing t do with the language. If I may say so. Then, again, when they are espousing the cause of Odia language, they are casting all kinds of aspersions around the horizon which only they seem to be capable of. They all at the same time feel that they cannot do without English. Even the protagonists of Odia language say like that. A man who is in two minds cannot do without English language, can never do any good to the Odia language. So I see no validity in their arguments. If it is decided that our language shall be developed then we should give up other language; we should take the consequence of going over to other languages; we shall sit and develop our own language, develop our own terminology; develop our language scientifically and everything that goes to develop a language. The language should be the vehicle of expression; of all that goes to build modern science. To my mind, it will take 15 years more time; it may be till that time we remain stunted. We cannot assimilate the knowledge of technology because we have decided to go back to the other language. If the House is prepared to do that, if the State is prepared for that and matters are improved I have not the slightest objection. But I am sure such a change-over will not be welcome outside. People today are not so much interested in the so-called language as in industries, as in scientific knowledge, as in roads, transport; people are more interested in these than the language issue which the protagonists are raising. Therefore, we have in our National Integration Council decided in the combined wisdom of all the national leaders that English should remain as an associate language of our nation, since it has been propagated for the last 150 years. If you can take a rich language and learn it, understand and assimilate through it the scientific and technical ideas, I think it would be wise to retain that language. The Hon'ble Members do, if I may say so, suffer under a terrible inferiority complex. We are an independent nation today. Language for us is a vehicle of thought and expression. Beyond that, I have no doubt, if I can assimilate English language, German language or Russian language and take advantage of their technological and scientific ideas and thought process, anything that goes to make our life richer and better, I would certainly assimilate like a machine, like a power-house which generates fuel and other conveniences. I do not feel sorry because I have learnt this language. I have got my mother-tongue. My mother-tongue too is a vehicle of thought and expression. It only happens that I was born and I learnt the language of my mother. Then, why don't you allow Shri Sonaram Soren to enrich his mother-tongue. His mother-tongue is completely different from Odia. It must be encouraged; the script should be developed and things must be printed in his mother-tongue. What arguments the protagonists of Odia would have against that? There are fifty *Adivasii* (tribal) languages; if they are brought into print and treated as modern language juts because there happens to be thirty-four Members present in the House out of 140 Members? What right have you to subjugate and not allow them to enrich the language that is their mother-tongue? By what right do you subjugate their right to their own mother-tongue of 34 Members in a House of 140? Therefore, it is not a question of language. It is not a question of number of majority over minority. It is a question of extolling the so-called mother-tongue. If it is done, if the pre-historic ill-conceived notion is done, it will not stand the test of modern times. Therefore, Sir, we say that language should be developed. To develop a language, we have to get words to make a language understandable. The Encyclopedia Britannica which has got crores of words, every year it imbibes and discard something like millions of words. Every year they take words from the languages all over the world, try to assimilate them in the English language and discard millions of words every year. That is the research on that. The language is to expand with language. English is no longer the language of Englishmen. In England, Sir, if you will go you will find what type of English we talk here, a small percentage of the inhabitants of Great Britain talk like that. In London you will find English is spoken in ten different forms. In Scotland, it is completely different, in Ireland it is completely different. Therefore, to say that English is the language of masters has no meaning. At one time it was the language of masters. Today it is not. It is a language of technology, it is an apparatus, it is a vehicle. We must use it in a better way, in a stronger way and in a fuller way as our erstwhile masters did. My language was the other day English. But history has taken a different turn. My culture was the culture of an Englishman. Bit it has taken a different turn. Shall I weep over that? Certainly not. The nation looks ahead. It does not look to the dim past. What I take is the strength from my glorious past history. All apparatus, all the vehicle, all the technology, I can gather from the world. Therefore, I have no complex, nor can I subscribe to the views expressed, by some of the Hon'ble Members. Nothing that is done in English should be detrimental to our own language Odia. What is required is that men of letters of Odisha should develop the language and the State can assist them in finance. That is being done through the Department of Cultural Affairs. It is for such men of letters to try to make a bigger language which can develop words into a scientific language, into a most modern scientific and mathematical language. Till such time, we out serve our children can use this language for technology and develop the modern science. Till such time we will use English, however limited use it might be in our great country, however few can learn in our country whatever little percentage of our population use this language, still it has to remain for talk in the world of science, mathematics, surgery, medicine, and so on. Here, what we are trying to do is merely that in this Legislative Assembly of ours, the use of English may continue beyond the 26th January 1965. But nothing prevents us to stop the use of English before or after that time. But we shall do so in our combined wisdom. That fact that it is extended is merely to remove the disabling clause that English will not be used after 26th January 1965. But nothing prevents us to abolish it now or after that. Therefore, let us try to think of the Odia language as a modern language. Let us try to make it modern language and expand it to take in the modern concepts within the four corners of the language. Let us expand it in the number of words. Let us make it a language of our future millions. Let our literary *pundits* try, let our grammarians try and let the Legislature support them. Till that time we may use the English language, or the German language or the Russian language. After that we can discard this language. Therefore, let us all combine our wisdom and try to develop our language which is a vehicle of sentiments and not give undue importance as mother-tongue or father-tongue. Let us use it in the modern concept as language is a vehicle and it is mobile, then only we can use a language for the betterment of our people. What our people require today is the abolition of poverty and they simultaneously recommend that Odia by itself as a vehicle is not competent to relieve us from our poverty. We shall not only have English and other languages to be used for our benefit for the masses for science, mathematics till our own people have got rid of the grinding poverty, I have nothing more to add. I have only tried in cogent terms to explain what I think of languages without any sentiments, purely in mathematical terms, as an instrument of utility and I do hope that my colleagues in this House who sympathize with this Bill will allow the passage of the Bill" (*OLA Debates*, Vol. V (21), 30.9.63; 37-40).

On the question of Odia type-writers, he said, "One issue was raised by the Hon'ble Member from Patnagarh regarding Odia typewriters. You know, Government had to do a great deal of work to bring out the typewriter to work satisfactorily. Great improvement had been made in it. A British firm, Remington & Co. is prepared to take up the work and prepare finally the key-boards, both for the type-writer and for lino-typewriters for Odia newspapers. Unfortunately, the emergency came and the foreign exchange required for the purpose was held up. We have reminded the Government of India several times and are pursuing it and when the foreign exchange will be released, the typewriters will be brought into operation in Odisha. It is an urgent necessary for work in the Panchayats, in the offices of Sub-Divisional

Officer, Collectorates and so on. The massive use of the Odia typewriter depends on Odia stenography like the Odia stenography which is normally done in the Assembly. To make it wide-spread, we have to establish more Odia stenography schools and we are doing so. Therefore, typewriter and lino-typewriter are essential factors for spreading the language.... The other point which the Hon'ble Member has raised is a point which is simplicity itself. He says that according to Article 210, Odia will be there or English. His contention is that nothing substantial has been done. That is true, Odia Bills have not come. It is optional for the Assembly, Department to print in English or in Odia. So, I do not know what he was arguing about. What the Hon'ble Member from Patna pointed out Government also considered to print in Odia in order to afford facilities to some Members who do not know English to study the Bills and know what are the implications of the Bills. But we are in difficulty because law books are in English. Our High Court and Supreme Court are using English law books. There are no Odia law books. So, we are in difficulty. The Legislature is making laws. No mistake is to be allowed in it. Every word of the law becomes important since interpretations of it will have far reaching consequences. Therefore, I do not know really when these Bills can be printed in Odia. I would like to point out to the Hon'ble Members that when the law books of the Nation can be printed in our language and when the interpretation of the words will be made in the High Court, then and then only this Legislature will print Bills in Odia" (*OLA Debates*, Vol. V (21), 30.9.63; 43-44).

On the subject of how to regenerate the spirit of the people of Odisha, he said, "Can we bring about a cultural renaissance, a cultural revolution? I am sure everybody wants to raise the people. The question is when we begin. The people from Khurda fought the British. But where are the ballads, where are the songs, where are the statues of heroes who fought the British? There is nothing for the sons of Odisha. There is nothing, but dust. You cannot raise people you cannot reconstruct a people only out of dust. It is only with memories that you can reconstruct a people. But when memories are lost, concept is lost, history is lost or your consciousness is gone, you are not people anymore. That is what Odisha suffers...... China today talks of the Chinese Emperors. China today demands the territories which the Emperors had. Whatever be the 'ism', we want conquest of mind. With the conquest of mind, you can melt a mountain in a steel plant with new technology, with new ideas. Today the feudal system is gone; the *Samrajyabad* (imperialism) is gone because the land is gone. But for the other conquest, you must have a mind for conquest. Today with our defeated mind, if we want to revive, then the arms that we have is our glorious history that we must capitalize to give us strength. Nothing will be gained only by changing the name of the state to Kalinga, or Utkal, or Odisha. The whole thing is poverty of mind. If you can destroy the poverty of mind, and collectively if this House can give a new direction, then it will be something worth doing (*OLA Debates*, Vol. V (10), 23.2.1973; 31-2).

On the issue of State giving funds for the maintenance of the temples, and the land reforms, he said, "In the name of religion, classes of people are exploiting the society. I strongly feel and believe that in between the State and the tenant there should not be any intermediary. If a temple has to subsist, the State should contribute to it and there should be a fund for the same and Government should give whatever they need for the welfare of the people or the temple activities or the religious activities of the people or the age-old habits of the people. But I do not understand why the Minister has side-tracked the fundamental issue and that too deliberately. It seems as if he is afraid of his electorate. I submit and that too strongly that we should move with the modern time which means drastic change. I do not want to use any harsh words against the Revenue Minister nor do I have any intention of using any word against Shri Biswanath Das. But what I wish to state that in Odia what we call *byabhichar* (cruelty) has entered into these religious institutions. I should say that this Paleolithic institution should be modernized and this Paleolithic practice should be modernized. Government should create a fund for it and contribute to it from the Consolidated Fund of the State. I do not see any reason why Land Reforms Bill should come into picture or land should come into the picture. The system which has degenerated should not lie like this and there should not be any intermediary between the State and the tenant in this sector" (*OLA Debates* Vol. V (8), 21.2.1973; 39-40).

On the issue of *Bali Yatra*, a cultural festival in Odisha, he said, "It is a revival. Emersion of a great history of Kalinga. It is inscribed that our traders were sailing from the river Mahanadi to the seas to far-flung foreign lands and bringing back costly jewels and other valuables and remembering it our Odia girls till today are sailing symbolic boats. This is our Kalinga heritage. It is a great feeling that we must feel collectively and to make that feeling strong, I insisted and trained young girl from our University, sent to Cochin to be trained by the Navy. When Navy gave her certificate that she is fit to sail, she was sent, nine thousand kilometers of sailing. It is not an easy task. This House has not yet given that girl felicitation. We have involved the sense of remembrance because we have forgotten our own great history. I wish we should not forget our history so easily, of two thousand years back. It is not too long back. We must feel proud of being the successor of those great Hindus. We should not forget that" (*OLA Debates*, Vol. X (3), 22.2.1993; 131).

He further exemplified by saying about the great prowess of the ancient Kalinga (modern day Odisha), "In this way, the empire of Kalinga was also built when we could conquer and this is our *buniyadi* or background. We have forgotten that. You talk of central assistance. I have to inform you, Sir, when Kalinga built his empire there was no central assistance. We assisted ourselves. We conquered nation after nation. We went to Java, Bali, and Sumatra to get built our empire. There was no Planning Commission. There was no one. We did everything of our strength, our own dreams 2000 years back. Now, if I would say this State has been devastated by floods, cyclone and droughts-God knows what, and we made a bill of ₹200 crores for devastation of houses, roads, power, hospitals and everything, with the hope that there would be some Central assistance. But it is pity not a single penny of so called Central assistance could come. I know, it cannot come. The Planning Commission function in such a way that Central Government has no money to give of its own.... The fiancés are so intertwined that no Prime Minister, no Finance Minister, nobody can change it. They can give you only advance from your own Plan. Nothing they can give of their own" (*OLA Debates*, Vol. II (3), 3.7.1995; 130).

Naxalite

On the prevalent social order, he said, "When I say that in the present society, the power must have the upper hand in the social order which is bound to be within a conflict with vested interests, whether in business sector or in any sector, we will have to wait. This is a big task. They control the executive, the bureaucracy and almost everything. Still, it is within the control. This has to be broken down carefully in a planned manner and I expect every Member of this House would bring about this in social order" (II (6), 7.6.1990; 193). He also said on the social order, "We want to change the present social order. We want to change the present administrative order. That we want. If you call us naxalite, then we are supper naxalite, because we want to change the social order" (*OLA Debates*, Vol. X (5), 13.9.1989; 85).

On the suppression of Naxalites by Odisha, he said, "The Governor also made very moving reference to the suppression of naxalites by the Government in the Koraput district. But he forgot that his party Government in Bengal, his party Government in Andhrta indulged in suppressing similar movement hundred times more and all this was done under the direct authority and direction of the Central Government. It seems the entire fact is not known to him and he is ridiculed due to his ignorance (*OLA* Debates, Vol. III (2), 4.1.1972; 42).

On the issue of combating naxalite menace, he said, "When it becomes a socio-economic and military problem, it becomes more complex. There is the socio-economic condition which is in a rotten stage for the inhabitants of that area. The position has become more and more complex. To help in removing the difficulties in that area, we had earnestly requested the Government of India with a plan programme of ₹165 crores, which includes roads, bridges, schools, hospitals and all manner of things which will mean civilized existence for those 151 villages. But I regret to tell this House that not one penny has been given by Government of India, although I repeatedly requested personally and in writing more than a dozen of times" (*OLA Debates*, Vol. VII (22), 25.3.1992; 48). He further said, "I have said the socio-economic and military aspects got into it and made it more difficult. In terms of socio-economic, we have failed in that area because we cannot reach there. You talk of PDS, how will you reach there? There is the biggest lake where many people died because the boat capsized. No teacher can go there; no doctor wants to stay there. It is not physically possible to do. So, they become easy targets for the naxalites, you call them revolutionaries, you call them whatever you can, so the villagers become easy prey of them. They forcefully collect tax and money by threat of force or by killing or by any other method, which of course the State resists to the hilt...That area will be a developed area and prosperous area so that the socio-economic attack of the naxalites to that extent would diminish" (*OLA Debates*, Vol. VII (22), 25.3.1992; 49).

He said on the naxalite setting up statues of their leaders, "Sri N. T. Rama Rao is opposing the naxalites. Sri Rao said that naxalite in some villages or somewhere wants to build the statue of their leader; I cannot stop it. If somebody wants to build memorial for their leader, how can you stop it. I have not stopped it. I do not think it an irresponsible statement.... I am telling you that the Government is not building it, the people wanted to build it. I cannot stop it. This is the habit of Congress Chief Ministers. Mr. Rama Rao wants to uphold the dignity of the citizens. In my opinion, they want a change in social order. They should be persuaded to change their methods. I would not take away the rights of any citizen" (*OLA Debates*, Vol. X (3), 11.9.1989; 134-5).

On the naxalite movement, he said, "I have said once, I am the first Naxalite. I claim to be naxal, because I want to introduce social justice at the lowest level. I believe Naxalites want to do the same thing. But I have said, I will not tolerate violence and killing. That is my only bar with Naxalites. I am with them. I am not with these people who are haves. They are well to do. They can have. But these poor people who are staying in Adivasi areas, they will not get wages fixed by the Government. Their land is taken away by *Sahukars*. If they can prevent this thing, then I am with them. They have introduced what I have said about the theory of *beating*. But there should not be any killings. I will lend full support to bring social justice. The ex-Chief Minister, when he projected these things that it is making law and order situation adverse, I am sorry, I cannot agree with him, because If I can think myself as a Naxalite to give social justice to the poorest, I have also to think of enforcing it. The law as it stands today in my country, the judicial practice is totally faulty as far as the poorest man is concerned, whoever the lawyer. To rich who can pay in the highest court of the country i.e., Supreme Court, for one appearance one lawyer charges one lakh. Who can pay that? Only rich can pay that. If you call it justice, then justice for whom? Justice for the poor? It is a negative factor. Any way, if Naxalites say, we want justice for the poor man, then I am with them. But one thing, I will not tolerate violence. That is all" (*OLA Debates*, Vol. XIV (13),16.3 1994; 119).

On an Adjournment Motion discussion on 'Alleged increase of Naxalite activities', he replied, "The Government is aware of the repeated incursions of the Kondapalli Sitaramayya group naxalites in the Malkangiri sub-division of the border district of Koraput. This incursion has started since 1982 and has recently increased. In order to escape from the actions of the Andhra Pradesh Police, these Naxalites are sometimes entering into the dense areas of Odisha and are engaged in illegal activities. But in recent past, they are trying to make this area as their permanent shelter. In June this year the Naxalites have distributed a 15 point demands in Chitakonda Police-Station limit. This has been claimed to have been distributed by *Adibasi Chasi Mulia Sangha* of Koraput district. They are inciting the tribals of Malkangiri area to solve different problems through the mediation of naxalites and not by Police or Courts. To arrest such illegal activities, the Government has decided to implement integrated socio-economic developmental plans along with Police action. Contact has been established with Government of India for educational, health, transportation, and other developmental works implementation on priority basis" (*OLA Debates*, Vol. II (17), 26.6.1990; 57).

Changing the perspective of the Naxalites towards administration and making it for people- friendly, he said, "The entire service needs to be changed from the oppression of the poor people to service to the poor. Violent change will only disrupt the things. Therefore, my attempt has been to talk, to discuss, to create some confidence in them that the people are not their enemies; the poor' are not their enemies. It is only the rich who have manipulated the police for their own purpose. This needs a lot of training by the senior police officials themselves and by the junior who should undergo thorough training course for the purpose. Therefore, this consciousness has to grow with not only our Police force but also in every branch of the administration" (*OLA Debates*, Vol. XVI (4), 21.9.1994; 71).

Citizens National Register

During the discussion on the continuance of the Proclamation of Emergency in Assam issued under Art. 356 of the Constitution by the President for a further period of six months with effect from 12 June 1980, Biju Patnaik initiated with the 1962 Chinese invasion, and said, "The important thing is that in 1962 when the Chinese invasion took place, a beaten Indian Army retreated, and Pandit Nehru made a statement that his heart went out to the people of Assam. A deep scar and wound was left in the hearts and minds of the people of all Assam, that was undivided Assam at that time including the present Assam, Arunachal Pradesh, Meghalaya and Mizoram. It was almost as if India had forsaken Assam. At that time all the sign-boards were eliminated from the whole of Assam. All the currency notes were burnt in all the banks. (*Interruptions*). You may belong to Assam, but I was in charge of looking after this area. I know a little more than you. Action was to be taken to blow up almost all the installations, which luckily was stopped at the last moment. Although at that time we were planning intense guerilla activity in the whole of Assam, a feeling swept over the people that India was prepared to forsake Assam-wrongly so, but it was so" (*Lok Sabha Debates*, 09.6.80; 320-21).

Analyzing the history of the Assam problem in the context of the National Register, and raising the 1951 issue, Biju Patnaik said, "1951 is the legal cut-off period when Nehru-Liaquat Pact was signed-31st December, 1951. From then, that was the agreement which was approved by Parliament and a National Register is supposed to be maintained from that time, not only in Assam, but in all neighbouring areas, like, Tripura, Mizoram, Manipur, etc. Unfortunately, this was not taken very seriously and infiltration in a very large scale took place into Assam and the adjoining areas, not only from Bangladesh, but also from Nepal and from other areas. There is a very large Nepal contingent in Manipur, where also there is some difficulty, in Arunachal Pradesh and Sikkim. This is the picture of the North-East. They have woken up twenty years late. Had they woken up 10 or 15 years before, something would have been done. They have woken up when three to four million people, who are aliens, are settled there. I put it to the House-How can any State accept such a huge number-three to four millions aliens? What would happen to the indigenous population of that State? Assam population is I believe, about 1 crore and of that about three to four millions, i.e. about 40 per cent is foreigners, who have come from a foreign country, originally East Pakistan and now Bangladesh. What would happen to the local population? Land is shared by all, business is shared by all, the future opportunities are shared by all. I would like this House to consider when the Hon. Minister said that these foreigners could be distributed all over the country, perhaps ha has a case there, if it could be all distributed. But I think, Mr. Home Minister, it will be very very difficult. Even in Bengal, to take back a few thousands of people, original Bengalis, who came from Bangladesh and who are settled in Dandakaranya. When they went back, they were shunted back with the Police force, (*Interruptions*). I am not misleading the House, I am saying that Bangladesh refugees, when they came, when the East Pakistan refugees came, a part of them were settled in Dandakaranya, but they did not want to stay there and they wanted to go back to Sundarbans. No State can accommodate these people. I am fully in sympathy with the Bengal Government. No State can really assimilate a very large number of outsiders. It is not possible because they cannot provide jobs to their own people; tens of thousands of their own young men are unemployed, the pressure from their own unemployed people is already there. They cannot take a very large number of outsiders. These are the physical difficulties before any Government. It is not a question of this party or that party. How do you propose to do that? I do not think that it is anybody's case, as far as I have understood, it is not the case of the students or the *Assam Gana Sangram Parishad* that the people who came there after 1951 should be thrown out. It is not the case. I believe so. I believe the Home Minister would corroborate my statement that in the discussions with him, they have not said that these people should be thrown out. They said, only record correct the National Register, you can allow them to settle down there. For people who came between 1961 and 1971, I believe, they have said, make a State list and give them work-permits. Work-permits are being given all over the world. Let them remain there and for those who came after 1971, as you are suggesting, they should be sent back to East Bengal or Bangladesh, or settle them elsewhere. I think this is the category-wise demand. What is the difficulty now? (*Interruptions*) Instead of that, what has the Government of India done? They have sent the Army there. What for? They have sent the *Border Security Force* also there. The BSF was created to protect the border. The Army is there to protect the border and to stop the infiltration. Inspite of that, you are sending the Army there to shoot down Indians or what. I would like to get a categorical answer from the Government to that....You now say that a parallel movement has been started by the so-called minorities. Who are the minorities? Are they foreigners or Indians? If they are foreigners, I have no sympathy with them. If they are Indians, yes, Indian minorities must be protected at all costs, but not foreigners who have infiltrated there. Instead of putting the cart before the horse, should you not settle as to who are the foreigners?" (*Lok Sabha Debates*, 09.6.80; 321-23). On the definition of "foreigner", Biju Patnaik said, "Those who have been infiltrating from East Pakistan or Bangladesh are foreigners. Should you not first settle whether a person is a foreigner or nor? The Home Minister himself has suggested that 300,000 foreigners have been asked to go out. Is it 3 lakhs or 30 lakhs? Has it been settled? I do not say that you throw all of them out. But first you must determine, as per the Nehru-Liaqat Ali Pact, which is the Constitutional position, who are the foreigners. You can allow them to settle there. You can give them Indian passports; you can give them work-permits or you can throw them out. That is for the future. Should you not first settle how many foreigners are there in the country?" (*Lok Sabha Debates*, 09.6.80; 323-24).

In this regard, Biju Patnaik gave the instance of Vietnam and said, "Even in Vietnam, they have thrown out 1 million Chinese people. They have not bothered whether they went by boat, whether they died on the sea or what happened to them. They did not care for them. But let us not do anything at the cost of the Assamese people, four million people settled in a small State of Assam" (*Lok Sabha Debates*, 09.6.80; 324).

On the question of minorities' protection and integrity in the State of Assam, Biju Patnaik said, "I agree with the Home Minister that genuine minorities, Indian minorities must be protected at all costs. I also agree that all steps must be taken by India to see that India is not disintegrated. I fully agree there. But where is the question of disintegration here....You find a suitable machinery, whatever machinery, to find out who are the foreigners. Then you decide what to do with them distribute them all over India; distribute them over the Bay of Bengal or whatever it is. It is for the Government and the Parliament to decide. Why these people should be landed only on a small State of Assam where the people have a feeling that they are not really a part of India.... I would ask the Home Minister to deal with this problem with great sagacity, with great patience, with great forbearance. There is no case for saying like beating a drum that India's integrity will be protected. It will be protected. It is not your business. It is everybody's business. The minority must be protected, of course. It should be protected; it is India's Constitutional business. But I have no sympathy for the multitude of foreigners who are allowed to pump in and flourish at the cost of India; this I will not allow" (*Lok Sabha Debates*, 09.6.80; 325).

Socialism

Speaking on the process of achieving socialism, he said, "We should steadily raise the lower order so that we can secure something precise. It is not radical. It is realism in society. This is the way to socialism. It is the removal of economy disparity. It is the rudiment of the modern society. They have already given out the slogan. Let us come down to solve this difficult task" (*OLA Debates*, Vol. II (2), 25.3.74; 28). He said, "Human factor is forgotten. I have heard saying India with its investment potentiality can sustain 30 crores of people, what about the balance? They will die otherwise you cannot have an affluent society. Theoretically correct. Investment and population go on never meeting at a point. Investment must be made to meet population at some point somewhere" (*OLA* Debates, Vol. II (2), 25.3.74; 29).

5

The Odia Identity

Conclusion

Biju Patnaik is an immortal personality only because of his determination to work for the people of Odisha and to develop the state of Odisha. He was the 'Odia identity' among all the Odias and his wisdom was not limited to a particular field or area. He commanded vast knowledge and wisdom, rarely found among the political class. He has special interest on international politics and science and technology, particularly defense technology. His prime concern was the development of the state of Odisha and through it, the holistic development of India. He did not adhere to the divisive politics on the basis of caste or religion, but adopted an inclusive strategy for the all-round social economic development. His brand of politics was mainly revolving around emphasis on industrial development for the economic properity of the people, also with a specific focus upon the disadvantaged section of the population. During the Question Hour on 24th February 1997, Biju Patnaik asked the then Defense Minister Mulayam Singh Yadav, about the crash of Indian Air Force Aircrafts, as it is being continuously causing death, and whether Defense Ministry would consider withholding the flight for this type of aircraft, particularly MIG-22. During the question, Biju Patnaik referred Shri Abdul Kalam as a competent person, but his competency is in the field of trajectory missile system. He does not know much about aircraft. Himself being a commissioned Pilot, he knew the intricacies of aircrafts much batter.

On the Odisha's progress, he said, "I have a feeling and indeed every Member of this House has a feeling that Odisha's destiny is on the march. No small minds can pull it back. Odisha's destiny is moving like a steam-roller and pebbles cannot stand in its way" (*OLA Debates*, Vol. VI (2), 18.2.1964; 45).

During the continuance of President's Rule in Assam discussion, Mr. H. K. L. Bhagat said, "Mr. Vajpayee and Mr. Biju Patnaik have one thing in common. Both of them are great Captains. They are not like the good old traditional Captains who sink, but they manage to save themselves. This has been the story of Lok Sabha elections; this has been the story of the Assembly elections" (*Lok Sabha Debates*, 09 June 1980; 328).

He was a person who looked to the future, and so he once said to Mr. Jyotirmoy Basu, "What is past is for you to dig up, I am interested only in the present and the future" (*Lok Sabha Debates*, 28 June 1977; 287).

Biju Patnaik once said that he was a resident of Cuttack town, to which the then Deputy Leader of Opposition Lokanath Mishra said, "You are a flying resident of Cuttack" (X (2), 1949; 51).

Sarat Kar, former Speaker of Odisha Legislative Assembly, once told in the Assembly, "The words of our Chief Minister Biju Patnaik in lines in stones, and not in water! Prime Minister of Jawaharlal Nehru was once asked in the Parliament as to who is the best Chief Minister in India at that time, and he replied Odisha Chief Minister Biju Patnaik. This was of 1961 period, and I was a student of Political Science at Allahabad" (II (20), 29.6.1990; 81).

Biju Patnaik was a staunch democrat and being as such was a great supporter of people for every cause. He said, "This is people, they are the Masters, do not please forget your MLAs and your Ministers are not masters. I am not master, people are masters. Do not irritate them, do not make them angry, do not make them lose confidence.....You did not get the vote, people have voted..... I do not have the dream, but people have dream, they expect so many things from you, because they have changed the Government, they expect much from you. If you cannot do it they will just throw you out like as hundreds have been thrown out, kicked out" (II (3), 1995; 133).

Being a magnanimous person, Biju Patnaik, always advised and wished all, including his opposition colleagues. In giving such an advice to the Government, he said, "you can only grow up when you will build up your Steel Plant, when you will build up your power plant, when you will build up your canals and other things and show to the world, here we are. I am Odisha that is what to do. I wish you luck, I wish the Government luck, whenever you need our support, the Opposition is there to support you for the development of the State and for the development of the people of Odisha" (*OLA Debates*, Vol. II (3), 1995; 134).

He said, "But the problem with the people is they think for themselves. For their own families, their own people, their own benefits. But I have habit of thinking and dreaming of my people. That is the difference" (XIV (3), 1994; 83). He continued to say, "I have said everywhere that Odisha will live only when my people have courage to say that I will not beg. I will not go for a job; I will do something for myself. Then only our State will become a different State. I feel in my tour and I find minimum people in every meeting, 20,000/50,000/3 lakhs in meetings. I saw their reaction and I feel this idea is catching up with them that people of Odisha will have to stand on their own legs. But not to beg. I don't want to wish them to depend on anybody and I think and I say when Biju Patnaik can do it, why not you?

Are you not born out of the same soil? I may not be better than you. You can do better than me. I hope and I think this is a catching thing for my boys, for the young people of my State" (*OLA Debates*, XIV (3), 1994; 84).

He said, "I have fought for the nation's independence and I went to jails alongwith Jayaprakash Narayan, Aruna and others. Do you think I enjoyed it? I have said it time and time again in National Development Council meeting. I said, why do not you control the population? This little Government showed one child business. Should it not be a national policy?.... It makes me ashamed that a nation for which we fought to bring freedom, we shed our blood, many of us shed our blood, has become servile" (*OLA Debates*, Vol. XIV (6), 1994; 98).

Becoming futuristic, he said, "You can only lead the future, if the people of Odisha rise to the heights where they were 2000 years ago. We have lost that. We have been reduced to nothing. We are mindless people begging all the time for a petty job, for this and that. That's all we do. That's all we think. How can this nation survive?" (*OLA Debates*, Vol. XIV (6), 1994; 99).

Biju Patnaik became remorseful of the system that has degenerated, and said, "System in which we live has destroyed our moral, destroyed our strength. We had a great thought when we were in Britisher's prisonfor 1000 days and nights that this Nation would be great when we will be coming out of the room. Since I had the privilege or honour or misfortune to live this long life to watch this Nation on the threshold of decay, I do feel sory for the future generation to come. I have no answer. I can condemn somebody. I can condemn myself before I condemn somebody else. Therefore, I have said I feel distressed. I said to the Radio, TV, that I am watching this thing down down and down..... We lost courage, confidence and self-reliance. Indian Doctors can exhibit their excellence in America, Engineers can produce many things outside. But here he has nothing. For what reason? Why? We must look to ourselves if the future generation of our country can think better, think stronger and can think collectively, I am sure some day our Nation will forget shore of Dunkel or of GATT as Japanese are doing today. America is begging Japan to come to terms. But Japan refuses. We are begging for terms. We cannot refuse. This is our problem. I am sorry. I had to intervene to go to the roots of the problems as the Nation suffers" (*OLA Debates*, Vol. XIV (6), 1994; 99).

On his ministerial assignment offers in Delhi, he said, "I have got many offers to go to Delhi. To become a Minister in Delhi. I said, I am sorry, I cannot. This is during the period of Pandit Nehru. So, this not a big deal for me. For me, Odisha is important. Whether I am in Government or not, important because here is a poverty-stricken State with 2-3 crores of people below the poverty-line, who do not have means to eat. How to raise them is an experiment. It is my mental experiment. Nothing doing with the Chief Minister, Prime Minister, whatever-whatever. This is my thinking right from the very beginning. When Nehru told me to come, I gave up all the industrial empire and took the Chief Ministership. At that time in 1961, I told Panditji to do Tikarpara, Paradip port, railway line, etc. In terms of capital investment, it was calculated at ₹12,000 crores. I also told Panditji that you do not have capital, I also do not have, and World Bank has money. For ten years, give me the RBI rules concessions. I will make Odisha one of the richest state in the country. At that time, Panditji said it was a good idea, but Morarji Desai. Lal Bahadur Shashtri, Gulzarilal Nanda, and other Ministers obstructed it. They said the country will disintegrate. The same fear is going on" (*OLA Debates*, Vol. V (8), 20.9.1991; 194).

On his personal matter, he said, "We are rebel Hindus. We rebel against expensive customs. I had my daughter's marriage with a very limited cost. I have invited my friends and colleagues" (*OLA Debates*, Vol. XI (2), 15.7.1993; 118).

To bring in rapid development for Odisha, he said, "Therefore, let us examine ourselves; before we die, let us examine ourselves, what good we have done to our people, what we have done ourselves. We are representatives of the people and we must see earnestly what we are able to do something for the toiling masses" (*OLA Debates*, Vol. IV (3); 21.2.1991; 171).

When Nandini Satapathy told in Assembly that Biju Patnaik recommended her name as a nominee for Rajya Sabha election only because Sanjiva Reddy, the then AICC President, said to recommend three names, Biju Patnaik rebuffed, "No Sanjib Reddy can order Biju Patnaik to send three names. I have not taken the names of three. Suppose I said 'No', had Sanjiva Reddy insisted on that?" (*OLA Debates*, Vol. X (3), 22.2.1993; 128).

He said, "Biju Patnaik is never behind anybody and will not be behind anybody; Biju Patnaik represents the people of Odisha and will continue to represent the people of Odisha" (*OLA Debates*, Vol. IV (16), 14.3.1991; 92).

He said, "If we do some sort of sacrifice for the good and future of Odisha, I say this sacrifice will be treated as that of heroes and statues will be made and at least our children will remember us" (*OLA Debates*, Vol. VII (28), 2.4.1992; 69).

For the development of Odisha, he said, "Therefore, we have to stand on our own legs. If I may say, if I may intrude on my colleagues here, forget everything, let us not bite each other, and let us fight for the sake of our people. Leave something for the future" (*OLA Debates*, Vol. VII (28), 2.4.1992; 70).

About his role at the national level with Nehru, he said, "At that time, Pandit Jawaharlal Nehru called me to assist him there during Chinese attack. At that time, I thought India was slightly more important than Odisha. I had to go to rescue the Government of India at that time. But this time however, I can assure the Hon'ble Members in this House and the people of the State that I will not go Delhi this time. That is why I did not stand for Parliament, and I have decided to stay here. And I have promised this time that for the rest of my life I will stay here, and serve the people of Odisha" (*OLA Debates*, Vol. I (4), 21.3.1990; 52).

He once said, "We come to power through election only. One becomes Chief Minister of the Government, not of his party. When I was Chief Minister and late R. N. Singhdeo was the Leader of Opposition. I made such a statement that *party is Government*. Late R. N. Singhdeo, the then Leader of Opposition, wrote a letter to Prime Minister Pandit Nehru. I was summoned to Delhi. Pandit Nehru told, 'Dam fool you said party is the Government'. Government is for everybody. Party is only implementing the policies through Government machinery. The administration must run just for every citizen. He told me 'Dam fool' – he is like my father" (*OLA Debates*, Vol. X (3), 11.9.1989; 138).

Speaking about his defeat at five constituencies, he said, "You have lost 5 bye-elections. I lost 5 elections. I was not in Government then. You have lost bye-elections while you are in Government" (X (3), 11.9.1989; 134). He also said, "Yes, I lost five elections at five places because we did not have enough candidates; I lost five, that was a national record. My driver said, *Saheb, Aap Hindusthan mein record kardiya*. Again, I created another record when I got elected from Rajnagar with a record margin of 59,000 votes. That was the maximum difference in India" (*OLA Debates*, Vol. V(2), 24.2.1987; 77).

He showed to the Assembly what the then Prime Minister opined on him in his letter dated 23 June 1986, where he writes about him, "Eminent citizens and patriots like yourself". The Governor of Odisha has said, 'Shri Biju Patnaik is an outstanding leader, gifted with dynamic qualities and his contribution during freedom struggle as well as during the post-independence era for the progress and development of our State and country are well known. As an industrialist, administrator, social and political leader, he has displayed indomitable courage, determination and confidence in diverse field of activity'. "I do not need these certificates. Neither do I need your certificate nor the certificate of your Prime Minister" (V (2), 24.2.1987; 76-7).

He sarcastically said in the House, "Now the Chief Minister is using helicopter. But I was born in helicopters" (*OLA Debates* Vol. I(2), 15.3.1985; 17).

To the remark of the Chief Whip that it is the same Congress whose leadership was taken by Mahatma Gandhi, thereafter Nehru ji, Indira ji and now Rajiv ji, he said, "I belong to Mahatma Gandhi's Congress and Jawaharlal Nehru's Congress. I do not belong to this Congress (I) or what-so-ever it may be. Before the birth of this Chief Whip, I was here the Congress Chief Minister" (*OLA Debates*, Vol. I, 30.7.1985; 84).

He reprimands the Congress party and said, "In some paper, I have seen Smt. Nandini Satapathy of whom the less I speak the better, made a statement that I sent words to Prime Minister about my eagerness to join Congress. To this she said 'no'. I do not know where from these ladies and gentlemen got this kind of information. I will remind my friends in the Congress party, how recently they have been knocked out in one, two, three, four, and five bye-elections. You should not see only your personal interest; you must see the interest of the State" (*OLA Debates*, Vol. III (2), 4.1.1972; 43).

During a discussion in the Assembly, Hon'ble Member Nityananda Mahapatra praised Biju Patnaik and said, "I never worry myself about *isms*. I believe that if the *ists*, whether it is a Democratist, Socialist, Communist, whosoever he may be, if he means well and if the means he adheres to is good to achieve a good end, he will early or later be able to achieve something positive. That is my firm faith Sir. Therefore, you find me here in the words of our beloved Chief Minister, a solitary figure in this House. He has said so very often here" (*OLA Debates*, Vol. V (10), 13.9.1963; 38-42). Biju Patnaik then said, "Sir, today, the Hon'ble Member is in great favour of me. He supports me, he associates with my feelings, he calls me beloved" (*ibid*). Hon'ble Member Nityananda Mahapatra, then said, "Sir, never before did I address the Chief Minister with these adjectives. But today I say so because I have found very few men who have for the good of the country, relinquished their offices willingly. Anybody who has got that spirit, I must thank him...." (*ibid*).

While participating in general discussion on the Budget of 1957-58, he said, "Now while we are faced with a very serious problem how to improve our State finance, how to implement our plan, how to reduce the unnecessary expenditure and how to increase our revenue by different methods......Sir, while the Chief Minister presented his Budget, I know that the man Mahtab must have been a very sad man. As the Industries Minister of the Central Cabinet, he had to handle hundreds of crores of rupee worth of trade and industry and a Governor of Bombay, he must have seen crores of rupees spent every day. But today he has come to the helm of a State where he cannot fine 1.6 crores of rupees to meet the deficit for the basic requirement of the Second Five Year Plan" (*OLA Debates*, 1957; 23).

He suggested to the people opposing him and said, "You can show black flag to Biju Patnaik, but that will not help you. You are welcome to do it. I have no objection. I know all of you. Your leader has told wherever you see show black flag and obstruct. Your Party will never come to power if you will go on fighting like this. You have to go to the people and convince them, then only they will want you and you can come to power. Only by obstruction and showing black flag, by this you will not come to power. Give me all the black flag clothes, I will do an umbrella factory. Whatever it may be, I as an Indian feel degraded" (*OLA Debates*, Vol. XIII (3), 24.12.93; 105).

Nilamoni Routray (1986; 706-7) writes about an interaction with the then Governor of Odisha, B. D. Sharma, just after the defeat of the Janata

(S) government under Charan Singh in January 1980. Governor Sharma told him that Biju Patanaik has expressed his desire to be the Chief Minister, and has told him to facilitate it by removing Routray. Governor Sharma was not inclined towards this proposal of Biju Patnaik, inspite of the fact that both of them were friends during emergency and shared the same jail. Routray narrates that Sharma told him that Biju Patnaik had attracted Nehru's attention even before he came to political power. However, his style of functioning as Chief Minister gradually eroded Nehru's attachment. Governor Sharma said that Biju Patnaik claimed to be the creator of the *Kamraj Plan*, and being influenced by it, decided to resign from Chief Minister to which others encouraged him. He said that Biju Patnaik was 'under control' till the time Nehru was alive, and that he was "highly courageous, but all his works are self-centered". However, Nilamoni Routray, differing from the last view, opines that "Biju Patnaik's unjustified adventurist nature is more responsible, and not jealousy or selfish attitude". "The greatest weakness of Biju Patnaik was that in many times he did not accept the status of others, and considered everybody inferior to him. The philosophy of his life was, he was the Managing Director of a company, and all others were labourers or daily-wage workers. Even though this philosophy of life has put in many difficulties, he was unable to change it till he breathed last" (Das, 2017; 194). Welles Hangen, the author of the famous book, *After Nehru, Who?* wrote (1963; 279):

> Bijoyananda Patnaik, the youthful millionaire businessman who retrieved Congress fortunes in Orissa, is a more sinister figure. He could embrace extremism of Left or Right with equal fervor. For tactical reasons he has opted for Menon's socialism, but principles will never interfere with his political mobility..... Patnaik still lacks national stature, but he is dangerous because he combines political cunning and a certain demagogic appeal with Menon-like drive and ambition. He is unscrupulous and autocratic without needlessly alienating his followers, as Menon does.

Biju Patnaik was always concerned for the welfare and development of the people, and had a people-centric approach in his governance style. Damodar Rout, former Minister, in an interview to *Odisha Live* TV (Youtube.com) said that once while travelling with Biju Patnaik, in tribal district of Keonjhar in 1988, many women labourers were walking, and seeing them, Biju Patnaik stopped and interacted with them. During interaction, Biju Patnaik came to know that the government minimum wage-rate was low for their subsistence. When he became the Chief Minister in 1990, he enhanced the government minimum wage-rate from ₹11 to ₹25. According to Rout, Biju Patnaik was 'extremely realistic, visionary and a statesman'. He said, Biju Patnaik would say, "if one's conscience is clear, don't bother for criticism". In another occasion, in 1990 at the Annual Day of The Law College, Cuttack, Late Prof Shreeram Chandra Dash, critically anlysed

Biju Patnaik's call for fiscal federalism and greater autonomy to states in development process *vis-à-vis* Constitutional limitations. Biju Patnaik, in reply, said, "Professor, what will happen if people will revolt, then what will the Constitution, state, government, other institutions do". This shows the immense concern he had for the people.

Biju Patnaik was an industrialist with a business empire of rupees 175 crores during the 1950s, which was a huge amount then (Biswas, 1993). His *Kalinga Airlines* had a fleet of 25 air-crafts. He started the Paradeep Port with an investment of ₹16 crores in 1962 which was later taken over by government in 1966. In 1992 he was asked what message does he want to give to the people of Odisha and he uttered these lines, "In my dream of the 21st century for the State, I would have young men and women who put the interest of the State before them. They will have pride in themselves, confidence in themselves. They will not be at anybody`s mercy, except their own selves. By their brains, intelligence and capacity, they will recapture the history of Kalinga" (www.iloveindia.com). President Sukarno presented him with an 100-acre estate in Palinbang, the seat of the Kalinga empire, which he returned, joking, "The King Of Kalinga doesn't accept gifts from his subjects" (Biswas, 1993). This was the persona called Biju Patnaik, the 'uncrowned emperor of Odisha', for whom "Odisha was a fascinating challenge with its unlimited natural wealth and poverty". Such was the life and deeds of this great person that on his death, the body was drape not only with our national flag but also of Russia and Indonesia, ·a rare distinction for any Statesman.

This is the enigma called Biju Patnaik who always cared for the welfare and development the people. He was a selfless person whose only desire was to see smiles in the face of all people, irrespective of any distinction. He never cared for his personal well-being but relentlessly fought for the right cause of the people. As one reaches the conclusion chapter, one realizes the great contribution made by him. His philosophy and thoughts were always for building India strong and powerful, and with it he wanted an industrially developed Odisha. This work is a humble attempt to bring the relentless effort of this charismatic personality before the people.

References

Anil Dhir, https://orissadiary.com/biju-patnaik-karunanidhi-untold-story/AnilDhir

Austin, Granville. (1991), *Working a Democratic Constitution*, OUP, New Delhi

Biswas, Soutik. (1993), "Biju Patnaik: Slapping people, berating colleagues", *India Today*, 31 May, https://www.indiatoday.in/magazine/profile/story/19930531-biju-patnaik-slapping-people-berating-colleagues-the-bull-of-kalinga-is-still-rampaging-811098-1993-05-31

Chandra, Bipan. (2003), *In the Name of Democracy*, Penguin, New Delhi

Chawla, Prabhu. (1990), "Mandal Commission: Political parties polarised along caste lines", *India Today*, https://www.indiatoday.in/magazine/special-report/story/19900930-mandal-commission-political-parties-polarised-along-caste-lines-states-rocked-by-violence-813092-1990-09-30, accessed 8 June 2021

Damodar Rout on Biju Patnaik-Memoir, 3 March 2016, https://www.youtube.com/watch?v=OmdQUQh-OTE, accessed on 20.06.2021

Das, Basanta. (2017), *Odisha Politics* (Odia), Media Academy, Bhubaneswar

Das, D. C. (2005), "Biju Patnaik: The Vision of a Patriot", *Orissa Review*, I&PR Department, Govt. of Odisha

Dilip Ray interview about Biju Patnaik, 6 March 2016, https://www.youtube.com/watch?v=dl8FbZxIoaU, accessed on 20.06.2021

Frank, Katherine. (2001), *Indira-The Life of Indira Nehru Gandhi*, Harper Collins, London

Hangen, Welles. (1963), *After Nehru, WHO?*, Harcourt, Brace & World Inc., New York

Kanungo, Pabak. (2005), "Biju Patnaik: A Profile", *Orissa Review*, February & March

Malhotra, Iqbal. Chand. (2021), *Red Fear*, Bloomsbury, New Delhi

Mukherjee, Pranab, (2016), *The Turbulent Years 1980-1996*, Rupa, New Delhi

Modi, Narendra. (2020), https://www.asianage.com/india/all-india/060320/pm-modi-cites-ib-letter-pays-tribute-to-biju-patnaik.html

Morris-Jones, W. H. (1969), "Candidate Selection: The Ordeal of the INC, 1966-67", in *Studies in Politics*, M. S. Rajan (ed.), Vikas, New Delhi

OLA (Odisha Legislative Assembly), *Biju Patnaik-The Great Parliamentarian*, Bhubaneswar

Pradhan, R. D. (1999), *Debacle to Revival: Y B Chavana Defense Minister 1962-65*, Orient Longman, New Delhi

Rudolph, Lloyd I. & Rudolph, Susanne Hoeber. (2008), *Explaining Indian Democracy: A Fifty Year Perspective*, Vol-III, Oxford University Press, New Delhi

Routray, Nilamani. (1986), *Smruti O' Anubhuti* (Odia), Grantha Mandir, Cuttack

Saba Naqvi. (1990), "Decision to implement Mandal Commission report stirs up protests across India", *India Today*, https://www.indiatoday.in/magazine/special-report/story/19900930-decision-to-implement-mandal-commission-report-stirs-up-protests-across-india-813545-1990-09-30, accessed 8 June 2021

Sable, Alan. J. (1967), "Education & the Polity in an Indian State", proceedings prepared for the *Conference on Education & Politics in India*, New Delhi 28-30 June (mimeo)

Sahu, S. N. (2021), "Biju Patnaik's warning against BJPs 'divisive nationalism' is still relevant today", https://thewire.in/politics/biju-patnaik-warning-bjps-nationalism-relevant-today, accession 6th June 2021

Taub, Richard. P. (1969), *Bureaucrats under Stress: Administrators & Administration in an Indian State*, University of California Press, Berkeley

Zachariah, Benjamin. (2004), *Nehru*, Routledge, London

https://frontline.thehindu.com/books/article24279733.ece, dtd 17.5.21

https://www.economist.com/obituary/1997/04/24/biju-patnaik, accession 6th June 2021

https://www.iloveindia.com/indian-heroes/biju-patnaik.html, accession on 6th June 2021

https://www.theweek.in/news/india/2019/08/07/when-biju-patnaik-saved-kashmir-pilot-politician-heroism-back-in-focus.html?__twitter_impression=true

https://parliamentofindia.nic.in/ls/lsdeb/ls10/ses4/0507089202.htm

Proeedings of Lok Sabha and Odisha Legislative Assembly

Lok Sabha Debates, 28 June 1977

Lok Sabha Debates, 10 May 1978

Lok Sabha Debates, 11 May 1978

Lok Sabha Debates, 09 June 1980

Lok Sabha Debates, 17 June 1980

Lok Sabha Debates, 12 September 1996

OLA Debates, 11 December 1948

OLA Debates, Vol. X, No. 2, 11 October, 1949

OLA Debates, Vol. XII, No. 22, 28 March, 1950

OLA Debates, Vol. XII, No. 24, 30 March, 1950

OLA Debates, Vol. VIII, No. 31, 7 April, 1956

OLA Debates, 1957

OLA Debates, Vol. II, No. 8, Part II, 26 March, 1958

OLA Debates, Vol. IV, No. 6, 25 February, 1959

OLA Debates, Vol. IV, No. 15, Part II, 10 March, 1959

OLA Debates, Vol. IV, No. 31, Part II, 29 April, 1959

OLA Debates, Vol. III, No. 3, 23 August, 1962

OLA Debates, Vol. III, No. 11, 5 September, 1962

OLA Debates, Vol. III, No. 29, 30 October, 1962

OLA Debates, Vol. IV, No. 4, 1 March, 1963

OLA Debates, Vol. V, No. 10, 13 September, 1963

OLA Debates, Vol. V, No. 13, 18 September, 1963

OLA Debates, Vol. V, No. 16, 23 September, 1963

OLA Debates, Vol. V, No. 18, 25 September, 1963

OLA Debates, Vol. V, No. 21, 30 September, 1963

OLA Debates, Vol. V, No. 22, 1 October, 1963

OLA Debates, Vol. VI, No. 8, 26 February, 1964

OLA Debates, Vol. VI, No. 2, 18 February, 1964

OLA Debates, Vol. VI, No. 17, 10 March, 1964

OLA Debates, Vol. VI, No. 26, 23 March, 1964

OLA Debates, Vol. VI, No. 55, 22 September, 1964

OLA Debates, Vol. VII, No. 25, 31 March, 1965

OLA Debates, Vol. VII, No. 30, 7 April, 1965

OLA Debates, Vol. VIII, No. 6, 28 September, 1965

OLA Debates, Vol. VIII, No. 7, 29 September, 1965

OLA Debates, Vol. IX, No. 3, 23 February, 1966

OLA Debates, Vol. III, No. 2, 4 January, 1972

OLA Debates, Vol. III, No. 6, 10 January, 1972

OLA Debates, Vol. III, No. 33, 6 April, 1972
OLA Debates, Vol. III, No. 23, 21 March, 1972
OLA Debates, Vol. V, No. 2, 12 February, 1973
OLA Debates, Vol. V, No. 8, 21 February, 1973
OLA Debates, Vol. V, No. 10, 23 February, 1973
OLA Debates, Vol. I, No. 2, 25 March, 1974
OLA Debates, Vol. I, No. 3, 26 March, 1974
OLA Debates, Vol. II, No. 2, 4 June, 1974
OLA Debates, Vol. II, No. 8, 17 June, 1974
OLA Debates, Vol. II, No. 9, 18 June 1974
OLA Debates, Vol. II, No. 10, 19 June, 1974
OLA Debates, Vol. II, No. 15, 27 June, 1974
OLA Debates, Vol. II, No. 24, 10 July 1974
OLA Debates, Vol. III, No. 1, 9 December 1974
OLA Debates, Vol. III, No. 6, 16 December, 1974
OLA Debates, Vol. III, No. 7, 17 December, 1974
OLA Debates, Vol. III, No. 8, 18 December, 1974
OLA Debates, Vol. III, No. 9, 19 December, 1974
OLA Debates, Vol. III, No. 10, 20 December, 1974
OLA Debates, Vol. III, No. 11, 20 December, 1974
OLA Debates, Vol. III, No. 13, 26 December, 1974
OLA Debates, Vol. III, No. 15, 28 December, 1974
OLA Debates, Vol. IV, No. 2, 19 February, 1975
OLA Debates, Vol. IV, No. 16, 13 March, 1975
OLA Debates, Vol. IV, No. 23, 24 March, 1975
OLA Debates, Vol. IV, No. 25, 26 March, 1975
OLA Debates, Vol. IV, No. 31, 9 April, 1975
OLA Debates, Vol. I, No. 2, 15 March, 1985
OLA Debates, Vol. I, No. 3, 18 March, 1985
OLA Debates, Vol. I, No. 6, 21 March, 1985
OLA Debates, Vol. I, 17 July, 1985
OLA Debates, Vol. I, 25 July, 1985
OLA Debates, Vol. I, 30 July, 1985
OLA Debates, Vol. I, 31 July, 1985
OLA Debates, 7 February, 1986
OLA Debates, 14 March, 1986
OLA Debates, 19 March, 1986
OLA Debates, 20 March, 1986
OLA Debates, 31 March, 1986
OLA Debates, 2 April, 1986
OLA Debates, 11 September, 1986
OLA Debates, Vol. V, No. 1, 23 February, 1987
OLA Debates, Vol. V, No. 2, 24 February, 1987
OLA Debates, Vol. V, No. 12, 12 March, 1987
OLA Debates, Vol. V, No. 13, 13 March, 1987
OLA Debates, Vol. V, No. 18, 23 March, 1987
OLA Debates, Vol. V, No. 27, 4 April, 1987
OLA Debates, Vol. V, No. 29, 9 April, 1987
OLA Debates, Vol. VI, No. 2, 10 September, 1987
OLA Debates, Vol. VII, No. 1, 24 February, 1988
OLA Debates, Vol. VII, No. 2, 25 February, 1988

OLA Debates, Vol. VII, No. 3, 26 February, 1988
OLA Debates, Vol. VII, No. 12, 14 March, 1988
OLA Debates, Vol. IX, No. 2, 22 February, 1989
OLA Debates, Vol. IX, No. 23, 27 March, 1989
OLA Debates, Vol. IX, No. 27, 31 March, 1989
OLA Debates, Vol. IX, No. 29, 4 April, 1989
OLA Debates, Vol. IX, No. 31, 6 April, 1989
OLA Debates, Vol. X, No. 3, 11 September, 1989
OLA Debates, Vol. X, No. 5, 13 September, 1989
OLA Debates, Vol. I, No. 4, 21 March, 1990
OLA Debates, Vol. I, No. 5, 22 March, 1990
OLA Debates, Vol. II, No. 17, 26 June, 1990
OLA Debates, Vol. II, No. 20, 29 June, 1990
OLA Debates, Vol. II, No. 6, 7 June, 1990
OLA Debates, Vol. II, No. 21, 5 July, 1990
OLA Debates, Vol. II, No. 22, 6 July, 1990
OLA Debates, Vol. III, No. 8, 17 October, 1990
OLA Debates, Vol. IV, No. 3, 21 February, 1991
OLA Debates, Vol. IV, No. 16, 14 March, 1991
OLA Debates, Vol. V, No. 8, 20 September, 1991
OLA Debates, Vol. VI, No. 3, 18 December, 1991
OLA Debates, Vol. VI, No. 5, 20 December, 1991
OLA Debates, Vol. VII, No. 22, 25 March, 1992
OLA Debates, Vol. VII, No. 23, 26 March, 1992
OLA Debates, Vol. VII, No. 26, 30 March, 1992
OLA Debates, Vol. VII, No. 28, 2 April, 1992
OLA Debates, Vol. IX, No. 9, 6 November, 1992
OLA Debates, Vol. X, No. 3, 22 February, 1993
OLA Debates, Vol. X, No. 7, 26 February, 1993
OLA Debates, Vol. XII, No. 6, 8 November, 1993
OLA Debates, Vol. XIII, No. 3, 24 December, 1993
OLA Debates, Vol. XIV, No. 3, 25 February, 1994
OLA Debates, Vol. XIV, No. 6, 2 March, 1994
OLA Debates, Vol. XIV, No. 13, 16 March, 1994
OLA Debates, Vol. XIV, No. 18, 22 March, 1994
OLA Debates, Vol.XIV, No. 29, 7 April, 1994
OLA Debates, Vol.XV, No. 2, 21 July, 1994
OLA Debates, Vol.XV, No. 5, 26 July, 1994
OLA Debates, Vol.XVI, No. 4, 21 September, 1994
OLA Debates, Vol.XVI, No. 8, 26 September, 1994
OLA Debates, Vol. I, No. 6, 29 March, 1995
OLA Debates, Vol. II, No. 3, 3 July, 1995
OLA Debates, Vol. II, No. 12, 14 July, 1995
OLA Debates, Vol. II, No. 22, 27 July, 1995
OLA Debates, Vol. IV, No. 1, 26 December, 1995
OLA Debates, Vol. IV, No. 2, 27 December, 1995
OLA Debates, Vol. V, No. 2, 14 March, 1996

*****

Index